Whispers
H*of*PE

365 Daily Devotional

Patricia M. Riggie

ISBN 978-1-0980-1729-3 (paperback)
ISBN 978-1-0980-1730-9 (digital)

Christian Faith Publishing, Inc.
832 Park Avenue
Meadville, PA 16335
www.christianfaithpublishing.com

Unless otherwise noted, Scripture taken from the New King James Version®. Copyright © 1982 by Thomas Nelson. Used by permission. All rights reserved.

Scripture quotations marked (NLT) are taken from the Holy Bible, New Living Translation, copyright ©1996, 2004, 2015 by Tyndale House Foundation. Used by permission of Tyndale House Publishers, Inc., Carol Stream, Illinois 60188. All rights reserved.

Printed in the United States of America

To my daughters, Yvonne and Jennifer.
2010

    Throughout the year, I have written words of encouragement to you, proclaiming God's promises in your life. I have captured these words spoken into your life in this journal. I pray that the seeds of encouragement and the promises of God's Word will grow deep within your hearts and the hearts of your children.

    May God richly bless you with His wisdom, understanding, and His love. Allow His Word to encourage you and build within your heart the faith to see yourself as He sees you. You are a precious child of God. He loves you very much and so do I.

With all my love,
Mom

Introduction

T hroughout my life as a mother, I've tried to be a good role model to my two daughters by sharing the heart of the Father to them and teaching them the importance of prayer in their lives. When my daughters awoke in the morning, they would often find me reading the Bible and spending devotional time with the Lord. I encouraged them to be good role models themselves, loving and respecting others, helping those in need and being good stewards with the blessings the Lord has given them.

My journey of writing encouragements to my daughters began in 2010 when I started sending them emails with scriptures and my thoughts of what the Lord wanted to speak into their lives that day. My audience grew as I began to include friends and co-workers as recipients of those emails. They in turn would forward the encouraging emails to their friends and family. Responses from many were very positive and uplifting. Having kept all the emails, at the end of the year, I decided to turn them into a devotional journal and have a copy made for my daughters as a keepsake.

I continued to write encouraging emails but limited them to once a week due to time constraints. Over the next four years, I was able to complete my second devotional journal and provide a second keepsake for my daughters. Throughout the next few years, I gave a copy to friends as birthday and Christmas gifts.

Being retired and not being around people in a work environment, I wondered how I could share the love of God to others and touch their lives like Christ has touched mine. A friend kept telling me that I needed to publish my work, that it would touch and enlighten many lives. Her persistence finally convinced me to pursue this adventure. I never dreamed in a million years that I would become an author, but God knew. He knew from the time when He gave me those first encouraging words to share with my daughters that He was going to have them published one day.

In the beginning of 2019, I decided to have the two devotional journals published so that others can be encouraged as I speak God's Word into their life. Now a grandmother, I wanted to make sure my grandchildren each had a copy of their own so that I could speak life into their lives as well. Having the devotional journals published will now make them available to future generations.

The journals I had bound for my daughters were titled "Encouragement for the Day." At the time, that's what they were, an encouragement for the day. Now that I was having them officially published, I wanted to think of a new title for them. I prayed about it, and one day while I was working out and thinking about what titles to use, I heard the words "Whispers of Hope" in my spirit. I loved it and felt the Holy Spirit was giving me one of the titles for the devotionals. As I continued to work out, the words "Whispers of Love" immediately came to me. I pondered on the titles and felt as if that was exactly what I was doing throughout the years but not even realizing it, imparting whispers of hope and love to my daughters. I asked them what they thought and they both loved the titles and so that is how the two devotional manuscripts got their names. *Whispers of Love* is currently in the publication process and will be available for sale in the near future.

No matter how young or old, devotionals can support us in strengthening our relationship with God. The ultimate goal is having a deeper, personal relationship with Jesus.

I thank the Lord Jesus Christ and His Holy Spirit for every inspired word He has spoken into my life to share with each of you. May each daily devotional bring enrichment to your soul and a closer walk with God. May you experience the depth of His love, mercy, and forgiveness as you proclaim His promises into your own life.

Patricia M. Riggie

JANUARY 1

Then He arose and rebuked the wind, and said to the sea,
"Peace be still." And the wind ceased and there was a great
calm. And they feared exceedingly, and said to one another,
"Who can this be, that even the wind and sea obey Him!"
—Mark 4:39, 41

How do you react when a storm comes your way? Is your first response that you will trust in God or do you panic like the disciples did and question whether God cares? No one likes to go through storms. When they do arise, it is an opportunity for you to use your faith and trust in God to get you through the storm. Sometimes the storm may be quick and sudden—it will cease and a great calm will come. Other times you may be called to ride out the storm for a little while before peace and victory comes. In these times God may be testing your faith to see if you are trusting Him. Whether the storm is quick or lingers on for a while, always put your faith in God who is with you in the midst of your storm.

Hurricanes will do major damage to objects in their path. Sometimes people have warnings that a hurricane is approaching and will have time to escape its path. Some people take the risk and refuse to leave the vicinity while others take heed to the warning. When the storm hits, there is no mercy for the just or the unjust, everything in its path is destroyed. There will be times the Lord will warn you that if you continue to live your life the way you are, danger is approaching and He gives you time to escape. If you heed to His warning, your life will be spared, but if you refuse to listen, destruction is sure to come.

Are you facing a storm right now? Is the Lord giving you a warning that a major hurricane is coming your way and you must leave now or face destruction. If so, by all means heed to his warning and remove yourself from the situation. If you put your trust in God, no matter what size the storm, when it is all said and done, you will be able to respond—I know this man Jesus—even my storm had to obey Him!

JANUARY 2

Peace I leave with you, My peace I give to you; not
as the world gives do I give to you. Let not your
heart be troubled, neither let it be afraid.
—John 14:27

Is the peace of God abiding in your heart right now, or are you allowing the cares and concerns of your day to rob you of that peace? It's so easy to become distracted by the events in your life that you lose focus of the great I AM who is in control of all circumstances. If you are troubled, worried, or afraid, your eyes are fixed on the situation and not on Jesus.

No matter what you are facing, if you focus your eyes on the Healer, the Comforter, the Almighty God, and believe that He will take care of your situation, then your heart will not be troubled or afraid. You may not always understand life's challenges and may question why you must go through the trials that you are faced with, but do not allow these challenges or your lack of understanding to rob you of our peace. Put your faith in Jesus and trust Him for your victory.

What is troubling you today? Are you faced with an important decision to make? Have you or someone you love been diagnosed with a terminal illness? Have you lost your job and can't pay the bills? Is a loved one high on drugs or imprisoned? Is your marriage in shambles and your spouse wants a divorce? No matter how small or how large your cares and concerns may be, give them to the Lord, our Helper. Surrender them to God and allow the great I AM to be in control. Fix your eyes on Jesus and believe in your heart that He is in control. Trust in Him, and let the peace of God guard your heart and mind through Christ Jesus (Philippians 4:7).

JANUARY 3

See then that you walk circumspectly, not as fools but as
wise, redeeming the time, because the days are evil.
—Ephesians 5:15–16

You can probably think of a million and one things you could be doing right now, but would you be investing your time wisely? Have the things you've done this past week brought honor to God? Review the way you spend your time regularly because the world is full of darkness and if you are not on guard, it would be easy to slip into it with your thoughts, words or actions without even realizing it.

God has a will and purpose for your lie. Be careful to live wisely, seeking God for direction on how He wants you to spend your time. Then after hearing from God, make the most of your time and opportunities He gives you. In this falling world, keep your standards high, act wisely, and do good whenever you can. God wants you to walk circumspectly, that is, being careful to consider all circumstances and their consequences.

God gives you many opportunities to share the Good News with non-Christians. You are to be good stewards of your time, using it wisely, sharing God's love whenever the opportunity arises. You are to "redeem the time," buying back every precious moment you wasted and investing it in sharing the love of Christ to others. God wants your time to be spent in some worthy endeavor. How are you investing your time? Are you walking circumspectly?

JANUARY 4

To everything there is a season, a time for every
purpose under heaven. I know that whatever
God does, it shall be forever. Nothing can be
added to it, and nothing taken away from it.
—Ecclesiastes 3:1, 14

Another year has quickly passed you by and a new year is beginning. Reflect on the things that have transpired this past year. What
challenges were you faced with and how did you overcome them?
How has the Lord blessed you this past year? Are there prayers that
still need to be answered? What awaits you this coming year and
what do you want God to accomplish in your life?

Many set goals or expectations throughout the year and when
they are not met, they become discouraged, give up, and let go of
their hope or dream. They quit right before their prayer is about to
be birthed. You may even be one of those people. Everything has
its time. To everything there is a season, a time for every purpose
under heaven. God has a purpose for each of us. For some, that
purpose has been established, but for many, you are a work in
progress. Destiny awaits you. You just have to do your part and
allow God to do the rest.

Trust God to answer your prayers in His timing. If you take
a cake out of the oven before it's finished baking, the cake will sink
into the pan and become a flop. If you try to birth your dream
before it's time, things may not turn out the way you planned and
it definitely won't be the way God had planned. When your prayer
seems to be taking a long time to be birthed, remind yourself that
God is in control. While you wait, you can be sure that whatever
God does, it shall be forever, and nothing can be added to it and
nothing taken away from it. May your dreams and destiny be fulfilled this coming year.

JANUARY 5

Therefore do not be like them. For your Father knows
the things you have need of before you ask Him.
—Matthew 6:8

Many times when you are faced with a difficult situation, you wonder if God can really provide what you need. Through your eyes it may seem hopeless, but that is when you must really trust in God. Your eyes need to focus on who He is and not on your situation. The very nature of God should give you reassurance that He will provide for your needs. God is omnipresent—He sees every situation and is at work making a way on your behalf. God is omniscient—He knows all your needs before you even ask. God is omnipotent—He has the power to change any situation and supply whatever you need.

Exploring the names of God will also bring you comfort and peace while you wait on God to supply your needs. He is Yahweh Yireh—the Lord will provide. Since the Lord sees the future as well as the past and present, He is able to provide whatever we need. He is Yahweh Rophe—the Lord who heals. God is the source to all healing. He is Yahweh Shalom—the Lord is peace. God is the source to all peace and will give you inner peace as you draw close to Him. He is Yahweh Roi—the Lord is my shepherd. God watches over you day and night and He will lead you safely on the path of righteousness. He will guide you to make the right decisions.

When you begin to lose faith because your situation or need looks too big—focus your eyes on the omnipresent, omniscient, and omnipotent God. Build faith and hope by exploring the many names of God throughout scripture and reflect on how the name connects to God's promises for you.

JANUARY 6

Thus says the Lord: "Let not the wise man glory
in his wisdom, let not the mighty man glory in his
might, nor let the rich man glory in his riches; But
let him who glories glory in this, that he understands
and knows Me, that I am the Lord, exercising
lovingkindness, judgment, and righteousness in the
earth. For in these I delight," says the Lord.
—Jeremiah 9:23–24

In this scripture, we are told not to glory in wisdom, power, or riches. When people have these things, they tend to become self-sufficient and forget who enabled them to obtain these things. They have a false impression that they are in control. But scripture tells us that the fool and the senseless person perish and leave their wealth to others (Psalm 49:10). It also warns us to let no one deceive himself. If anyone among you seems to be wise in this age, let him become a fool that he may become wise. For the wisdom of this world is foolish with God for He catches the wise in their own craftiness (1 Corinthians 3:18–19).

You are not to glory in your possessions, but you are to give glory to God for providing them to you. You are to put your confidence in God alone and not in your wisdom, power or riches. Becoming a fool that one may become wise means that you let go of the world's wisdom and you become wise by applying spiritual truth to one's life. It all starts by having a fear of the Lord (Psalm 111:10). It is only fools who despise God's wisdom and instruction (Proverbs 1:7).

The Lord delights when you give glory to Him for it is then that you truly understand and know the Lord. Delight yourself in the Lord today. Give glory to God for His mercy, forgiveness, and loving kindness. Give glory to God for enabling you to have the wisdom to do your job, the strength to persevere, and the finances to live and bless others.

JANUARY 7

*A new commandment I give to you, that you love
one another; as I loved you, that you also love one
another. By this all will know that you are My
disciples, if you have love for one another.*

—John 13:34–35

When Jesus spoke these words, His disciples had no idea how much Jesus really loved them and what He was about to do for them. Jesus knew this love would require His death—an ultimate sacrifice on the cross. We are required to love the way Jesus loved. Loving the way Jesus loves means that we seek and do the Father's will no matter what the cost. Loving the way Jesus loves means that we love unconditionally. Jesus commands us to love with a brotherly love, to be willing to lay down one's life for his friends (John 15:13). If we don't do things out of love, it profits us nothing (1 Corinthians 13:1–3).

We all know how complicated, challenging, loving, and unloving people can be. Being with other people presents us with great opportunities to demonstrate the love of the Father to every person we encounter. Because living with people can be complicated and very challenging at times, it is vital that we seek the love of God in our own lives so that the love of our Father may penetrate through us and touch those around us. Are you challenged with difficult, unloving people in your life? Shower them with the Father's love. Love suffers long (1 Corinthians 13:4). Be willing to suffer a little to bring healing in relationships or to lead others to Christ. Unconditional love has a way of changing the hardest of hearts and initiating changes in people's lives.

JANUARY 8

The Lord is my shepherd, I shall not want.
—Psalm 23:1

No matter what your need may be, God shall supply it. Do you believe that? In Psalm 23, David speaks of the Lord as his heavenly Shepherd. David being a shepherd himself took care of all the needs of his sheep. Knowing that He could fully trust in the Lord, the heavenly Shepherd, he had no doubt that God would provide for him. Thus David said, "I shall not want." Although his needs were not being met yet, He knew they would be in God's timing.

Remind yourself that Jesus is the good shepherd who will meet your needs as well (John 10:11). But what if you pray and pray and that need is not met? Will you still believe that God will supply that need? You may be tempted to lose hope or think that God really doesn't care. You may become desperate and even be tempted to try to meet that need yourself. But deep down inside you come to the realization that only God can fulfill that need.

So what do you do when your need is not being met? Persevere! Don't lose hope. Keep the faith. Know that God is on your side. Keep your eyes focused on Jesus and believe that He is working on your behalf. Hold onto the promises of God. Hear Him say to you, "For I know the plans I have for you, plans to prosper you and to not harm you, plans to give you hope and a future" (Jeremiah 29:11). Keep saying to yourself—God shall supply all my needs. Have the faith like the psalmist had and declare "I shall not want." Witness God's love as He meets your need. The Lord is your shepherd, you shall not need!

JANUARY 9

So God created man in His own image; in the
image of God He created him; male and female
He created them. Then God saw everything that
He had made, and indeed it was very good.
—Genesis 1:27, 31

The first chapter of Genesis is the history of creation. After God was finished with His work for the day, He sat back and said…it was good. The last of creation was mankind. After mankind was created, everything that God made was not only good, but very good. Think about it. When God created us, He made us in His own image. Why do you think He did that? By creating us in His own image, He made it possible for us to have a deep personal relationship with Him. This is His ultimate desire for us. It should be our ultimate desire for Him.

Have you really thought about this? God not only created you, but He created you in His image. Does your life resemble God? Are you walking in love and humility? Do you aim to live a Christ-like life? Daily you need to examine yourself and ask, "Am I living in the image of God?" Allow the Holy Spirit to reveal things to you that need to be changed so that you are walking in the image of God. This year, make it your ultimate desire to learn what it means to walk in the image of God. Elohim, God the Almighty Creator, created us in His image to have a deep intimate relationship with Him. Make it your desire to walk intimately with Him.

JANUARY 10

And He said, "My Presence will go
with you, and I will give you rest."
—Exodus 33:14

With the busyness of our schedules, it's no wonder we are all so tired. Everyone and everything is demanding our time and we wonder if we will ever get everything accomplished that we need to get done. Just the thought of it can make us weary. Some even lose sleep worrying about what they need to do the next day. Where do we find peace in the midst of it all?

Peace comes only by spending time with God. A moment in God's presence can seem like hours of natural rest. If we would take the time to be in the Lord's presence, He will restore rest and peace in us. He will show us how to better our time and let go of things He never called us to do. We are not to be a God to everyone else's problems or situations, trying to fix things that God wants individuals to fix on their own. It is okay to say "no" when asked to help someone and you feel in your heart God has not called you to do it.

Start your day in the presence of the Lord, allowing Him to order your day, and to give you the strength for the tasks at hand. Take the time in your busy schedule to be still and quiet your soul. Meditate on the goodness of the Lord and thank Him for what He has done for you. Meditate on His Word and allow it to give you strength, hope, and peace. When you do these things, then you will be able to say "I have calmed and quieted my soul" (Psalm 131:2).

JANUARY 11

Stand fast therefore in the liberty by which
Christ has made us free, and do not be
entangled again with a yoke of bondage.
—Galatians 5:1

What does freedom mean to you? Is it temporary or is it permanent? Who gives you the freedom? When people commit crimes and are imprisoned, they serve their time and then are set free. For some, they have learned their lesson and remain out of jail. For others, it's just a matter of time before they repeat the crime and are faced with jail time again. The source of true freedom comes from Jesus. When Jesus sets us free, we are not only liberated from the punishment of sin but also from the power that sin has over us.

Freedom is a choice. We can walk in the bondage of sin or choose to allow Christ to set us free. Once free, we are to stand firm in our freedom and not look back and become yoked in that bondage again. Many become free but turn around and fall into the same trap again, because they don't have the strength or courage to say no to that sin. We have to want freedom. The only way to continually walk in freedom is to go back to the source that gives us strength to not entangle ourselves with the yoke of bondage.

Jesus is here to set us free from anything that holds us in bondage. Do you need freedom today from something that holds you in bondage—fear, rejection, low self-esteem, anger, worry, doubt, or a bad habit? Give it to the Lord. Ask the Lord for forgiveness and then ask Him to set you free in this area of your life. Choose to stand firm in your freedom. Daily remind yourself, "The Son set me free and I am free indeed" (John 8:36) and rejoice in your freedom.

JANUARY 12

*Blessed is the man who walks not in the counsel of the
ungodly, nor stands in the path of sinners, nor sits in
the seat of the scornful; But his delight is in the law
of the Lord, and in His law he meditates day and night.*
—Psalm 1:1–2

We all want to be blessed by the Lord and one sure way of being blessed is by reading God's Word. There is no better way to gain wisdom and insight about God than by reading His Word with reverence, and then taking the time in silence to hear God speak to you on what you have read. God will speak His Word into your heart if you will allow Him.

What is your delight? What are you consumed with? Is it watching television, playing/watching sports, socializing on the Internet, pursuing a career or reading the Bible? God's Word says we are blessed if our delight is in the law of the Lord and we meditate on it day and night. To meditate means to contemplate, to ponder, to engage in deep mental exercise directed toward a heightened level of spiritual awareness. If you are not reading and meditating on the Bible in this manner, you should be.

When you read the Word of God, read it with the expectation that the Holy Spirit will speak specifically to you. When He does, be obedient to what He asks you to do and thank Him for the knowledge and insight He is sharing with you. Be blessed—let the Word of God be your meditation day and night.

JANUARY 13

The Lord is my rock and my fortress and my deliver;
The God of my strength, in whom I will trust; My
shield and the horn of my salvation, my stronghold and
my refuge; My Savior, You save me from violence.
—2 Samuel 22:2–3

What do you do when the storms of life shake the foundation of your day? Where do you run for peace and shelter? Is your refuge talking with friends or using social media as an outlet? Do you ignore the issue hoping the storm will pass over or do you find shelter under the protective shadow of God?

When the storms of life come your way, run to the Lord for your strength and refuge. He will be your shield no matter what comes your way. Despite your moments of doubt and unbelief, trust in your sovereign Lord. He is the one who keeps His promises and will walk with you through life's challenges.

In the very midst of your weakness, He will shield you and give you strength. Believe this and take action to keep moving forward and trusting in God. No matter how rough the storm may get, there is always peace that follows the storm. What challenge or storm are you facing today? Whatever it is, God has promised to be your refuge and deliverer when you put your trust in Him. Know that the Lord is your rock, your fortress, and your deliverer and the gates of hell will not prevail. Trust in Him to walk you through whatever storm has shaken your foundation. Take refuge in Him.

JANUARY 14

*Whatever my eyes desired I did not keep from them.
I did not withhold my heart from any pleasure, for my
heart rejoiced in all my labor; And this was my reward
from all my labor. Then I looked on all the works
that my hands had done and on the labor in which
I had toiled; and indeed all was vanity and grasping
for the wind. There was no profit under the sun.*
—Ecclesiastes 2:10–11

In the second chapter of Ecclesiastes, we are told of all the great accomplishments of Solomon. He built houses, planted vineyards and gardens, possessed flocks and herds, and acquired much gold and silver. He searched in his heart how to gratify his flesh with wine while guiding his heart with wisdom. Whatever he desired, he made sure he got it. He did not withhold his heart from any pleasure. Then he looked on all the works that his hands had done and the labor in which he had toiled and realized it was all in vanity—it did not make him happy.

Richness does not have to be gained in material things. Solomon had all the riches he could imagine and yet the result of all his accomplishments was emptiness. The richest moments of our lives are spending time with people and God. A child won't remember how clean the house was, but will remember the special moments you spent with him. Enjoy the moments you have raising up your children, caring for an elder parent, or helping someone in need. These are the priceless memories that you will be able to reflect upon.

What do you base your richness on? Is it based on personal gain and accomplishments or is it based on spending quality time with God, family, and friends? The richest moments in life are not the most expensive—the smile of a child or stranger, walks with a spouse or friend, holding someone in your arms, a surprise call to someone. Be a blessing to others and fill your life with richness by touching the lives of others.

JANUARY 15

*If we confess our sins, He is faithful and just to forgive
us our sins and to cleanse us from all unrighteousness.*
—1 John 1:9

Daily we must seek the Lord and ask the Holy Spirit to reveal our sins to us. Our hearts are deceived so easily and what may appear okay in our own eyes and hearts may be displeasing to the Lord. Honest confession of sin with a sincere heart brings power to our life and victory over sin.

Confession means that you not only tell the Lord of your sin and ask forgiveness, but you also hand it over to Him, trusting Him to take it away. Have sincerity and determination to never want to do that sin again. Without sincerity and determination, you will fail and fall right back into your sinful nature. Without the power of the Holy Spirit, you are too weak, unwilling, and incapable to conquer sin on your own.

By an act of faith, depend on God to deliver you. Believe that there is great power in the confession of sin and that God will cleanse you from all unrighteousness. I know that when I confess my sins to God and ask for forgiveness, there is such a weight lifted off my shoulders knowing that my sins are forgiven. After all, that is why He died on the cross, for you and me, so that our sins may be forgiven. Blessed are we for our transgression is forgiven and our sin covered by the blood of the Lamb (Psalm 32:1).

JANUARY 16

May the Lord give you increase more
and more, you and your children.

—Psalm 115:14

The Lord desires that we live a happy and fulfilled life. He had established plans for us long before we were even born. "For I know the plans I have for you," declares the Lord, "plans to prosper you and not harm you, plans to give you hope and a future" (Jeremiah 29:11). God wants you to prosper and grow, not only in material things, but also in the wisdom and knowledge of Him.

What you do in life will have an impact on your children. God is jealous over you and when you turn away from Him and live in sin, the consequences of your sin will be handed down four generations (Exodus 20:5). God honors faithfulness and when you are faithful to Him, He will bless you a hundredfold (Genesis 26:12). The Lord has been mindful of you. He will bless you. He will bless those who fear Him, both small and great (Psalm 115:12–13). These blessings are passed down to your children. The Lord will increase you more and more, you and your children.

Pray and desire spiritual increase. Jesus increased in wisdom, stature, and in favor with God and men (Luke 2:52) because He continually sought the heart and will of the Father. You too will increase in wisdom, stature, and in favor with God and men as you seek the heart and will of God. Let it be your passion, let it be your desire. I pray blessings upon your life today. I pray that you will prosper and grow as your years increase in the wisdom and knowledge of God. May God's favor be upon you and your family in Jesus's name.

JANUARY 17

Ponder the path of your feet, and
let all your ways be established.

—Proverbs 4:26

Sometimes we fall into sin, not because we plan to, but because we are not looking at where we are going. It's so easy to become sidetracked not even realizing we are headed down a wrong path. If we are not careful, others can also misguide us. God wants us to be spiritually alert at all times and that includes taking regular inventory of our life's direction. We are to ponder the path of our feet and carefully consider where our pathway of life is leading us.

Are you carefully examining the path your feet are travelling? Are you allowing the Holy Spirit to help you establish your ways? When God reveals an issue that needs to be dealt with in your life, immediately take action. Repent of your sinfulness and ask God for forgiveness. No matter how small or how big the stronghold, God has the power to break any yoke of bondage that controls you. When conviction comes upon you, it is because God wants to help you in some area where you have gone astray.

When you examine carefully your steps and allow the Holy Spirit to establish your ways, there is an inner peace that will come over you. Your life will radiate with His presence. Your path will be like the shining sun, that shines brighter and brighter each day until that perfect day comes when you meet Christ our Savior face-to-face (Proverbs 4:18).

JANUARY 18

As the Father loved Me, I also have loved you;
abide in My love. If you keep My commandments,
you will abide in My love, just as I have kept My
Father's commandments and abide in His love.
—John 15:9–10

Not feeling loved has got to be the worst experience anyone has ever felt. You can be the richest person in the world but if you don't feel loved or love others, of what value is it? Relationships depend on the love that each one has for one another. Marriages end up in divorce because one or both spouses fall out of love for the other.

Our relationship with Jesus depends on love as well. God is love and everything He does is out of love. What value is the knowledge and zeal in God's work without the knowledge and experience of Christ's love? Many people know about Christ's love but few actually experience it. Jesus desires that each of us come to not only know about His love, but to experience it as well. What a blessing to daily abide in Christ's love.

Read about God's love in His Word and allow it to sink deep into your heart. Get to know Him personally more and more each day and allow His love to abide in you. The greatest feeling one can have is to know that they are loved by Christ! Know that Christ loves you. You are precious in His sight. Abide daily in His love.

JANUARY 19

*Let him know that he who turns a sinner
from the error of his way will save a soul
from death and cover a multitude of sins.*

—James 5:20

What a great feeling it is to be a part of winning a soul from everlasting death. When Christ takes possession of our hearts, He pours His love into us so that we in turn will pour out that love to others and bring others to Christ. Everyone who has the love of Christ is commissioned to tell others of that love.

Why is it so easy to talk to others about the football game, a vacation trip or the problems of others but it's so hard to witness about Christ and what He has done in our lives? We must overcome the fear of man and stop worrying about what people think. There are many hurting people who are waiting on us to share with them what we have received.

If we don't share the love of Christ to others, are we really experiencing Christ's love? Jesus's ultimate goal was to reach the lost, heal the sick, and proclaim the good news to the world. We need to embrace Jesus's ultimate goal to reach the lost as well. Have you shared the love of Christ to someone? Be a witness for Christ and help win a soul today.

JANUARY 20

And You shall remember that the Lord your God led
you all the way these forty years in the wilderness, to
humble you and test you, to know what was in your heart,
whether you would keep His commandments or not.

—Deuteronomy 8:2

There will be times that the Lord allows circumstances to happen in our lives to test us, to humble us, to see whether we will obey Him and lean on Him when things get difficult. None of us like the discomfort it brings but we sure do like the victory in the end.

Many times when the circumstances arise, we are quick to share our burdens with others, but the Lord wants us to depend on Him and not on others. He is the great burden-bearer and will listen as we cry out to Him. He wants to lead us, guide us, and give us wisdom to make the right decision. He is training us to hear His voice and not depend on the voice of man.

The next time something comes up in your life, hold back from sharing it with others and share it only with the Lord. Give God the freedom to shape the circumstance and depend on Him to give you the strength and wisdom to make the right decisions. When you do, it not only builds your faith but you shall remember that it was the Lord your God who led you out of your circumstances and into your promised land. To God be the glory.

JANUARY 21

*So they watched Him closely, whether He would heal
him on the Sabbath, so that they might accuse Him.*
—Mark 3:2

Do you ever feel like you are constantly being watched so that another can have the satisfaction of showing you your mistake? You may not ever be doing anything wrong but they will still find something to criticize you about. Living with critical people can be very difficult and discouraging at times. So how do you deal with a critical person? I want to share with you what I learned from a health minister. How we respond to a critical person determines how long we stay in that dysfunction or how quickly we come out of it.

A negative thought left unchecked gives you a negative decision that leads to negative actions. Negative actions lead to negative habits which lead to a negative character that leads one to a negative destiny. A Positive thought gives you a positive decision which leads to positive actions. Positive actions lead to positive habits which lead to a positive character which leads one to a positive destiny.

Respond to the negative words of a critical person with positive thoughts and actions. Don't take their words personally. More often it's an issue with them and not you. Jesus did not let the critical spirit of others or their accusations stop Him for doing good and fulfilling His destiny. Don't allow the critical spirit of others to cause you to not fulfill your destiny.

JANUARY 22

And I have declared to them Your name, and
will declare it, that the love with which You
loved Me may be in them, and I in them.
— John 17:26

Have you ever been or are you now in a relationship where it seems like you are the only one putting any effort into the relationship? It makes you wonder if the other person really cares or loves you. Now look at your relationship with Christ. Is Christ putting all the effort into the relationship with little effort or correspondence from you? Do you give the impression that you don't care or love Him? Love relationships work both ways. If only one side of the relationship puts all the effort into it, the relationship will fail. Christ came from heaven to love us with the love that the Father loved Him. He suffered and died to win our hearts for this love. What Christ wants in return is for us to have that same deep personal love for Him.

We can do all the right things—go to church, be in ministry, follow the Lord's commands, help those in need, all these things are good, but what the Lord values most is still missing—He wants US, that special one-on-one time with our Savior. The Lord wants you. Hear Him speak to your heart right now: "Come, my beloved, I've been waiting for you"—and then go and spend some intimate time with your Savior. It doesn't take much to touch the Father's heart. Words spoken from your heart will melt His heart. Speak to Him throughout your day and tell Him how much you love Him. Let Him know how much you appreciate Him and thank Him for always being there for you, tending to all your needs.

JANUARY 23

He brought me to the banqueting house, and his banner over me was love. "O my dove, in the clefts of the rock, in the secret places of the cliff, let me see your face, let me hear your voice; For your voice is sweet, and your face is lovely."
—Song 2:4, 14

God's greatest gift to us is His love. Yet it is one that most of us have a hard time receiving. Why? Because we don't understand the depth and quality of pure love. We want to believe He loves us the way we love others, but His love goes deeper, much deeper. God's love is not based on emotions. Our performance does not determine the amount of love He has for us nor is it based on the amount of love we have for Him. His love is unconditional.

God is love (1 John 4:8). Since it is impossible for Him to do anything contrary to His nature, His love will always remain forever faithful. Just as black is black and white is white, God is love and nothing will change that, no matter what. We can live a holy life or be the worst sinner, and His love for us remains the same.

God always loved you and always will. Every day, walk under the banner of His love. The more you come to know His love, the more you begin to love yourself and others unconditionally. It is in the secret places that you will see His face, hear His voice, and come to know and feel His unconditional love. Go there often and bask in His love.

JANUARY 24

*"Therefore I say to you, do not worry about your
life, what you will eat or what you will drink; nor
about your body, what you will put on. Is not life
more than food and the body more than clothing?"*

—Matthew 6:25

Do you have the peace of God in your heart right now? At
times this may not seem easy to have because of situations at work
or the cares and concerns of life. But you are to give every situation, care, and concern to the Lord and trust that He will take care
of the matter. The number one killer of peace is worry. The Bible is
filled with scriptures telling us not to worry. Instead we are to cast
our cares upon the Lord (1 Peter 5:7).

Jesus will not take your cares from you, you have to give
them to Him and He wants them all. Until you give your cares
to Him, his hands are tied and you will not have peace. Once you
give them to Him, He is free to work on your behalf. Jesus said,
"Peace I leave with you, My peace I give to you; not as the world
gives do I give to you. Let not your heart be troubled neither let it
be afraid" (John 14:27). Jesus does not want your heart to be troubled with the cares of this world. It is peace He wants to give you.

Do you want the peace of God to rule in your heart? Cast
your cares upon Him, all of them. Trust in Him to resolve every
care and concern you have. Be anxious for nothing but in everything by prayer and supplication, with thanksgiving, let your
requests be known to God; and the peace of God, which surpasses
all understanding will guard your heart and mind through Christ
Jesus (Philippians 4:6–7).

JANUARY 25

*Lord, who may abide in Your tabernacle? Who may
dwell in Your holy hill? He who walks uprightly, and
works righteousness, and speaks the truth in his heart.*
—Psalm 15:1–2

God honors those who seek after Him, walk in His ways, and do not follow the crowd. Our Christian walk should be uncompromising. When the voice inside of you is telling you to do one thing, but someone else wants you to do just the opposite, chances are, it is God's Spirit giving you insight into what He wants you to do. Be strong and do not give in to the pressures of others to just "fit in."

There are other ways you compromise your walk as well—by keeping silent when you know the voice of the Lord wants you to speak up. The fear of what people will think keeps you from saying anything, so you just keep silent. Decide which is more important, to abide with man or abide with the Most High.

The more you love God, the easier it is to follow His ways. You do it out of your love for Him and not because of His commands to us. When you love someone, you go the extra mile for them. Go the extra mile in your walk with Jesus today. Walk uprightly, work righteously, and speak the truth in your heart so that you may abide in the tabernacle of the Most High.

JANUARY 26

The Lord God is my strength; He will make my feet like deer's feet, and He will make me walk on my high hills.
—Habakkuk 3:19

God delights in upholding the weary and bringing hope and life to the faint heartened. When you feel emotionally and physically drained, turn to God whose supply never runs out. He is the source of all power and strength. When the outlook of your circumstance looks grim, Christ is your strength. When the economy is shaky and everything around you seems to be collapsing, God is your stability.

When you try to do things in your own strength and power, they usually do not turn out the way you had planned. Trust in God to get you through the dark valleys. Trusting God means looking beyond what you can see and view the situation through God's eyes. Trusting God means looking beyond your own strength and stamina and relying on God's power to get you out of the valley and onto the top of the hill. The Lord gives power to the weak and increases strength to those who have no might (Isaiah 40:29). Put your trust in God today.

Although the road you're travelling on may seem difficult, your circumstances will change as you put your hope in God. The Lord is your strength and He will make your feet like deer's feet to conquer any mountain that lies before you.

JANUARY 27

The other disciples therefore said to him, "We have seen the Lord."
So he said to them, "Unless I see in His hands the print of the
nails, and put my finger into the print of the nails, and put my
hand into His side, I will not believe."…Jesus said to him,
"Thomas, because you have seen Me, you have believed.
Blessed are those who have not seen and yet have believed."
—John 20:25, 29

Thomas was a doubter. He had to see things for himself in order for him to believe. Jesus came and stood in the midst of His disciples. Knowing the heart of Thomas, Jesus said to him, "Reach your finger here, and look at My hands; and reach your hand here, and put it into My side. Do not be unbelieving, but believing" (John 20:27). Jesus is saying that to us now—do not be unbelieving, but believing.

Are you believing in your miracle or dream or must there be signs before you know for certainty that God is meeting your dream. Doubt is the opposite of faith and can creep into your mind when you do not see God in action. You do not know what God is doing behind the scenes. Hold onto the faith that He is working on your behalf. Jesus calls you blessed when you have not seen but yet still believe.

Jesus did many other signs in the presence of His disciples which are not written in the Bible; but those that are, are written that you may believe that Jesus is the Christ, the Son of God, and believe you may have life in His name (John 20:30–31). When uncertainties begin to enter your mind, remember the power of the Almighty God we serve. Choose the path of faith and declare your victory that lies ahead. Believe in your miracle, believe in your dream. Simply believe!

JANUARY 28

He has not dealt with us according to our sins,
nor punished us according to our iniquities. For
as the heavens are high above the earth, so great
is His mercy toward those who fear Him.
—Psalm 103:10–11

Many are not living in freedom because they are held in bondage from their past sins. They have not forgiven themselves for their past mistakes and continue to hold onto past failures and disappointments. Instead of learning from their mistakes and moving on, they allow the guilt, shame or regret to rule their lives. If our Creator is merciful towards us, then who are we to not extend that same mercy towards ourselves?

Forgiving yourself is essential. When the Bible talks about forgiving others, that includes forgiving ourselves. Forgiving oneself does not justify what you have done nor does it make a wrong action right. Forgiving yourself is simply letting go of what holds you in bondage so that you can move forward in God's mercy and love.

Is there something from your past that holds you in bondage? Stop seeing yourself through the eyes of guilt, shame, and condemnation. The Bible tells us that "there is therefore now no condemnation to those who are in Christ Jesus, who do not walk according to the flesh, but according to the Spirit" (Romans 8:1). It is time to let go of old disappointments and regrets. They are old and do not represent who you are today. Give them to the Lord. Symbolically place them in your hand, stretch your hand up to Almighty God and give them to Him. Then receive His mercy and set yourself free.

JANUARY 29

*Not that I have already attained, or am already perfected; but
I press on, that I may lay hold of that for which Christ Jesus
has also laid hold of me. Brethren, I do not count myself to have
apprehended; but one thing I do, forgetting those things which
are behind and reaching forward to those things which are ahead.*
—Philippians 3:12–13

None of us have reached the ultimate goal God has for us. No matter where you are in your walk with God, never settle for past blessings and yesterday's best. Instead, press forward that you may grab hold of what God has for you today.

Many fall short of their destiny because of adversity in life. They do not press through the battles of life. God does not glory when He sees us suffer with pain or sorrow, but He allows adversity to come our way so that we will draw close to Him. God always has something in mind when He allows us to face difficulty. We just need to press through and ask God to show us what we are supposed to learn from the situation.

Are you facing adversity? Turn to God. Keep your eyes focused on Jesus and not on the circumstance. Never forget that God knows your future and He is using that adversity to shape your destiny. Forget those things which are behind you and reach forward to those things which are ahead. Press forward that you may obtain all that Christ Jesus saved you for and wants you to be.

JANUARY 30

*"Ask, and it will be given to you; seek, and you
will find; knock, and it will be opened to you.
For everyone who asks receives, and he who seeks
finds, and to him who knocks it will be opened."*
—Matthew 7:7–8

Faith has a part of God responding to our needs. If we do not have the faith that He is willing and able to meet our needs, then chances are He won't. In Matthew 8, a centurion came to Jesus pleading with Him to heal his servant. The man not only had faith, he had great faith. Jesus responded to those around, "Assuredly I have not found such great faith, not even in Israel." Then Jesus said to the centurion, "Go your way, and as you have believed, so let it be done for you." His servant was healed that very hour (Matthew 8:13).

Jesus tells us to ask, seek, and knock, but He expects us to do it with faith that He will respond to our requests. It takes an action on our part for there to be a reaction on His part. We may not have the great faith that the centurion had, but if we have faith even the size of a mustard seed, it will cause God to move mountains on our behalf and nothing will be impossible for us (Matthew 17:20).

What do you have need of today? Ask Jesus in faith and it will be given to you. Is there an answer you are waiting for? Seek Him in faith and it will be found. Do you just need someone to talk to? Knock on the door of His heart in faith and it will be opened to you.

JANUARY 31

*Since you are precious in My sight, you have been
honored, and I have loved you...Everyone who is
called by My name, whom I have created for My
glory; I have formed him, yes, I have made him.*

—Isaiah 43:4, 7

To think, the God of Heaven, the creator of this universe formed
and created us to bring Him glory. We were created to serve, worship, and glorify God. Have you ever thought about what would
bring glory to Him? Jesus gives us a roadmap for achieving that
purpose. Everything we do must not be done for the purpose of
man or self, but for the purpose of glorifying God.

I asked the Lord how I can give glory to His name and this
is what He spoke to me. My child, you bring glory to My name
by showing the love of the Father to those around you. There is no
other commandment greater than this, that you should love your
neighbor as yourself. I am love and my love flows through you.
Allow the love of the Father that is in you to flow through others.

And so I pray that the love of the Father that is in me is flowing through me and touching your life. You are precious in the eyes
of God and He wants to let you know how much He loves you and
how special you are to Him. You are very precious in His eyes. You
too were made to love and bring glory to His name. Spend some
time alone with God feeling His love and ask Him how you can
give glory to His name.

FEBRUARY 1

Do not love the world or the things in the world.
If anyone loves the world, the love of the Father
is not in him. For all that is in the world—the
lust of the flesh, the lust of the eyes, and the pride
of life—is not of the Father, but is of the world.
—1 John 2:15–16

If you think about it, we live in a dangerous world. I'm not referring to the dangers that come from terrorist groups or evil people
who want to take innocent lives, I'm referring to the hidden lusts
of wealth and enjoyments of the world. This world offers so many
attractions to entertain us, some are healthy but many come with
deception. The world offers riches, beauty, fame, luxury, and love
but at what cost? There is so much to allure and occupy our eyes
and heart and if we are not careful, they will soon become lusts of
our flesh and eyes and the pride of our life.

That is why it is so important to be strengthened by the
Word of God and allow the Holy Spirit to help you shun away
from the world and its attractions. Temptations are all around. If
you think you can conquer the temptations on your own, you are
only fooling yourself. The Bible warns us in Romans 12:2, "Do
not be deceived. Do not be conformed to this world, but be transformed by the renewing of your mind, that you may prove what is
that good and acceptable and perfect will of God." You renew your
mind by aligning your thoughts with God's thoughts and reading
God's Word to know what is good and acceptable in His eyes.

All that is in the world—the lust of the flesh, the lust of the
eyes, and the pride of life—is not of the Father but is of the world.
And the world is passing away, and the lust of it; but he who does
the will of God abides forever (1 John 2:16–17). Do you want to
abide with God forever? Pray with a sincere heart and ask the Holy
Spirit to reveal all deception and lusts that may be hidden in your
heart and then give them to the Lord.

FEBRUARY 2

But put on the Lord Jesus Christ, and make
no provision for the flesh, to fulfill its lusts.
—Romans 13:14

What are you wearing today? Were you prepared for the wintry weather that may have hit the area in which you live today? What about the storms of life? Are you prepared for the bad weather or do they catch you off guard?

Christians must daily put on the Lord Jesus Christ. Just as my clothing protects me for the extreme weather conditions, the spiritual clothing I wear guards me from the winds and storms of life. Have you ever noticed how people dress? You can visualize that person by observing the style of clothing he wears. Just as a man may be characterized by the clothes he wears, Christians ought to be recognized for putting on Christ and exhibiting His life and character in them.

Are you putting on Christ in a way that exhibits Christ? Sometimes the weather catches us off guard and we are not clothed or prepared for the storm that creeps up on us. How often do we fall into sin because we don't plan for it. Dress for the occasion. Put on the Lord Jesus Christ daily and you will be able to weather out any storm that catches you off guard.

FEBRUARY 3

*Finally, my brethren, be strong in the
Lord and in the power of His might.*
—Ephesians 6:10

If you think about it, Christians should have all the strength and power to do that which God has called us to do. But many lack power because they rely on their own wisdom and strength instead of Christ's strength in them. The same power that raised Christ from the dead is available to us every moment of our day.

We must pray that God through His Spirit would teach us to believe in His almighty power and that we may experience this power in our lives. A person only gains physical strength by lifting weights. We can only gain spiritual and emotional strength by lifting up God and spending time in His presence. That is where our strength and power will come from. Believe in God's divine power working in you. Hold onto the promises that God will manifest His power within you.

Be strong in the Lord and in the power of His might. As Paul prayed in Ephesians 3:16, so also I pray for you that God would grant you, according to the riches of His glory, to be strengthened with might through His Spirit in your inner man.

FEBRUARY 4

*Blessed are those who keep His testimonies,
who seek Him with their whole heart. With
my whole heart I have sought You; Oh, let
me not wander from Your commandments!*
—Psalm 119:2, 10

When we want to be successful, we put our whole heart and soul into the matter. An athlete going for the gold will put all the time and energy practicing to be the best athlete in their specialty. Do we do the same with our spiritual conditioning? Do we put our whole heart and soul into living and serving God? Is He not worth the prize?

We spend a lot of time taking care of our physical needs and little time conditioning our spiritual needs. Do you not want to be the best spiritual athlete you possible can be? How important it is to condition yourself daily with prayer, reading God's Word, striving to do His will, and spending time alone with God?

It's a heart matter. Desire to seek Him with your whole heart. Give God permission to take complete control of your heart so that you can learn and train to love Him with your whole heart and soul. Blessed are they who keep His testimonies and seek Him with their whole heart.

FEBRUARY 5

The Lord is my light and my salvation;
whom shall I fear? The Lord is the strength
of my life; of whom shall I be afraid.

—Psalm 27:1

Fear is not from God and yet there are many Christians walking in fear—fear of the unknown, fear of sickness, fear of failing, fear of losing their jobs, fear of not finding a job…the list goes on and on. When fear enters our heart, we lose focus of who our God is and settle our heart on the issue at hand. But our God is bigger than any situation we face and we must put our trust in Him.

When fear strikes you, take authority over it right away and speak to your inner soul and tell yourself that God is in control. His rod and staff moves before you clearing the way of the enemy's snares. You don't need to fear the dark days when He is our Light. You do not need to fear the enemy when you walk in the power of God's Spirit.

When fear tries to take control over you, keep repeating to yourself, "Though I walk through the valley of the shadow of death, I will fear no evil for the Lord is with me (Psalm 23:4). The Lord is my strength and I will not be afraid. The Lord is my Light and my salvation." As God sees your confidence in Him He will move on your behalf. Cast fear forever from your heart.

FEBRUARY 6

Delight yourself also in the Lord, and
He shall give you the desires of your heart.
Commit your way to the Lord, trust also
in Him, and He shall bring it to pass.

—Psalm 37:4–5

Do you commit your ways to the Lord? To commit our ways to the Lord is to entrust God with everything—our lives, our desires, our jobs, our possessions, our health, our family, everything…and believe that He can care for us better than we can care for ourselves. God knows our heart's desires and He delights in seeing us happy and prosperous in life. He really cares about us.

Commit your ways to the Lord and your thoughts will be established (Proverbs 16:3). If you trust in Him, He will not disappoint you. In the midst of adversity, commit your ways to the Lord, cast your burden on Him and He shall sustain you. He shall never permit the righteous to be moved (Psalm 55:22). The more you trust in Him, the easier it is to let go and let God be God. Many times, you are the obstacle that keeps God from moving.

Have you committed your ways to the Lord, not just some of them but all of them? If not, why not? God will not disappoint you. Commit your way to the Lord and trust in Him. Delight yourself in the Lord and He will bring to pass the desires of your heart.

FEBRUARY 7

But He was wounded for our transgressions,
He was bruised for our iniquities;
the chastisement for our peace was upon Him,
and by His stripes we are healed.

—Isaiah 53:5

The Bible doesn't say that we may be healed. The Bible says that by His stripes we *are* healed! Jesus took on all our sins, all our infirmities, all our sicknesses and carried them to Calvary. Jesus who knew no sin took on our sins and infirmities so that we might be made right with God.

So why are so many people not being healed? Many miracles and healings do not take place because of unbelief. It is faith that moves Jesus. Unbelief is telling Jesus I don't think you have the power to remove my sickness from me. Jesus fulfilled prophesy by healing people. They brought many to Him who were demon-possessed and He cast out the spirits with a word and healed all who were sick (Matthew 8:16). Have you ever wondered what that one word was that He spoke? Jesus had so much power that all He had to do was speak and spirits and sickness had to obey. Now that's power.

Jesus is the same yesterday, today, and forevermore. What He did for one He can do for all. Do you need a physical, emotional or spiritual healing? Give it to the Lord and claim your healing. Jesus, you died for my infirmities, I command [name the illness] to leave my body in Jesus name. By Your precious blood I *am* healed. I claim my healing now in Jesus's name. I walk in freedom free from [name the illness] because it is by Your stripes, I *am* healed.

FEBRUARY 8

*For we do not wrestle against flesh and blood, but against
principalities, against powers, against the rulers of the darkness
of this age, against spiritual hosts of wickedness in the heavenly
places. Therefore take up the whole armor of God, that you may be
able to withstand in the evil day, and having done all, to stand.*
—Ephesians 6:12–13

The Lord tells us that it is not people we struggle with. Instead, we
wrestle against spiritual powers from on high. It's hard to win a battle
when we are caught off guard and not prepared for the attack. In the
remaining verses of Ephesians 6, the Lord gives us a warrior's prayer
that we should pray daily for our protection. So today, let's proclaim
victory over the enemy by putting on the whole armor of God.

I am strong in the Lord and in the power of His might. I prepare
for battle by putting my trust in Jesus and by clothing myself with the
full armor of God so that I can stand against every satanic scheme. I
put on the girdle of truth. May I live a life of integrity standing firm in
Your truth so that I will not be deceived and fall into the trap of Satan's
lies. I put on the breast plate of righteousness. May my heart remain
pure and protected from the evil forces of this world. I put on the
shoes of peace. May I stand bravely and walk with tranquility knowing
that I am victorious because the battle has already been won by the
precious blood of Jesus Christ. I take the shield of faith. May I be ready
to quench all the fiery darts of Satan. I put on the helmet of salvation.
May I guard my mind from all spiritual attacks and keep my thoughts
focused on Your truth. I take the sword of the Spirit. May the two edge
sword of Your Word be in my hands so that when Satan tempts me
with twisted cunning words, I can answer as Jesus did, "It is written…"

By faith I have put on the whole armor of God. I stand alert,
watching and praying in the Spirit with all perseverance. Through
Your armor, I live my life with integrity, purity, tranquility, certainty, and with a sound mind. I am strong in the Lord and in the
power of His might and am prepared to live this day in spiritual
victory through Christ Jesus.

FEBRUARY 9

For I will set My eyes on them for good, and I will bring
them back to this land; I will build them and not pull
them down, and I will plant them and not pluck them up.
Then I will give them a heart to know Me, that I am the
Lord; and they shall be My people, and I will be their
God, for they shall return to Me with their whole heart.
—Jeremiah 24:6–7

The Lord has a destiny for each of us. His eyes are upon us, watching over us and making plans and provisions for us to reach our destiny. The Lord rejoices over us to do good. He puts His whole heart and soul into the matter so that we can prosper (Jeremiah 32:41). His plans also include a desire that we would know Him and that He would be the God of our life. He gives each of us a heart to know Him and it is up to us to accept the invitation and to love Him back with our whole heart and soul.

God is gathering His people giving them one heart and one way—that they may fear Him forever, for the good of them and their children after them (Jeremiah 32:39). He will make an everlasting covenant with us, that He will not turn away from doing good; but will put His fear in our hearts so that we will not depart from Him (Jeremiah 32:40).

God will not force Himself on you. He gives you the freedom to choose whether you will follow Him or follow the things of this world. Your decision impacts your children. If you accept the invite, He is there to build you up, to plant hope and dreams into your life and the lives of your children. He is there to plant love and nurture you and not pluck you down. He has given you a heart to know Him. The question is, do you desire to truly know Him?

FEBRUARY 10

As in water face reflects face,
so a man's heart reveals the man.
　　　　　　　　　　　　　　—Proverbs 27:19

W e may lie with our lips but our heart never lies. What is in our heart is who we really are no matter what we tell ourselves or what others may think we are. What is your heart revealing about you? Look deep inside and see what it is saying. Do you dislike some of the things you say or do? Then look deeper into your heart and find the root cause that makes you say or do those things. Deal with that issue. Deal with the hurt, pain, disappointment, fear or whatever the emotion may be that you are feeling, and your attitude towards the situation will change.

Let the love of God enter deep into the wounds of your heart and bring emotional healing to you. Allow God to reveal the true condition of your heart. Seek forgiveness and then allow Him to fix the wounded pieces. Ask God to create a new heart in you and renew a steadfast spirit within you (Psalm 51:10). Respond positively to what the Holy Spirit tells you to do. As you do, you will begin to see a new person develop inside of you. Hear the heartbeat of the Father and let it beat in you and transform you. He will give you a new heart and put a new spirit within you. He will take the heart of stone out of your flesh and give you a heart of flesh (Ezekiel 36:26).

FEBRUARY 11

And the Lord God said, "It is not good that man should
be alone; I will make him a helper comparable to him."
—Genesis 2:18

Feeling lonely does not feel good, in fact, it can make one really depressed. We all feel lonely at some point in our lives. I can be in the same room with someone and yet not feel connected with that person. Emotionally and spiritually we are not united together. We can attend a church service and still not be connected with the people there. We all tend to put on masks to cover our true feelings and emotions. When someone asks you how you are doing, do you tell them the truth? Or do you mask your feelings and pretend everything is okay? If you hide your true feelings, are you really connected with that person?

If you think about it, we can put on that same mask before God. Do you really let God know what's in your heart? If He asks you a question, are you truthful with your answer? You may not feel like being truthful to yourself or to God, but remember that God knows all and He wouldn't ask if He didn't care about you. Do you feel connected with God in church services or are you disconnected because your thoughts are with someone or something else and not on our Lord? Give your full devoted attention to Him and He will take care of the rest.

God is always with you (Matthew 28:20). It is not that He left you but you have not been attentive to His Holy presence. Christ is all and in all (Colossians 3:11). Christ is all you need to get you through your day. He wants to let you know that even though you feel alone, He is always with you. He knows what it feels like to be alone. He experienced it once too when He was on the cross and cried out, "My God, My God, why have you forsaken Me?" (Mark 15:34). He felt alone but He was never really alone, the Father was always with Him. And the Lord wants you to know that He is always with you too.

FEBRUARY 12

Love suffers long and is kind; love does not envy;
love does not parade itself, is not puffed up; does
not behave rudely, does not seek its own, is not
provoked, thinks no evil; does not rejoice in iniquity,
but rejoices in the truth; bears all things, believes all
things, hopes all things, endures all things.
—1 Corinthians 13:4–7

This scripture tell us a lot about the virtues of love, what love is and what love is not. We all want to think that we are loving and caring people, but are we really as loving as we think we are? One way to find out is to read the above scripture again and put your name in place of the word "love." Chances are you hold many of the characteristics of what love is but fall short in a few areas. Those are the areas that the Lord wants you to work on so that those virtues of love will be manifested in you.

Examine your words, actions, and motives to see if you truly walk in love. Everything you do, do out of love. You can give to the poor, have faith to move mountains, speak words of wisdom or literally extend your life to another, but if it is done without love, it is all done in vain. It profits you nothing (1 Corinthians 13:2–3). What is the motivation behind what you do and say? I would suspect that the majority of the time it is all done in love. Each night, examine yourself and see if your day aligns with these verses. If they do, then you can honestly say that you have served the Lord with love for the day. If not, then you need to seek the Lord for forgiveness and strive to do better the next day.

Love never fails (1 Corinthians 13:8). What the world needs is the Father's love and it is our responsibility to share the love of the Father to others. What does God's love look like? Read the above scripture again and this time replace the word "love" with "Christ" and that is what God's unconditional love looks like. Touch a life today. Share the love of God with everyone you encounter.

FEBRUARY 13

Blessed be the Lord, Who daily loads us with benefits,
the God of our salvation! O God, You are more awesome
than Your holy places. The God of Israel is He who gives
strength and power to His people. Blessed be God!
—Psalm 68:19, 35

When you go grocery shopping, you load up your shopping carts with items you have on your list to buy. More likely than not, you have placed items in the shopping cart that were not on your original list. You either needed the items and forgot to add them to the list or your taste buds told you to grab them. Sometimes you add some delights to the cart to surprise a loved one with their favorite snack.

Daily the Lord fills His cart with items that He wants to bless you with. Some of the items were on His original list but as He stuffs your cart, He throws in other blessings that He knew you would need. Other times He just adds an item or two out of pure love, for He knows the joy it will bring you. You will never know how much the Lord daily blesses us with His benefits. If you think about it, we really take so much for granted.

He blesses you with food, water, clothing, shelter, health, jobs, finances, friends, and family. He protects you from accidents, sickness, and harm, many times when you are not even aware of it. He provides you with strength, power, and protection from the forces of darkness. He blesses you with peace, wisdom, and insight and most of all He extends His mercy, forgiveness, and love to you. Take the time today to thank the Lord for all He has done for you and to praise Him for who He is. Daily give back to Him a cart loaded with praise, worship and thanksgiving.

FEBRUARY 14

Be anxious for nothing, but in everything
by prayer and supplication, with thanksgiving,
let your requests be made known to God;
—Philippians 4:6

How can anyone be anxious for nothing and yet that is what we are commanded to do. Think about it…be anxious for nothing. With all the demands and stresses of life can you really be anxious for nothing? Seems impossible doesn't it? When anxiety hits you and you allow it to take over your thoughts, the anxiety brings on worry and you end up believing that God is not able to take care of your need. So how do you not be anxious when circumstances in your life are crumbling down? The answer is by prayer and supplication, bringing your needs before the all-powerful and Almighty God. The power of prayer changes everything. You have to believe that. When you do, the peace of God which surpasses all understanding will guard your heart and mind through Christ Jesus (Philippians 4:7).

There is a peace that comes when you spend time with the Lord for He reassures you that all is in His hands. When you humble yourself under the mighty hand of God, He will exalt you in due time (1 Peter 5:6). The opposite of anxiety and worry is faith. Faith says that although I don't see the results yet, I know they're coming, for my God is bigger than my circumstance. What is on your heart today? Is there a special hardship or concern that needs to be answered? Take it to the Lord who has the power and the wisdom to take care of that need and believe that He always has our best interest at heart. Lord, I ask that you would grant the wishes to those who seek your face today. Grant them the thing that they long for in Jesus's name, I pray (Job 6:8).

FEBRUARY 15

But at midnight Paul and Silas were praying and singing hymns to God, and the prisoners were listening to them. Suddenly there was a great earthquake, so that the foundations of the prison were shaken; and immediately all the doors were opened and everyone's chains were loosed.

—Acts 16:25–26

Paul and Silas did not let their circumstance rob them of their joy or faith in God. At midnight they lifted up their voices in prayer and sang hymns of praise to God and suddenly an earthquake shook the prison and set all the prisoners free. They did not let their situation get the best of them and instead trusted in God and gave Him praise before they even had victory. As a result, not only were they set free, but everyone around them was set free as well. There is something about praise and worship that causes God to move.

Though your situation may be different, you too must have that same faith and sing your way to victory. Be willing to trust God in your circumstances. As you sing a melody in your heart, see the Lord shaking the prison walls of your situation and opening the chains that hold you in bondage. Lift up your voice, sing hymns of praise and see the King of Glory come in and not only set you free but also those around you. To God be the honor, glory, and praise.

FEBRUARY 16

Therefore let us not judge one another anymore,
but rather resolve this, not to put a stumbling
block or a cause to fall in our brother's way.
—Romans 14:13

There is an old saying, don't judge a book by its cover. The same applies to us whenever we start to criticize or judge another by what we see on the outside without examining the whole story. We can take this thought one step further and say that we should not judge the whole story of a person's life by the page they are currently on. We are all a work in progress and the Lord uses circumstances in our life to build character in us to prepare us for our season. When we criticize or judge another, we put a stumbling block in their path and may cause them to fail or lose hope. How many times have we caused ourselves to stumble because of our own critical spirit towards ourselves?

When the urge to judge oneself or another comes to your mind, remind yourself that you or the other person is a "work in progress." Say a prayer for the person. Never judge someone by the page they are currently on, but see the person through the eyes of God and you will discover that their story in life has a different ending. We all shall be like a tree planted by the rivers of water, we shall bring forth fruit in our season and whatever we do shall prosper in Jesus's name (Psalm 1:3).

FEBRUARY 17

"To him who overcomes I will grant to sit with
Me on My throne, as I also overcame and
sat down with My Father on His throne."
—Revelation 3:21

Jesus was an over-comer. Despite the challenges and opposition He faced, He obeyed His Father unto death. Upon the cross, victory over Satan was finally won. You are to be an over-comer in your life as well. Although opposition and challenges will come your way, you must be strong in the Lord. Do not become discouraged with the trials you are facing today, for the Lord sees all and is making intercession on your behalf (Romans 8:34). Do not let complacency, compromise or temptations defeat you; it is not worth the value of your soul.

Continue to walk in the favor of the Lord and remember that Satan is already defeated (John 16:33). Use challenges and opposition to build your character and faith in God. Let the peace of God sustain you as you face adversity, for Christ Himself is our peace (Ephesians 2:14). Let your faith triumph in trouble. You are more than a conqueror through Christ who loves you (Romans 8:37). You are an overcomer because He who is in you is greater than he who is in the world (1 John 4:4). Christ in you, the hope of glory (Colossians 1:27). And when your tribulation is over, you too will be able to say—the enemy is defeated, victory has been won.

FEBRUARY 18

"But where can wisdom be found?
And where is the place of understanding?"
And to man He said, "Behold, the fear
of the Lord, that is wisdom, and to depart
from evil is understanding."
—Job 28:12, 28

Where do you find wisdom? Job asked himself that question and then pondered on it. He told himself that man does not know its value (Job 28:13). Job goes on to say that it's so valuable that it cannot be purchased with gold, silver, and precious stones nor can it be exchanged for jewelry. The price of wisdom is far above all of these (Job 28:15–19). Then Job asks himself the question again, from where then does wisdom come from and where is the place of understanding (Job 28:20)? Job answered his question by saying it is hidden from the eyes of all living but God understands its way and He knows its place (Job 28:21, 23). To man God said, behold the fear of the Lord, that is wisdom, and to depart from evil is understanding.

In Proverbs 3, Solomon knew where wisdom came from and gave us some guidance. We are to trust in the Lord with all our heart and lean not on our own understanding. In all our ways acknowledge God and He shall direct our paths (Proverbs 3:5–6). Happy is the man who finds wisdom, and the man who gains understanding; for her proceeds are better than the profits of silver and her gain than fine gold. Wisdom is more precious than rubies, and all the things you may desire cannot compare with her (Proverbs 3:13–15). Wisdom is a tree of life to all who take hold of her and happy are all who retain her (Proverbs 3:18).

You need not search for answers to many of the mysteries of life, but only trust in God and follow Him in obedience. God does not require you to understand His will, just obey it. Understanding comes as you walk in obedience. If you make the Lord your highest priority in life, wisdom shall be given to you each day as needed.

FEBRUARY 19

For I consider that the sufferings of this
present time are not worthy to be compared
with the glory which shall be revealed in us.
—Romans 8:18

Are you fully convinced that what God has promised you, He is able to perform? Or do your current trials and tribulations cause you to doubt and lose hope? You should not allow God's timing of things to discourage you or cause you to lose faith because your promise has not been fulfilled yet. The sufferings of this present time are not worthy to be compared with the glory which shall be revealed in you.

In His wisdom, God sets an appropriate time for everything. Put your complete trust in God regardless of how long He decides to fulfill it. For your light affliction, which is but for a moment, is working for you a far exceeding and eternal weight of glory (2 Corinthians 4:17). Trust God and hold onto this promise as you wait on His timing.

There is a season for everything (Ecclesiastes 3:1). If an apple is picked too early, it may taste bitter or sour and not sweet like it's supposed to taste. Likewise, if your promise is fulfilled before its season, the taste of its fruits may not be what you expected. Allow God to nurture your promise until it is at its prime and you will not only see the beauty, but you will also taste the sweetness of the fruits of His promise to you.

FEBRUARY 20

The word of God is living and powerful, and
sharper than any two-edged sword, piercing
even to the division of soul and spirit, and
of joints and marrow, and is a discerner of
the thoughts and intents of the heart.

—Hebrews 4:12

If you ever watched a movie where there were soldiers fighting with swords, one can see how a sword can easily penetrate through the body and bring death to the one being pierced. If a soldier loses his sword in the midst of the battle, it is just a matter of time before his life will come to an end for he has no weapon to defend himself. You face many battles in life but are you using the right weapon to defend ourselves? God gives you a weapon that is far more piercing than a sword. He gives you His Word. The Word of God is living, powerful, and sharper than any two-edged sword.

The Word of God will reveal the true condition of your heart if you allow it to. When you pursue God's Word as your daily wisdom, God is able to work His will in your life. Everything in your life will be judged and brought in line with His Word. Allow His Word to pierce the very depths of your soul and spirit, bringing to death those things that are not from God. His Word helps you discern whether your motives are right or selfish. It convicts you when you are wrong, and teaches you how to live right. Not only read God's Word, but apply it to your life as well; otherwise, you are only deceiving yourself. It would be like a soldier holding his sword in battle but never using it. The Word of God will only be as powerful and piercing in your life as you allow it to be.

There is no creature hidden from His sight, but all things are naked and open to the eyes of Him to whom we must give account (Hebrews 4:13). You can never be without the Word of God, for like a soldier in battle with no sword, so it will be to you—it will only be a matter of time before you are destroyed.

FEBRUARY 21

*"Heal the sick, cleanse the lepers, raise the dead,
cast out demons. Freely you have received, freely give.
Therefore whoever confesses Me before men, him I
will confess before my Father who is in heaven."*
—Matthew 10:8, 32

God blesses you so that you can be a blessing to others. By God's grace you have received the gifts of salvation, forgiveness, freedom, healing, restoration, and much more. It must now be your mission to give out to others what God has so richly blessed you with. Be concerned about the hurts of those around you, whether it be family, friends, or strangers. You are to continually reach out to help others, allow them to see Christ in you, and let them know that what God has done for you, He will do for them.

You are the hands and feet of Jesus, and you must go about doing the works that Jesus did. Be willing to pray for someone in their time of need and not just when it's convenient for you. Take authority over sickness and disease and command them to leave in Jesus's name. Be God's spokesman and decree miracles in people's lives. Bring restoration to those who have been held in bondage to the lies and deception of Satan. Freely you have received, freely give. Confess Christ before others and let them know that they can have the same freedom as you do. Jesus came to save those who were lost. Bring salvation to those who are lost by leading them to Christ.

Your life on earth is but a vapor and is passing away quickly (James 4:14). What are you doing with the time you have left? Continue the works of the Father and share the love of Christ to them. Ask the Lord to put someone in your path today who needs a touch from Him. Then allow the Lord to use you to show the Father's love to that person.

FEBRUARY 22

For our light affliction, which is but for
a moment, is working for us a far more
exceeding and eternal weight of glory.
—2 Corinthians 4:17

God never said He would take away all your difficulties or sufferings. But if you wait out the storms of life, the anguish you feel will be a light affliction, compared to the rewards that accompany your faith and the weight of His glory that follows. Just as a woman in labor forgets the pains of her labor after the baby is delivered, so too it will be when you labor through the affliction and bring new life into the situation. When a baby is aborted, there is no new life, only death. If you abort the labor of affliction, you will kill the new life that God is forming within you. Press on and not abort the labor of His love. Your light affliction is but for a moment, but the reward and weight of His glory is for eternality.

Are you facing a storm in your life right now? Do not lose heart. Wait out the storm. Seek comfort and strength by reading God's Word. God is the one who gives power to the weak. To those who have no might, He increases strength (Isaiah 40:29). Renew your strength in Him, and you shall mount up with wings like eagles, you shall run and not be weary, and shall walk and not faint (Isaiah 40:31). The sufferings of your present time are not worthy to be compared with the glory which shall be revealed to you.

FEBRUARY 23

I will bless the Lord at all times; His
praise shall continually be in my mouth.
—Psalm 34:1

We all have habits, some are good while others not so good. But one good habit to acquire is to praise the Lord at all times no matter what your day may bring. Just knowing that the Lord loves you will bring comfort in the hours you need it the most. The Lord must become your source of life and joy. Through your difficulties, the Lord tests your love for Him.

God's love is constant and you should never question His love for you. His love should not be based on your own happiness or unhappiness. Many people blame the Lord for their circumstances and their unhappiness. If you are unhappy, it is because of your own wrong reactions. One way to restore peace, joy, and happiness in your life is to raise up your voice and give praise to God throughout your day. Praise Him when you wake up, praise Him when you eat, praise Him when you leave for work, praise Him at work, praise Him before you put your head to rest. Praise, praise, praise Him. Continually praise Him.

If you will get into the habit of continually praising God, your heart will be filled with peace and joy no matter what the day may bring. I release the joy of the Lord into your heart today. Bless the Lord, O my soul for all the marvelous works you have done for me. Let all breath that is in me praise Your Holy Name.

FEBRUARY 24

"However, when He, the Spirit of truth,
has come, He will guide you into all
truth; for He will not speak on His own
authority, but whatever He hears He will
speak; and He will tell you things to come."
—John 16:13

The Bible promises us that God will instruct us, teach us, and guide us into all truth. But the ultimate decision is ours. Just like the saying—you can lead a horse to water but you can't force it to drink—the same applies to our lives as well. The Holy Spirit can lead us to what we should do, but never controls or forces us to do anything against our will. Life would be much simpler if the Holy Spirit did control us, especially when we have important decisions to make or when we are being tempted by the enemy. But that is not the case.

That is why it is so important to pray that the Holy Spirit aligns your will to the Father's will. Command your soul to submit to your spirit and your spirit to come to the forefront. Then command your spirit to submit to the Holy Spirit. The Holy Spirit is there to guide you, to help you discern what is truth and what is a lie, to show you where you are compromising your walk with God, to steer you into choosing the narrow path and avoiding the way that leads you into destruction. As you develop more sensitivity to His presence, it becomes easier to know the will of the Father and what He wants you to do. You will worry less about the decisions you make, and trust that the Holy Spirit is guiding you.

Will you make mistakes? Of course you will. But when you do make mistakes, God will use them as an opportunity to learn and become more sensitive to His guidance. Holy Spirit, open our spiritual ears to hear Your voice. Guide us into all truth and show us the path that we should follow. Instruct us and teach us in the way we should go and guide us with Your eye.

FEBRUARY 25

Jesus answered, "You could have no power
at all against Me unless it had been given
you from above. Therefore the one who
delivered Me to you has the greater sin."

—John 19:11

As children of God, we are never victims of our circumstances. Many things can happen to you, but only if God allows them to. You may not understand why God allows sickness, suffering or delays to your prayers, but you just have to trust in Him to know what is best. God will allow situations or events to happen to draw you closer to Him or to bring glory to His name. Many times you struggle, when you could be resting in the arms of our Father. You concern yourself with the actions of others, become anxious, and then react in a way that is ungodly. You forget that man has no power over us unless it had been given from above.

Unrest comes when you take your focus off God. Negative reactions come when you move before God is ready, or when you take things into your own hands and move without God. Positive reactions come when you move with God. Positive results come when you put your trust in God and allow Him to work on your behalf. Trusting in God brings peace into any situation. Your prayer must be "In God I put my trust; I will not be afraid. What can man do to me?" (Psalm 56:11) Although men will fail or disappoint you, God is faithful and true to His Word. To believe in the Word of God is to trust in the Word of God. Simply believe and trust.

FEBRUARY 26

And God said to Noah, "The end of all flesh
has come before Me, for the earth is filled with
violence through them; and behold, I will destroy
them with the earth. Make yourself an ark of
gopherwood; make rooms in the ark, and cover it
inside and outside with pitch. Thus Noah did;
according to all that God commanded him, so he did.
—Genesis 6:13–14, 22

When Noah was commanded by God to build an ark, he ventured out to do exactly what God had told him to do. His neighbors, friends, and family must have thought he was crazy but that did not stop Noah. There was no sign of a great storm approaching; and as each day passed, one can only imagine the ridicule and mockery he received. Even so, Noah continued to build the ark. He believed and trusted in God, and did what God asked. Noah's obedience led to God's blessings and rewards. In the end, it saved him and his family. As God fulfilled His promise to destroy all mankind, He wiped out the remaining people by the great flood while Noah and his family were safe in the ark.

Is God asking you to do something out of the ordinary? Are you holding back from carrying out what God has told you to do because of fear, ridicule or reasoning from man? No matter how out of the ordinary it may seem to man, if God has put something in your heart, then have the faith like Noah and the willingness to obey God no matter what people may think or say. God may not be calling you to build an ark, but whatever He is calling you to do, it has a purpose in His great scheme of things. Step out in faith and obedience and watch God's plan unfold.

FEBRUARY 27

Thus says the Lord, your Redeemer,
the Holy One of Israel: "I am the Lord
your God, who teaches you to profit, Who
leads you by the way that you should go."
—Isaiah 48:17

In order to be taught by someone, you must possess a teachable spirit—one that is willing to learn and willing to let go of old mindsets. You also must trust the person who is instructing you. Everyone wants to profit in life. Some are successful, while others are not. Some are misled by others and end up losing their entire life savings because they trusted in the wrong people. God will never lead you astray. He will instruct and teach you the way you should go in order to be successful in life (Psalm 32:8). It is God who teaches you to profit.

God wants you to work hard, to be wise with your spending and to remember to count your blessings, for it is He who gives you the power to gain wealth (Deuteronomy 8:18). It is the blessings from the Lord that makes one rich (Proverbs 10:22). When you fail to recognize that, chances are you will end up losing it. That is what happened to the Israelites. They did not recognize that it was God who gave them the grain, wine, oil, and multiplied their gold and silver. When God saw their ungratefulness and pride, He returned and took it away (Hosea 2:8–9).

No job is secure. I learned this first hand when I was terminated from a company after working there seventeen years; my position was outsourced to a company in India. No savings or retirement is secure. They can be here one day and gone the next. Thank the Lord He gave me wisdom to profit those years when I was employed. Nothing is secure in life except your relationship with God. Everything you possess is a blessing from Him, and you need to thank God for what you have. Take the time today to thank God who gives you the power to get wealth, and then pray for those who are in need of work.

FEBRUARY 28

At Gibeon the Lord appeared to
Solomon in a dream by night; and God
said, "Ask! What shall I give you?"
—1 Kings 3:5

The Lord appeared to Solomon in a dream and God said, "Ask! What shall I give you?" Solomon asked for an understanding heart to judge people, that he might discern between good and evil. The Lord was very pleased with the thing Solomon had requested. Because Solomon did not ask for personal wealth, long life, and the destruction of his enemies, the Lord did according to what Solomon asked for and more. The Lord not only made him the wisest king of all time, but He also gave Him riches and honor. The Lord promised to give him a long life if Solomon obeyed His commandments and walked in His ways (1 Kings 3:5–13).

God expects you to ask. Many times He wants to bless you or answer a need you have, but you never go to Him with your request. Instead you go about your business trying to work things out on your own. God wants you to ask Him to meet all your needs, not just when a crisis comes, but all the time. When you ask, ask in faith, believing that He has your best interest at heart. You may not always get what you ask for, but God does respond in ways that always benefit you most. When you have a heart like Solomon, oftentimes He will give you things you didn't even ask for because He just wants to bless you and demonstrate his love for you.

Is there something you need from God today? Go boldly before God and let your requests be known to Him. Jesus said, until now you have asked nothing in My name. Ask in faith and in Jesus's name, and watch God move on your behalf. Ask and you will receive, that your joy may be full (John 16:24).

MARCH 1

Then he said to me, "Do not fear, Daniel, for from the first day that you set your heart to understand, and to humble yourself before your God, your words were heard; and I have come because of your words."
—Daniel 10:12

Do you believe God is able to meet all your needs? It's easy to say yes to this question when everything is going well. But when you are in your lowest valley, are you still able to say yes? When life throws you a few blows and knocks you down, gain the strength to pick yourself back up. God is committed to meeting your needs. He has all the wisdom, power, and ability necessary to change any situation. God is faithful to His Word. He is the same yesterday, today, and forever (Hebrews 13:8).

When God has not met our need, we begin to look for reasons why and question if He is the God He says He is. Many make the error of saying that God has not lived up to His promises. Who are we to question God? Remember that nothing is too great or too powerful to stand in God's way if He chooses to act. The questions we should be asking are: What does God want to change in me as I wait on Him? What am I saying or doing in the midst of my circumstances? Continually seek God to see if there is anything you are doing or not doing that is keeping God from meeting your need.

Only God knows the circumstances that led to your situation and only God knows what it will take for Him to act on your behalf. Just because it seems like God has not moved in your favor, it does not mean that God has not heard your prayers, or that God will not meet your need. You do not know what God is doing behind the scenes. God asks you to trust Him and obey Him no matter what may become of your circumstances. Trust God to meet your every need, in His timing, and in His way.

MARCH 2

The Lord will guide you continually, and satisfy
your soul in drought, and strengthen your bones;
You shall be like a watered garden, and like a
spring of water, whose waters do not fail.
—Isaiah 58:11

No matter how down and out you feel, no one can fill the void you feel in your soul. People may temporarily fill the gap, but eventually it wears off and the void returns. Why? Because it is the longing in your soul to draw close to God. He is the companionship that you long for. Nothing and no one but God will satisfy that void. It is only God who can satisfy the longing you feel in your soul to draw close to Him. If you draw Him close to your heart, He will satisfy every longing and fill your hungry soul with goodness (Psalm 107:9). The more you reach out to God, the less you depend on yourself or others. What others provide is only temporary and will not last very long. It is the Lord's presence that will sustain you.

Only the Lord can take a drought land, continually water it, and make it into a spring of water. That is what He wants to do for you. He is the only One that can satisfy the drought you feel in your soul. He is the only One that will stir up the waters within you and bring forth renewed life. Is your soul thirsty or longing for something? Draw close to God. He will guide you continually and satisfy your soul in drought. In the midst of your drought, it may only feel like droplets are falling, but remain in His presence and soon you will be like a watered garden, like a spring of water whose water never fails.

MARCH 3

And the Lord restored Job's losses when he prayed
for his friends. Indeed the Lord gave Job twice as
much as he had before. Now the Lord blessed the
latter days of Job more than his beginning.
—Job 42:10, 12

God expects you to be obedient to Him no matter how you may feel or how things may look. We all know the story of Job and how all his possessions and family were taken away from him (Job 1:13–22). Then God allowed Satan to attack his health, but he was not allowed to take his life (Job 2:6). In the midst of Job's misery, there came three of his friends. Instead of comforting him, they judged his pitiful situation. They insisted that his misery was because of his wickedness, for surely God would not allow this to happen to the righteous (Job 2:11, Job 36:33).

From the time that Satan first attacked Job until the very end, God had his eye on the whole situation. In the end, the Lord had the final say. He rebuked Job's three friends and had them go to Job and offer up for themselves a burnt offering. The Lord already saw the heart of Job and knew that he would pray for his three friends for He said, "My servant Job shall pray for you and I will accept him." Had Job not prayed, the Lord would have dealt with them according to their folly (Job 42:7–8). This should be a warning to you to not judge others. You can bet that after all the critical things these men said to Job, the last thing Job felt like doing was to pray for his friends. But he did. He obeyed God and because of his obedience, Job was restored twice as much as he had before (Job 42:10).

God allows things to happen to the just as well as the unjust. The fact that you are a Christian does not mean you will have a life free from adversity. When adversity comes, believe that God is still in charge. If you are obedient to Him He will bless your latter days more than your beginning. Do not allow your emotions to cause you to react ungodly. Do what is right and pray for those who persecute you.

MARCH 4

The rich rules over the poor, and
the borrower is servant to the lender.
—Proverbs 22:7

Americans have fallen into the trap of buying what they want instead of what they need. We have fallen into the trap of buy now and pay later because we do not have the finances to pay for it now. In this scripture, God tells us how He feels about debt and warns us that we will become a slave to the lender. Yet millions of Christians and non-Christians alike believe that the time is now to purchase something, whether they have the money for it or not. With the changes in law regarding credit card companies, many are going to find out real soon what it really cost them to purchase their wants with credit.

It would be nice to live debt free but for many there are certain debts that cannot be avoided: mortgages, car payments and unexpected medical bills. It's not our needs that get us in trouble, it's the luxuries in life that we think we must have. Our government is even worse off. We have borrowed and borrowed until we now have a national debt in the trillions of dollars. We would not think to sell our children into slavery, but that is exactly what the government has done with our children and grandchildren, for it is they who will ultimately be responsible for paying our national debt.

We and our government need to get back to the basic principles of life and not spend unless the money is there for us to purchase the product. We must seek the Lord for His wisdom on how we can be good stewards of His money. After all, God is the one who enabled us to have a job and become financially blessed. Avoid borrowing when possible. Be a good steward of His money and invest and spend wisely.

MARCH 5

Keep your heart with all diligence,
for out of it spring the issues of life.
—Proverbs 4:23

You are to guard your heart and keep it pure, for out of it will spring the issues of life. Many speak words but their hearts are hollow. They say things that people want them to say instead of being honest and speaking from their hearts. Many will speak from their emotions and then regret later what they have spoken. You can usually tell when someone is being genuine and speaking from his heart.

You need to ask the Holy Spirit to be a guard to your lips and to guide you in the words that need to be spoken. How you say something will have a great impact on how another will receive the words you speak. Speak in love. Your intentions may be good, but the way you present it may not be. Instead of degrading someone when you confront him, speak to him in a manner which will encourage him to change. Think about how you would want to be confronted with an issue. Would you appreciate someone addressing you with the same words and demeanor you use for others?

Listening with a pure heart is just as important. Emotions, circumstances, and weariness are interferences that can cause you to not hear correctly. When listening to others, tune out those things that are causing interference and listen to the person with a pure heart. Your words and reactions to things spoken will be quite different when you first listen with a pure and sincere heart. Keep your heart with all diligence, for out of it spring the issues of life.

MARCH 6

For you are the temple of the living God. As God
has said: "I will dwell in them and walk among them.
I will be their God, and they shall be My people."
—2 Corinthians 6:16

God's greatest desire is for you to have a personal relationship with Him. God fills you with His Holy spirit that He may dwell within you and be with you constantly. Just like He walked and talked with Moses and others in the Bible, so He desires to walk and talk with you. He wants to help you with your daily struggles and share His love and joy with you.

God calls you to come out from among the ungodly and separate yourself unto Him (2 Corinthians 6:17). Those whom God walked with throughout the Bible were those who were people after God's heart. Do not engage in things that are immoral, unclean or impure. Instead, you are to seek after and embrace the things that are on God's heart. When you live righteously, God will receive you and will be a Father to you, and we shall be His child (2 Corinthians 6:18). Having these promises, cleanse yourself from all filthiness of the flesh and spirit, perfecting holiness in the fear of God (2 Corinthians 7:1). Having these promises, this should motivate you to pursue a lifestyle of holiness.

Your body is the temple of the Holy Spirit, who lives in you and was given to you by God. God bought you with a high price. So you must honor God with your body (1 Corinthians 6:19–20). You must keep yourself pure for Him to abide in. God is not looking for perfection. He is looking for those who want a relationship with Him and are willing to allow Him to move in their lives. If you do not know God on a personal level, ask Him into your heart today. Ask Him to fill you with His Holy Spirit and to be the Lord of your life.

MARCH 7

The eyes of the Lord are in every place,
keeping watch on evil and the good.
—Proverbs 15:3

The eyes of the Lord are on the righteous and His ears are open to their cry (Psalm 34:15). Righteousness is not based upon how you follow man's laws. Righteousness in God's eyes is based upon how you live in accordance with God's standards (Genesis 6:9). God is the ultimate standard that must be followed to define justice and righteousness (Ezra 9:15). You will be judged based upon His standard. There is no creature hidden from His sight, but all things are naked and open to the eyes of Him to whom you must give account (Hebrews 4:13).

The eyes of the Lord are in every place, keeping watch on the evil and good. God sees everything you do, both the good and the bad. Nothing escapes Him. Even your thoughts are heard by Him. His eyes are on all your ways; they are not hidden from His face, nor is your iniquity hidden from His eyes. He will repay double for your iniquity and your sins (Jeremiah 16:17–18). You will be held accountable for your actions as well as for your inactions. The Lord will give everyone according to his ways and according to the fruit of his doings (Jeremiah 32:19).

The eyes of the Lord run to and fro throughout the whole earth to show Himself strong on behalf of those whose heart is loyal to Him (2 Chronicles 16:9). The Lord delights when you do good and bless others. The Lord looks for hearts who are loyal to Him. He hears every kind word you speak and sees every hidden act of kindness you show to others. These things reveal the love of the Father to others. Today, take some time to bless someone. Buy a cup of coffee for the person in line behind you or leave a generous tip to a waitress who is having a bad day. Brighten up someone's day and your heart will be touched too.

MARCH 8

Behold, I set before you today a blessing and a curse:
the blessing, if you obey the commands of the Lord your
God which I command you today; and the curse, if you
do not obey the commandments of the Lord your God.
—Deuteronomy 11:26–28

From an early age, you were taught by your parents that there are rewards for obedience and consequences for disobedience. As you grew older, you braved the risk of getting caught by doing something you knew you should not. Sometimes you got away with it. Other times you faced the unpleasant consequence of your disobedience as well as observing looks of disappointment on your parents' faces. Knowing you disappointed your parents hurt worse than the punishment you received.

As Christians, we know that we are supposed to be obedient to our Heavenly Father. What drives you to be obedient? Some are obedient for the sole reason of not having to face the consequences of their disobedience. Others are driven by the fact that they know it pleases God and anticipate the blessings that follow for their obedience. But obedience is really a heart matter. You have to get to the point that knowing you disappointed your Heavenly Father hurts worse than the consequence of your sin. The closer you draw to God and the deeper your love grows for Him, the more you will desire to be obedient for the sole reason that you love Him. Rewards and consequences will no longer be the driving force for your actions. Your love for Him is what will drive you to be obedient.

Small choices in life may seem insignificant, but put them all together and they lead to a lifestyle of constant obedience or disobedience. What lifestyle are you choosing?

MARCH 9

"Watch and pray, lest you enter into temptation.
The spirit indeed is willing, but the flesh is weak."
—Matthew 26:41

Children learn quickly that if they play with fire, they will get burned. A child touching a hot stove burner learns to never touch it again. The Lord warns us throughout scripture that if we play with fire, we will get burned. It's a shame we have not learned from childhood that once we have been burned by something, stay away from it. Why is it that we think we can get away with something that burned us in the past?

Temptations are all around you. If you give in to the pleasures of life, eventually you will get burned. Many times you pray too late. Your careless choices have placed you in a fire and then you want the Lord to save you before you get burned. You can't expect God to rescue you from the consequences of your sins. God desires to help you, but you need to seek His face before the temptation to sin comes knocking at your door. God warns you that even though your spirit may be willing, your flesh is too weak to bypass the temptation.

The Lord tells us to watch and pray for we really don't understand ourselves. We want to do what is right, but we don't do it. Instead, we do what we hate (Romans 7:15). If you do not watch and pray, you will not be able to resist the flesh's nature to sin against God. You want to do go, but you don't. You don't want to do what is wrong, but you do it anyway. It is not that your spirit wills to do it, but it is because sin dwells in you (Romans 7:19–20). Take heed, watch and pray! Watch for those things that want to lure you into sin and flee from them before the temptation takes over and your flesh is too weak to resist. Lord, give us the strength to resist any temptation that may come our way. May we learn from our mistakes and like a child, stay away from those things that will burn us.

MARCH 10

My soul thirsts for God, for the living God.
When shall I come and appear before God?
—Psalm 42:2

Does your soul thirst for God? Is there a yearning in your spirit that cries out to God, "I need more of you"? Do you feel a void in your life, a void that no one or anything can fill? This void that you are feeling can only be met by the Lord. Deep down in your soul you are thirsting for more of God. Your heart and flesh are crying out for the living God. So how do you fill that void? It's really not that difficult but it does require time on your part. In order to draw near to God and fellowship with Him, give God the time to make Himself known to you. When you approach God, usually you approach Him in prayer with all your needs, all your desires, and all the cares of others who have asked you to pray for them. Your heart is not set on waiting on His presence and hearing what He has to say, but it needs to.

Communication is a two way street. You need to talk less, sit quietly, and wait upon the Lord to speak. It is not the volume of words in prayer that have the power, but it is your faith in action believing that God hears your prayers and desires to commune with you more than you do with Him. Take some time today to sit quietly before the Lord. Meditate on a scripture, fix your eyes on Jesus, and then spontaneously journal what the Lord is speaking to you.

MARCH 11

There is a way that seems right to a
man, but its end is the way of death.
—Proverbs 14:12

Be aware of false peace that may enter your heart. Usually this happens when your spirit is not sensitive to the Holy Spirit. You build false hope because of the comfort you feel. It would be similar to a person living in a house that has carbon monoxide leaking inside. The gas is odorless and cannot be detected unless one has a carbon monoxide detector. If carbon monoxide builds inside the home and the detector fails to go off, the person inside the house soon dies in a peaceful sleep.

The way of a fool is right in his own eyes, but he who heeds counsel is wise (Proverbs 12:15). Fools will listen to their own hearts and not listen to wise counsel. They despise wisdom and instruction (Proverbs 1:7). Don't be a fool! Seek counsel from God and He shall direct your paths. Do not be wise in your own eyes but fear the Lord and depart from evil. It will be health to your flesh and strength to your bones (Proverbs 3:6–8).

In Luke, we read about the parable of the Pharisee and the tax collector. The Pharisee was wise is his own eyes. When he went to the temple to pray, he thanked God that he was not like the extortioners, unjust, adulterers or even the tax collector who was also in the temple praying. He had a self-righteous attitude and bragged how he fasted and gave his tithes. The tax collector on the other hand would not so much as raise his eyes to heaven, but beat his breast, and asked God to be merciful to him for he was a sinner. This sinner, not the Pharisee, went home justified, forgiven of the guilt of sin and placed in right standing with God (Luke 18:9–14).

Be certain that the peace you feel is the result of walking in obedience to God and being in His will. Holy Spirit, may Your wisdom lead me down paths of righteousness and avoid paths of evil. Warn me when danger is approaching.

MARCH 12

A merry heart does good, like medicine,
but a broken spirit dries the bones.
—Proverbs 17:22

Our countenance not only has an effect on our spirit, but also the spirits of those around us. Hang around a negative critical person for long and his downiest spirit will muster up inside of you as well. People who have drama in their lives, where everything is a crisis, wear other people down to the point that their spirits are broken. You have to choose wisely with whom you want to spend your time.

Oftentimes your heart is sorrowful because you have not laid your carnal man aside. Many of your sorrows and grief are caused by unmet fleshly desires. You place unnecessary weights upon your heart that are directly related to worldly affections. As a result, anxiety sets in and causes depression. Carnal sorrow can really tear a man down and eat at the very core of his being. Relinquish those things that break your spirit and give them to God. It is Godly sorrow, repentance and pure actions of heart that makes one's heart cheerful. A merry heart makes a cheerful countenance (Proverbs 15:13).

What is the condition of your heart today? Is your countenance cheerful or dried up like bones? If your heart is not merry, seek the Lord with godly sorrow and true repentance. The purification will make your heart cheerful. Surrender all to Him. It will bring you relief and anxiety will melt away. A merry heart does wonders to your soul and disposition and will also affect those around you. Be a person whom others want to be with because they feel the peace that is within you. Be medicine to their broken spirits and dry bones.

MARCH 13

But the Lord said to Samuel, "Do not look at his
appearance or at his physical statue, because I have refused
him. For the Lord does not see as man sees; for man looks
at the outward appearance, but the Lord looks at the heart."
— 1 Samuel 16:7

Man tends to judge a person's character by his appearance but we have no idea what is hidden in a person's heart. I view this similar to when I buy apples. I bring some very nice looking apples home from the grocery store only to find out that some of the apples are rotten in the inside. How deceiving the appearance of those apples were, especially when they blended in with some good ones. The same is true with people. They look so convincing that they are pure and genuine but later we find out that their outward appearance and demeanor fooled many people. We may have been fooled, but the Lord was not fooled, and He will refuse them.

What does the inside of your heart look like? Is your appearance deceiving and your heart filled with some decay? All sin is a result of the condition of your heart, whether it be resentment, jealousy, lust, rebellion, pride, lying…you name it…it all originates in your heart. Sin is a heart condition that must be dealt with from within. One way to change your heart is to fill it with the Word of God. When you saturate your heart with God's Word, His Word reveals your sinfulness. When you sin, it is God that you sin against, not man. Allow God's Word and the Holy Spirit to cleanse you from the inside out. You don't want the Lord telling someone to not look at your appearance because your heart is not right and He has refused you. Get your heart right before God. What is hidden in your heart? Your Word Lord I have hidden in my heart that I might not sin against You (Psalm 119:11).

MARCH 14

And He said to me, "My grace is sufficient for
you, for My strength is made perfect in weakness."
Therefore most gladly I will rather boast in my
infirmities, that the power of Christ may rest upon me.
Therefore I take pleasure in infirmities, in reproaches,
in needs, in persecutions, in distresses, for Christ's
sake. For when I am weak then I am strong.
—2 Corinthians 12:9–10

Sometimes the Lord has to break you so that He can use you in a greater way. When you humble yourself before the Lord, it is then that you realize that weakness is strength. For it is during your weakness that you learn to lean on God. You cannot handle the situation on your own but must depend on God.

God is a merciful God and He will give you the grace that you need to be victorious in every circumstance. God uses adversity as a bridge to a deeper relationship with Him. Be willing to walk across that bridge and embrace His love. Take pleasure in infirmities, in reproaches, in needs, in persecutions, in distresses, for Christ's sake. Allow the power of Christ to rest upon you.

If you are reproached for the name of Christ, blessed are you, for the Spirit of glory and of God rests upon you (1 Peter 4:14). You are to glory in your tribulations, knowing that tribulations produces perseverance; and perseverance, character; and character, hope (Romans 5:3–4). Allow the adversities in your life to produce perseverance, character and hope.

MARCH 15

My soul, wait silently for God alone,
for my expectation is from Him.

—Psalm 62:5

What God says undoubtedly has more worth than what man says. Yet when we go before God in prayer, we are quick to tell Him our desires and needs without allowing Him to speak to us. In our prayer time, we need to spend more time being silent before God. We must wait on Him to speak what is on His heart.

I don't know about you, but waiting for things to happen can be challenging at times. If I have somewhere to go and need to be there at a certain time and someone is delaying me, or if I have to wait in a doctor's office for an extended period of time, I can become impatient. I feel my time is valuable and it could be spent doing other things that I need to get done. I have to be careful that I don't become impatient before God too. God does not spring into action on my timetable but on His. As I wait upon God in silence, I have to give Him His time. After all, His time is valuable too. God often waits until the last minute to intervene, and if we leave too early, we will miss out on His presence and His blessing. Waiting on God builds and strengthens our faith.

Do you struggle with waiting? In your silence, meditate on His love, His holiness, His power, and His glory. As you reverence God and worship Him, your heart will be open for Him to impart into you. Such time in worship is not a waste of time. You should not turn away from it even if it feels different at first. As you become more accustomed to it, His presence will abide with you throughout your day. I will wait on the Lord, my soul waits, and in His Word I find hope (Psalm 130:5). Wait on the Lord, and you will find not only hope, but peace as well.

MARCH 16

Make Your face to shine upon thy servant;
Save me for Your mercies' sake.
—Psalm 31:16

Everyone looks forward to those bright sunny days. When you see that sun beaming in the morning, you expect it to be there throughout your day. But that may not always be the case. There are many days when the sunshine is pushed away with clouds of darkness, and soon after the downpour of rain begins. Your life is very similar to the weather. It can start out shinning bright, bringing sunshine to your heart, but then the circumstances in life have a way of clouding your day. When things are getting stressful at work, I look forward to taking a walk outside and letting the sun shine upon my face. There is another Son who wants to shine upon us as well, and if we allow Him to, His countenance will be upon us all day long, no matter what weather we have to face in our lives.

As you begin a new day hoping that the sun will be shining, meditate on this scripture until you feel the radiance of the Lord resting upon you. Take the time necessary until you feel His light penetrating into your heart. Then when the clouds of life start to surround your day, you can rest in the knowledge that the Son is still there lighting your path. No darkness can penetrate through the Light of God that resides in you.

MARCH 17

Ho! Everyone who thirsts, come to the waters; and
you who have no money, come, buy and eat. Yes, come,
buy wine and milk without money and without price.
—Isaiah 55:1

Picture yourself walking along the shoreline of the beach, the coolness of the water washing over your feet. It's very hot outside and the sun is penetrating through you. You become very thirsty but the only water around is the salt water from the ocean. You continue along your journey, and all you can think about is water. You are so thirsty for water that you say, "I must have water or I will die."

Now that I have you thirsting for water, the Lord tells us that He who is thirsty, come to the waters—the Living Waters. The picture you just imagined is the same desperation your soul should have in thirsting for God. Your cry ought to be—"I must have more of the Living Water or I will die." Water meets your physical needs by stabilizing and cooling your body. Water transports nutrients, dilutes food, and carries waste from your body. It washes and bathes every cell and hydrates your skin. If you do not drink water throughout the day, your body begins to cry out for it. When it is not supplied, your body will try to find the source in some unhealthy way.

The Living Water meets all your needs—physical, emotional, and spiritual. When you spend time with the Lord, your thoughts are stabilized and your soul is refreshed. The Living Water transports nutrients throughout your body and brings healing. As you spend time reading the Word of God, it dilutes the impurities in your body, and through repentance, dispels all waste from your inner being. If you allow God to speak to you, the Living Water will wash and bathe every cell, renewing and refreshing your mind, body, and soul. Jesus said, those who are thirsty come. Come to the Living Waters. It is a free invitation to an abundant life. How thirsty are you?

MARCH 18

He has made everything beautiful in its time. Also He has
put eternity in their hearts, except no one can find out the work
that God does from beginning to end. I know that nothing is
better for them than to rejoice, and to do good in their lives.
—Ecclesiastes 3:11–12

At times, it may not feel like God is in control of things, but
He is. He sets an appropriate time for everything and in its time,
everything will be made beautiful. God had His eyes upon you
even before you were conceived. It was God who made all the deli-
cate inner parts of your body and knit it together in your mother's
womb (Psalm 139:13). It is He who has chosen the exact time of
your existence and the exact time when you will depart from this
earth and reach your eternal destiny.

From the very moment you were born, the Lord had eternity
in mind for you. You will never know the full works of the Master's
hands behind the scenes orchestrating your life. He has placed you
at your job and with the people you have become close with for
one purpose—that all may come to know His saving grace and
to share the love of the Father with others. There is no greater joy
than knowing one is saved.

If you have already accepted Jesus Christ as your personal
Savior, then rejoice in your salvation and help others who are not
saved to find the freedom and joy in one's salvation. If you have
not received Jesus Christ as your personal Savior, the Lord is putting eternity into your heart right now and wants you to accept
His calling upon your life. Won't you accept Jesus into your heart
today? The Lord has caused our lives to cross paths for such a time
as this. He has made everything beautiful in its time. He has placed
eternity in our hearts.

MARCH 19

"O house of Israel, can I not do with you as this potter?"
says the Lord. "Look, as the clay is in the potter's
hand, so are you in My hand, O house of Israel!"
—Jeremiah 18:6

Like clay being molded and shaped into a beautiful piece of art by a potter, so our Lord wants to mold and shape you into a beautiful masterpiece too. As the clay is being spun on the potter's wheel, the clay is at the mercy of the potter and does not know what its final destiny will look like. At times, the potter is not happy with what he sees, so he starts over and forms it into another vessel. The clay does not have any say in the matter, he must trust the potter's hands to finish the work that was started.

Being formed by the Master's hands does not happen overnight, but takes a lifetime, for you are being molded into the likeness of Christ. Being molded and shaped into Christ's image can only happen if you surrender yourself to the mercy of the Potter and trust His hands to finish the work which He has started in you. Like the clay, you must not have any say in the matter, but rely totally on the Master's hands to form your life. You may not be able to discern your final destiny, and the Potter may need to water you down and start all over again, but whatever the Potter decides, do not resist His work.

The Lord may be spinning and molding you right now or putting the final touches on your life. Whatever stage you are in, know that the Potter's gentle hands want to mold you into His masterpiece. Allow Him to take whatever time He needs to fulfill His destiny for your life.

MARCH 20

And the Lord your God will circumcise your heart and the heart of your descendants, to love the Lord your God with all your heart and with all your soul, that you may live.
—Deuteronomy 30:6

Bottom line is—the Lord desires all of your heart. It is He who puts the desire in your heart to love him and to want to know Him (Jeremiah 24:7). The Lord will circumcise your heart, cutting away those things that separate you from His love if you allow Him to. The Lord will fill you with a desire to love Him with all your heart and soul. The Lord wants to be your God. It is He that will give you a heart to fear Him. It is He that will make an everlasting covenant with you and will not turn away from doing good. It is the Lord that will put fear in your heart so that you will not depart from Him (Jeremiah 32:38–40).

Have you ever been passionate about someone or something? The Lord is passionate about you and that's what He wants from you; to be passionate about Him. He does not want part of you. He wants all of you. He is jealous for you with godly jealousy (2 Corinthians 11:2) and will not allow anything to take His place. Do a Bible search on "jealous God" and you will see how jealous He is for you. Are you as jealous for God as He is for you? Do you allow other passions to take His place? Be jealous for God with godly jealousy and remove those passions so that Christ is first in your life.

The Lord wants to deliver you from all uncleanliness. He wants to remove the gods you've placed in your heart that cause Him to take second place. Are you ready to have your heart circumcised? Are you ready for the Lord to put a new spirit within you and remove the stony heart and replace it with a heart of flesh? Ask the Lord to circumcise your heart and fill you with a deeper desire to know and love Him. Ask Jesus to remove those things in your life that steal your love away from Him.

MARCH 21

Do not be deceived, God is not mocked; for whatever a
man sows, that he will also reap. For he who sows to his
flesh will of the flesh also reap corruption but he who sows
to the Spirit will of the Spirit reap everlasting life.
—Galatians 6:7–8

Many people do not realize the old saying, "You sow what you reap" is biblical, but it is, and the saying is so true. When you show acts of kindness and reveal the heart of the Father to others, God blesses you in return. The same is true when you sin. You may get away with a sin once or twice, but eventually it comes back to haunt you. God warns you to not be deceived. God's judgement is righteous. When you become stubborn and refuse to turn from your sin, you are storing up terrible punishment for yourself. A day of wrath is coming, when God's righteous judgment will be revealed. He will judge you according to what you have done (Romans 2:5–6).

It is a very dangerous thing to give in to the flesh. Instead, sow seeds of love into people's lives. If you treat others with respect, they will treat you with respect. If you want to be treated kindly, treat others with kindness. Whatever you want for yourself, be willing to do the same for others. Do not be deceived, God is not mocked. Whatever a man sows, that he will also reap. What are you sowing into the lives of others? Are you sowing seeds of love, peace, kindness, faithfulness, hope, gentleness, and forgiveness? Do you build up another or are you tearing others down? Are you holding back the seeds of corruption and enduring all things for the love of Christ? Follow the footsteps of Christ and sow a seed of love into someone's life today.

MARCH 22

Return to the stronghold, you prisoners of hope.
Even today I declare that I will restore double to you.
—Zechariah 9:12

The Lord is in the restoration business. He desires to see His people whole and living in freedom. Many times adversity comes our way and we question God. Why did You allow this to happen? Why didn't You hear my prayers? There is always a purpose for everything, and in the midst of our circumstances, God will turn every situation around for His glory. Sometimes restoration comes right away; other times it may take years.

My husband loves to restore older cars. There were times he had the entire engine and body of the car torn apart. He knew what pieces needed replaced and which pieces were still in good shape. Other parts of the car just needed some sanding to get rid of some rust. He would put the car back together and drive it for a while and discover other parts that needed adjustments to fine tune it. Eventually the car was totally restored.

Your life is the same way. God knows every detail of your life. There will be times that it feels like your life is torn apart. There is a reason for this. The Lord is bringing restoration to your life. He knows the damaged areas of your life that need repaired. Only God can repair the deep wounds of your heart. His gentle hand removes the rusty particles from your past that seem to cling to you and corrode your life. There are some parts of your life that need a little oil applied to them. As you journey in life, the Lord lets you discover other areas that need fine tuning. He will take some people out of your life and replace them with people who will help you reach your destiny. Layer by layer, piece by piece, the Lord touches every area of your life and keeps refining and tuning you until you become totally restored. If the Lord's hand is upon you right now, and you feel like you are falling to pieces, be not discouraged for He is bringing restoration to your life.

MARCH 23

My beloved spoke, and said to me: "Rise up,
my love, my fair one, and come away"...
"Rise up, my love, my fair one, and come away!"
—Song 2:10, 13

In any relationship, time must be spent alone with the other person in order for the relationship to last or have any meaning. When couples do not spend quality time with each other, their love eventually fades away and they drift farther and farther apart. They may be living together but their love is far from the love thy once had for each other. The same is true with your relationship with God. Your relationship with the Lord will not blossom and grow unless you spend some time alone with Him.

The Lord is calling you to rise up and go away with Him. Let Him spark a flame in you to rekindle a fire of His love within you. Feel the tender love of His invitation as He calls you His love, His fair one, His beloved. Feel the tender love of His invitation to go away with Him. Embrace His hand, step away, and receive all that He wants to pour into your life this very moment.

The Lord longs to see your face and to hear your voice (Song 2:14). Feel your heart beating against His as you lose yourself in Him. His love dispels all fear, all worry, and all the cares you hold close in your heart. Hear Him say—give them to Me my beloved and I will take care of them for you. Receive the invitation and give all to Him as you rest in His arms. Allow His peace to rest upon you today, knowing that you are His beloved, His fair one, His love.

MARCH 24

Set up the standard on the walls of Babylon; Make
the guard strong, set up the watchmen, prepare the
ambushes. For the Lord has both devised and done what
He spoke against the inhabitants of Babylon. You are
My battle-ax and weapons of war: For with you, I will
break the nation in pieces; with you I will destroy kingdoms.
—Jeremiah 51:12, 20

You are called to be a watchman and to prepare for the ambushes when the Lord calls you to engage in battle. If you think about the damage an ax does when chopping wood, image the damage you are doing in the spiritual realm when the Lord calls you to be His weapons of war. With you He will break the strongholds of this nation in pieces.

Are you facing battles right now in your life? Are there strongholds in your life that you can't seem to get rid of? Do you hate the evil you are seeing around you? Then go to war in your prayer closet. Set up a standard in the walls of your prayer closet and be the battle-ax and weapon of war. Man the fort. Strengthen your flanks! Fortify your power mightily (Nahum 2:1). Call upon Almighty God to break the strongholds in pieces and destroy the enemy's kingdom. Symbolically chop off those strongholds that hold you or others in bondage. Instead of complaining about situations or allowing the enemy to rob your peace, take them to your battleground and be a weapon of warfare against them. Chop off that circumstance and declare things that are not as if they were.

What you do symbolically has great ramifications in the spiritual realm. I hear the Lord saying, stay alert My people. My battle cry is sounding. Set up an army, for every purpose of the Lord shall be performed. For the Lord has devised and will do what He has spoken against the spirits of darkness. For with you, He will break strongholds in pieces, and with you, He will destroy demonic kingdoms.

MARCH 25

For the eyes of the Lord run to and fro throughout
the whole earth, to show Himself strong on behalf
of those whose heart is loyal towards Him.
—2 Chronicles 16:9

No matter where you are or what you are doing, the eyes of the Lord are always upon you. Nothing is secret from the Lord. He sees all, hears all, and knows the condition of your heart in everything you say and do. None of us will ever be perfect but we must try to do our best each day. To have a loyal heart means that you will live your life being devoted to God, keeping His commandments, walking in truth, and obeying His statutes. It means that you have yielded your whole heart to do God's will.

We read an example in scripture of how God was loyal towards Hezekiah in the book of 2 Kings. Hezekiah was sick and near death and the profit Isaiah told him to set his house in order for he was going to die. Hezekiah turned his face toward the wall and prayed. He asked the Lord to remember how he had walked humbly before Him in truth, and with a loyal heart, having done what was good in the Lord's sight. Then Hezekiah wept bitterly. Before Isaiah had gone out into the middle court, the word of the Lord came to him and told him to return to Hezekiah and speak to him once again and tell Hezekiah: "I have heard your prayer, I have seen your tears; surely I will heal you." And the Lord extended Hezekiah's life fifteen more years (2 Kings 20:1–6).

You cannot expect God to move on your behalf when you have not humbled yourself and walked uprightly before Him. But oh the joy and encouragement that 2 Chronicles 16:9 should be to you when you do. It assures you that His eyes are upon you and that He will show forth His mighty power for you. Expect by faith that His power is working for you, in you, and through you. When you hear bad news, turn your face toward God. Pray to the Lord and remind Him how you have walked in truth and with a loyal heart. Weep bitterly for redemption, and see God move on your behalf like he did with Hezekiah.

MARCH 26

My flesh and my heart fail; But God is the
strength of my heart and my portion forever.
—Psalm 73:26

God is omnipotent. He is our Stronghold. Your strength must come from Him if you are to have sustaining strength throughout your day. Most of the time when I think about strength, I think of it in a physical sense having the ability and energy to accomplish my daily tasks. But it goes far beyond that. God wants to be the strength of your heart. He wants your heart to be filled with faith that He is working in you and through you. He wants you to realize that in His strength, His will shall be accomplished through you. When you find your strength in God, your weakness turns into strength. His strength will give you the ability to say no when temptation comes your way.

In Ephesians 1:19, Paul prayed that believers would have spiritual wisdom, that through the Holy Spirit, believers might realize the exceeding greatness of His power toward those who believe, according to the working of His mighty power. This is the secret to your strength—to fully realize the power and strength that is within you through Almighty God. Is your heart troubled or weakened today? Encourage yourself in the Lord. Fill your heart with faith in what God can and will do for you. God is your refuge and strength and He will strengthen your heart.

MARCH 27

"Blessed are those who are persecuted for righteousness'
sake, for theirs is the kingdom of heaven. Blessed are
you when they revile and persecute you, and say all
kinds of evil against you falsely for My sake."
—Matthew 5:10–11

J esus tells us to rejoice and be exceedingly glad when we are persecuted for righteousness' sake. Great is your reward in heaven when
you do (Matthew 5:12). It helps you to take your eyes off earthly
rewards and focus your eyes on kingdom rewards. The thought of
sacrificing all, because we know our reward awaits us in heaven,
should strengthen everyone's faith. God wants you to be faithful to
Him. Are you being faithful to Him even if it means persecution
for your beliefs?

Does your conduct reflect the convictions and belief you
have in Christ? Do you remain silent when you should take a
stand? Do you blend into the culture and beliefs around you, or
would people recognize that you belong to Jesus? Do you pursue
righteousness, or do you hold back out of fear of being persecuted?
These are tough questions you need to be asking yourself. Are you
truly getting involved for righteousness' sake or are you on the
sidelines watching to see what happens?

Take a stand for your religious beliefs, for righteousness and
faithfulness to God. Speak truth in love and take a stand on issues
of righteousness. Instead of blending in with society and compromising your own convictions, put your trust in God and know
that He will be with you no matter what persecution you may
face. I would rather face trouble standing for what's right than to
succeed in what's wrong or allow injustice to prevail. Your attitude
through persecution serves as an example to others. Allow others
to see Christ in you, even if you are mocked, and persecuted, and
lied about because you are a follower of Christ. God will bless you,
and great is your reward for faithfulness.

MARCH 28

No temptation has overtaken you except such as is common
to man; but God is faithful, who will not allow you to be
tempted beyond what you are able, but with the temptation will
also make the way of escape, that you may be able to bear it.
—1 Corinthians 10:13

We all face temptation but we all do not respond to temptation in the same way. Satan knows each of your weaknesses and looks for the right moment to attack—when you're discouraged, upset, weak, sick, or lonely. Jesus was led by the Spirit into the wilderness to be tempted by the devil. When He had fasted forty days and forty nights, He was hungry and the tempter made his attack (Matthew 4:1–3). But Jesus was able to overcome the temptation and win the battle. Jesus was purposely led by the Spirit to be tempted by the devil to give us an example of how to respond to temptation.

So how did Jesus overcome temptation and win the battle? He spoke the Word. Three times Jesus was tempted with cunning words by the devil and three times Jesus responded to him with the words, "It is written" (Matthew 4:4, 7, 10). When you are tempted, first recognize that it is an attack from the devil and then use the Word of God to fight off the attack. Endure every temptation for God says that He will not allow you to be tempted beyond what you are able to handle. The problem is you give in to the temptation instead of calling on God to give you the strength to resist the invitation to sin.

Are you being tempted? Call upon the Lord and He will make a way for you to escape. Respond to the devil like Jesus did. Endure the temptation by using the power and authority of God's Word and eventually the tempter will leave. Blessed is the man who endures temptation; for when he has been approved, he will receive the crown of life which the Lord has promised to those who love Him (James 1:12).

MARCH 29

Peter answered and said to Him, "Even if all are made
to stumble because of You, I will never be made to stumble."
Jesus said to Him, "Assuredly, I say to you that this night,
before the rooster crows, you will deny Me three times."
Peter said to Him, "Even if I have to die with You, I will
not deny You." And so said all the disciples.
—Matthew 26:33–35

Jesus always had a way of knowing what was on people's hearts and He predicted that Peter would deny Him three times. Not realizing the true condition of his heart, Peter immediately told Jesus He was wrong, that he would never deny Him and that he would even die for Him. But just a short time later, it was a different story. Three times Peter denied Christ, cursing and swearing that He never knew the Man. Immediately the rooster crowed. Jesus looked at Peter. Remembering the words that Jesus had spoken to him, Peter went away and wept bitterly (Matthew 26:69–75).

At the very end, what caused Peter to deny Christ? After all, he was one of His beloved disciples. He followed Jesus, was taught by Jesus and saw all the healings and miracles that had taken place by Him. It was not that Peter disbelieved in who Christ was, or what Jesus could do that made him deny Christ, but he denied Him because of his fear. He feared what man could do to him.

Fear is one spirit that may be hidden inside of you without you even knowing it until you are faced with a situation. Picture yourself in Peter's shoes. How would you have responded? Are you willing to die for Christ? A question you need to ask yourself is, "Am I denying Christ in my life?" Are there things that I am saying or doing or not saying and not doing that are signs of me denying Christ? Be willing to seek the Lord with a pure heart to find the answer to these questions. If the Lord reveals to you that you have denied Him, weep bitterly with a sorrowful heart and become right with God. Reaffirm your love for Him and deny Him no more.

MARCH 30

"I have glorified You on the earth. I have finished the
work which You have given Me to do. And now, O
Father, glorify Me together with Yourself, with the glory
which I had with You before the world was."
—John 17:4–5

If your boss told you he had an important assignment for you
to do but in order for you to fulfill it, he had to demote you and
cut your salary, how would you respond? Would you accept the
offer? Like most people, you probably wouldn't. But that is exactly
what Jesus did. He was already royalty, deity, and glorified with the
Father, but in order to fulfill a request from His Father, He humbled Himself and took the form of flesh. Jesus emptied Himself
completely of royalty in heaven that He might bring glory to His
Father on earth.

From the time of His birth to the time of His death, Jesus had
one mission in mind. He set out to reconcile heaven with earth, to
make atonement for the wages of our sins. He paid the price for our
salvation. Without His death on the cross, there would be no eternal life with the Father for us. In John 17:4, Jesus told the Father,
"I have glorified You on the earth. I have finished the work You
have given Me to do." How did Jesus glorify the Father? By living a
life of total dependence and obedience to the Father. Jesus only did
what He saw and heard the Father do (John 5:19). Jesus finished
the work which the Father had called Him to do—He sought to
seek those who were lost and gave Himself up as a ransom for the
penalty of our sins. On the cross Jesus cried out—"It is finished"
(John 19:30). He had truly conquered sin and death.

Jesus brought the Father glory. Does your life bring glory
to God? Are you doing the work the Father has asked you to do?
Reflect on your life and see whether you bring glory to the Father.
When your life comes to an end and you meet your Heavenly
Father, be able to say to the Father what Jesus said to Him, "I have
finished the work You have given me to do."

MARCH 31

He went a little farther and fell on His face, and prayed,
saying, "O My Father, if it is possible, let this cup pass
from Me; nevertheless, not as I will, but as You will."
—Matthew 26:39

Three times in the garden of Gethsemane Jesus prayed that the cup of suffering and separation from His Father would be removed, but only if it was the will of the Father to do so. Jesus faced anguish and agony to the point of sweating blood (Luke 22:44). He said to His Father, "Abba, Father, all things are possible for You" (Mark 14:36). He knew His Father had the power to stop the torture and ridicule that was about to occur. During the most difficult hour of His life, Jesus made the decision to accept His Father's will and drink the cup which His Father had given Him. He did not let anything or anyone come between Him and that cup He was to bear. Even when Peter tried to ward off the high priest, Jesus said to Peter, "Put your sword into the sheath. Shall I not drink the cup which My Father has given Me?" (John 18:11)

You will never have to endure the cup that your Savior was given but you will be given cups to bear. Respond and pray the way Jesus prayed—not my will but Yours. Jesus learned obedience by the things which He suffered (Hebrews 5:8). Allow your sufferings to teach you obedience as well.

If you've offered up prayers and are still faced with your circumstance, ask God to give you the strength and grace to endure the cup that you must bear. It may not be what you expected or even what you had hoped for or wanted, but God is the One who should determine the path you walk. If your soul is troubled, speak the words that Jesus spoke, "Now my soul is troubled and what shall I say? Father, save Me from this hour? But for this purpose I came to this hour. Father, glorify Your name" (John 12:27–28). Make the decision to accept the Father's will and He will give you the grace to drink the cup.

APRIL 1

And about the ninth hour Jesus cried out with a loud
voice, saying, "Eli, Eli, lama sabachthani?" that is,
"My God, My God, why have You forsaken Me?"
—Matthew 27:46

Have you ever felt lonely and abandoned? Just when you need a friend, they are nowhere to be found or they have totally turned their back on you. In desperation, you cry out to God and He feels a million miles away. Jesus knew more about feeling abandoned than we will ever know. For nine hours He was separated from His Father. For a moment, God turned His back on His Son when He became sin for us. Jesus didn't cry out because of the physical pain. Instead, His cry expressed the pain, anguish, and intense feeling of abandonment He felt while separated from His Father. The price Jesus paid for our sins!

The next time you question whether the Lord has forsaken you, remember the cross and what Jesus endured! Why would He forsake someone He paid a ransom for? Although you may feel like He is a million miles away, the Lord is right there with you and He will see you through. Jesus said He would never leave you nor forsake you (Hebrews 13:5). God is with you and will keep you wherever you go (Genesis 28:15). As He was with Moses, so He will be there with you. He will not leave you or forsake you (Joshua 1:5). No matter what you face in life, you can count on Him to never forsake or abandon you.

APRIL 2

Knowing that you were not redeemed with
corruptible things, like silver or gold, from your
aimless conduct received by tradition from your
fathers, but with the precious blood of Christ, as
of a lamb without blemish and without spot.
—1 Peter 1:18–19

Jesus came as the Lamb of God to lay down His life for all mankind. It is the blood of Jesus Christ that cleanses you from all sin (1 John 1:7). He was the ultimate sacrifice that took away all sin. He laid down His life as a substitute for you. God accepted His blood sacrifice, pure and unblemished, as an atonement for your sins. Nothing can wash away your sins but the blood of Jesus. It is through His Blood that you have reconciliation with God. The blood of Jesus will continually cleanse you. There is no sin that Jesus's blood cannot wash away. His Blood has a cleansing purifying power that penetrates to the deepest roots of iniquity. But in order to experience the victory over iniquity, apply the blood of Jesus to your life.

Oh, the power of His blood that makes you white as snow (Isaiah 1:18). Jesus died that you may have eternal life with Him. Christ has given you the victory. His shed blood unleashed the power of God upon hell, taking from the devil the keys of authority over earth and mankind. Jesus's blood conquered the devil. By His shed blood you are called to a place of authority and you need to use that authority. The power to overcome is in the blood. The power to love is in the blood. The power to forgive is in the blood. Oh, the power of the precious blood of Jesus Christ.

What situation are you dealing with today? Apply the blood of Jesus over it. Apply Jesus's blood over your mind, body, emotions, and will. Apply the blood of Jesus over yourself, your family, your church family, and your community. Apply Jesus's blood over your struggles and watch your struggles go away. What can wash away your sins? Nothing but the blood of Jesus. Oh the power of His blood!

APRIL 3

My son, give me your heart,
and let your eyes observe my ways.
—Proverbs 23:26

What is on your heart today? What are your eyes observing? Usually the two go hand-in-hand. You will focus your eyes on whatever is captivating your heart. Your heart is the place that harbors the fruits of your being, whether for good or evil. The Lord wants you to give Him your heart and let your eyes observe His ways. Throughout the Bible the Lord calls you to carefully observe His statues, judgments and commandments. When you do, then He will make your way prosperous and you will be successful in all you do (Joshua 1:8). When you don't, you will pay the consequences for your disobedience.

Jesus said, "You will know them by their fruits" (Matthew 7:16). Jesus spoke to the multitudes and to His disciples, saying: "The scribes and the Pharisees sit in Moses's seat. Therefore, whatever they tell you to observe, that observe and do, but do not do according to their works; for they say, and do not do (Matthew 23:1–3). That is why the Lord wants you to carefully observe His ways and not the ways of man. If you give Him your heart and let your eyes observe His ways, you will live by them. The Lord is the only one who can take away the fruit of unrighteousness and replace it with the fruit of the Spirit which is love, joy, peace, long-suffering, kindness, goodness, faithfulness, gentleness, and self-control (Galatians 5:22–23). You cannot produce this fruit on your own. It is the Holy Spirit who helps you to bear this fruit. What fruit is harboring in your heart? Is it for good or evil? Give your heart to the Lord, observe His ways, and He will produce in you good fruit.

APRIL 4

Now behold, an angel of the Lord stood by him,
and a light shone in the prison; and he struck
Peter on the side and raised him up, saying,
"Arise quickly!" And his chains fell off his hands.
—Acts 12:7

Have you ever wondered about angels and what role they play in your daily life? I have heard that we are assigned at least one guardian angel. Angels have a ministry to the saints of God to strengthen, comfort, warn, and protect. All throughout the Bible, angels have had a part in God's relationship with man. An Angel of the Lord freed Peter from prison (Acts 12:1–11)

God's is the same yesterday, today, and forever more. He used angels in the past to minister to His people, and He will use angels now to minister to us. They stand at their command post ready to take action, ready to heed to the voice of the Lord and to His Word. It is important to speak the Word and proclaim the blessings of God. When you proclaim that the Angel of the Lord encamps around you, you are inviting the Angel of the Lord to do just that—to surround you and protect you (Psalm 34:7). Don't talk yourself out of a blessing with negative words. Just believe.

When the Israelites cried out to the Lord, He heard their voice and sent the Angel, and brought them up out of Egypt (Numbers 20:16). I ask You Lord to hear the cries of Your people and send forth Your angels to minister to them. Allow the Angel of the Lord to bring strength, hope, and healing to those in need. Just as the Angel of the Lord struck Peter on his side and caused the chains to fell off, send forth the Angel of the Lord to come and break the chains of bondage that hold your people captive. I decree that the Angel of the Lord encamps all around us bringing strength, healing, and deliverance to all who fear You, Lord Jesus.

APRIL 5

But he said to them, "Do not be alarmed. You seek
Jesus of Nazareth, who was crucified. He is risen!
He is not here. See the place where they laid Him."
—Mark 16:6

In John 10:17–18 Jesus said, "Therefore My Father loves Me, because I lay down My life that I may take it again. No one takes it from Me, but I lay it down Myself. I have power to lay it down, and I have power to take it again. This command I received from My Father." Jesus paid the ultimate price for the wages of our sins. God gave Jesus the authority both to offer His life as a sacrifice for our sins and to rise from the dead in power and glory.

The chief priests and scribes may have believed that they had taken the life of Jesus, but they didn't. Jesus willingly laid down His life. Jesus knew the power within Himself and knew that He would rise again. And now He sits on the right hand of the Father making intercession for you and me (Romans 8:34).

You need to remind yourself who you are in Christ. Christ lives in you and you have the same resurrection power that raised Christ from the dead living inside of you. The works of the devil were defeated at the cross. When the devil comes knocking at your door, demonstrate the resurrection power of Jesus in you and put him in his place. Walk in the victory that Christ gave you. Walk in the resurrection power of Jesus. Just believe in the resurrection power of Jesus to take away that stronghold, that fear, that doubt, that depression, that doctor's report, or whatever struggle you are facing today. Receive your freedom and victory.

APRIL 6

Ah, Lord God! Behold, You have made the heavens and
the earth by Your great power and outstretched arm.
There is nothing too hard for you. You show lovingkindness
to thousands, and repay the iniquity of the fathers into the
bosom of their children after them—the Great, the Mighty
God, whose name is the Lord of hosts.
— Jeremiah 32:17–18

Many times we will tell our co-workers or our children what a "Great" job they did. People like to be encouraged and told how well they are doing. Throughout scripture, we are told how great and mighty is the Lord we serve. We use the word "great" so freely that we lose the true understanding of God's greatness. How superficial is our knowledge of God's greatness. Let us take the time to know and adore His greatness.

Oh God, You made the heavens and the earth by Your great power (Jeremiah 32:17). You laid the foundations of the earth and laid each star in its place. You commanded the morning since your days began and caused the dawn to know its place. You cause it to rain on land where there is none and tender grass to spring forth on the desolate waste. You lift up your voice to the clouds that an abundance of rain may cover us. You send forth the lightning. You have put wisdom into our minds and given us understanding (Job 38).

You show loving kindness to thousands. You are great in counsel and mighty in work, for your eyes are open to all the ways of the sons of men. You brought your people out of Egypt with signs and wonders (Jeremiah 32:18–21). You are the ruler over all the kings of the earth. You washed us from our sins with Your own precious blood. You are the Alpha and Omega, the Beginning and the End, who is, who was, and is to come. You are the Almighty (Revelation 1:4–8). Take some time to ponder on the "Greatness" of God.

APRIL 7

So Samuel said: "Has the Lord as great delight in burnt offerings and sacrifices, as in obeying the voice of the Lord? Behold, to obey is better than sacrifice, and to heed than the fat of rams. For rebellion is as the sin of witchcraft, and stubbornness is as iniquity and idolatry. Because you have rejected the word of the Lord, He also has rejected you from being king."
—1 Samuel 15:22–23

God places a high value on obedience. He even prefers it more than sacrifices. If you fast, but are living a life of rebellion and stubbornness, your sacrifice is in vain, it will be worthless. The Lord compares your rebellion to that of witchcraft. When you become stubborn in your ways and do what you want and not what the Lord asks you to do, God compares that sin to idolatry. We all know the importance of keeping the covenant of a marriage and the damage in the relationship that occurs once that trust is broken and infidelity sets in. When you choose to ignore the words of the Lord and follow your own love and passion, it damages your relationship with the Lord. Infidelity will soon set into your heart because you have lost your first love.

Many people choose not to read their Bible. But if we don't read it, how are we to know how God wants us to live? Ignorance is no excuse when you have the resources at our finger tips. Obedience is a form of worship. Stir up a passion in your heart to obey God. Stir up a passion to live in righteousness. Living in righteousness is doing what is right before God, keeping His commandments, and turning away from sin.

If you are reading the Word, have faith and trust that God is leading you and will show you how to walk in His ways. Daily walk in His presence, and He will remove those things in your life that displease Him. Let the passion kindle inside of you the desire to do right. The more we desire to be right with God, the more we will want to listen to His voice and walk in obedience. What are the desires of your heart?

APRIL 8

And Joshua said, "Alas Lord God, why have
you brought this people over the Jordan at all—
to deliver us into the hand of the Amorites, to
destroy us? Oh, that we had been content, and
dwelt on the other side of the Jordan!"

—Joshua 7:7

Why is it that when trouble arises, we question God and want to blame Him for our circumstances? Are you as quick to question God when the outcome of your prayers turns out in your favor? Or do you just assume that God is supposed to respond on your behalf so you may take the things His does for granted?

Joshua was quick to question God. Why Lord, why did you allow the enemy to defeat us? When he was finished complaining and accusing God, God responded back—it was because of sin, for Israel has transgressed against Me (Joshua 7:11). Like Joshua, we too are quick to complain and accuse someone else, including God, when the outcome of our situation does not turn out in our favor. When you go before God in prayer, ask God what you may have done wrong and what can you do to fix the situation. In Joshua's case, it was sin in his camp that caused them to be defeated. Sin will cause you to lose the favor of God. You have to remember that the consequences of your sin may not only affect you but may also affect the people around you.

As you pray, listen with a pure heart and be willing to hear what the Lord has to say about the matter. If He reveals sin in your life, then you need to confront that sin, get right with God, and with any other person involved. Take action to resolve the situation.

APRIL 9

I spoke to you in your prosperity, but you said
'I will not hear.' This has been your manner
from your youth, that you did not obey My voice.
—Jeremiah 22:21

God is always speaking to you. He speaks when you are prosperous and when you are in hardships. Jeremiah repeatedly reminded the people that God was speaking to them but they would not hear Him. It makes me wonder how many times God has spoken to me and I have failed to hear Him. None of us intentionally purposes in our hearts to tune God out, but yet, we fail to hear what God is saying.

There are many obstacles that can block you from hearing God's voice. One of the obstacles is your busyness. You don't take the time to quiet your mind and heart to hear from Him. You may be spending time with the Lord, but your mind is somewhere else. Another obstacle is when your mind is convinced that you have already heard from God, when it was your own flesh and desires that you have heard. How many times have you rationalized what you have heard from the Lord in order to justify your desires? You compromise your walk by doing what you want instead of what the Lord desires. Compromise will eventually destroy your relationship with God.

Do you really want to hear from God? Do you want Him to be the Lord of all areas of your life? Humbly go before God with a sincere heart. Depend on the Holy Spirit to reveal God's truth and His will for your life to you. Write the words that the Lord has spoken to you on the scrolls of your heart. Listen attentively and do what the Lord asks you to do.

APRIL 10

*According to their deeds, accordingly He will repay, fury to
His adversaries, recompense to His enemies; the coastlands He will
fully repay. So shall they fear the name of the Lord from the west,
and His glory from the rising of the sun; when the enemy comes in like
a flood, the Spirit of the Lord will lift up a standard against him.*
—Isaiah 59:18–19

Have you ever had one of those days when it feels like everything is going wrong—the alarm never goes off and you're late for work; someone stole something that belongs to you; your best friend lied about you or broke your trust; you were blamed for something you didn't do; someone else gets the credit for something you did—the list can go on and on. If today is one of those days, just remember this—when the enemy comes in like a flood, the Lord will lift up a banner against him. The Lord is on your side and will restore to you that which the enemy has taken from you. It is just a matter of time when He will repay.

The Lord will pay back his enemies for what they have done. In Romans 2, God warns us, "But because you are stubborn and refuse to turn from your sin, you are storing up terrible punishment for yourself. For a day of anger is coming, when God's righteous judgment will be revealed. He will judge everyone according to what they have done. He will give eternal life to those who keep on doing good, seeking after the glory and honor and immortality that God offers. But he will pour out his anger and wrath on those who live for themselves, who refuse to obey the truth and instead live lives of wickedness. There will be trouble and calamity for everyone who keeps on doing what is evil—for the Jew first and also for the Gentile" (Romans 2:5–9, NLT). Continue to do good, even if everything is going wrong. Your reward will be great in the day of wrath.

APRIL 11

Blessed be the God and Father of our
Lord Jesus Christ, who according to His
abundant mercy has begotten us again
to a living hope through the resurrection
of Jesus Christ from the dead.

—1 Peter 1:3

Who or what are you placing your hope in? Many place their hope in winning the lottery so they can quit their job, pay off debts, and have lots of money to spend on luxuries. Although many people gamble in hopes of winning the lottery, very few do win, and when they do, they soon find out that they have won a lot more than money. They find out that people will take advantage of them, they are targets for lawsuits and scams, they have to fight off a host of long-lost family members and friends, relationships fail, and because of poor money management they have to file bankruptcy. In the end, they discovered that money did not buy them happiness. They had placed their hope in the wrong thing.

Paul said his hope was in the Lord Jesus Christ (1 Timothy 1:1) and that is where you should place your hope. Paul thanked Christ for considering him trustworthy and appointing him to service even though he was formerly a blasphemer, a persecutor, and a rude man. God had mercy on him so that Jesus Christ could use him as a prime example of His great patience with even the worst sinners. Then others will realize that they, too, can believe in Him to receive eternal life (1 Timothy 1:12–16).

It doesn't feel good when you go through trials and tribulations, but God uses these times to mature you and make you stronger Christians (Romans 5:3–4). He is building your character as you put your trust and hope in Him. Are you facing a difficult situation right now? Know that God sees your difficulty and is present to strengthen you during this time. Persevere and allow the experience to make you a stronger person. That is how you grow in faith and build your character. Let the resurrection of Jesus Christ be your living hope.

APRIL 12

For we brought nothing into this world, and it is
certain we can carry nothing out. And having food
and clothing, with these we shall be content.
—1 Timothy 6:7–8

It is amazing how many unhappy people there are in the world. Sadly, many of the discontent people are Christians. Why is that? Part of the problem is trying to keep up with the demands of life and wanting the best for our children. The worldly attractions cause you to desire more than what you can afford or need for that matter. Another reason is that Satan tries to steal your joy by directing your focus on things you don't have or things you wished you had done in life. You know those thoughts like…"if only" or "if I could" or "if I had only."

When the enemy tries to get your attention on things you don't have, focus your attention on the things you do have. Everything you have is a blessing from God. It is Christ who enabled you to have the finances to purchase your needs and luxuries. We take so much for granted. We need to remind ourselves that we came into this world with nothing—and look how the Lord has blessed our lives. You need to be thankful for what you do have because when you depart from this world, you will not be taking anything out with you.

You also become discontent when you lose focus on who your provider is. When you strive for things and try to do things on your own, you set yourself up for failure. The more you realize that God is your Provider, the more content you will become. As you get older, you begin to realize how unimportant material possessions are in life. You gain an awareness that what is really important are relationships with God, family, and friends. Lord give me a spirit of thankfulness, and let me be content with what You provide me. I brought nothing into this world and I will carry nothing out. May I be content knowing that my basic needs of food and clothing are met, and focus my attention on my relationship with You and others.

APRIL 13

But the fruit of the Spirit is love, joy, peace,
longsuffering, kindness, goodness, faithfulness,
gentleness, self-control. Against such there is no law.
—Galatians 5:22–23

The Spirit of God lives in us and we are to walk in the fruit of the Spirit. Believers who walk in the Spirit will be different than other Christians for they will be genuine and sensitive not only to the Holy Spirit but to others around them. Nonbelievers will say to them, "You are different than most Christians I know. Why?" The answer is simple, the Father's love is in their heart and they want others to experience that same love. They do not approach others with a condemning or judgmental spirit, but approach them in love. Walking in the fruit of the Spirit takes discipline and is a choice. Pray that you will choose to walk in the Spirit.

Lord, help me to love those who are difficult to love. I refuse to let circumstances rob my joy, but I will use them as an opportunity to see You in motion. I will be still and know that You are God. I will allow You to make the best of each moment in my day. I will replace those moments of frustration with moments of prayer, praise and thanksgiving. Allow me to see the root of unkindness in a person's heart that I may treat that wound with kindness. I will be honest in all my ways and encourage others and not condemn them. I will keep my promises and be true to my word. I will be tender and caring when engaging with others. I will lift others up and not cast them down. Anger is far from me and I will respect the opinions of others. I will not give in to fleshly temptations or engage in things that will damage my relationship with You. I will ask the Holy Spirit to help me walk away and to be influenced only by His Spirit.

Life is full of choices. Today Lord, I choose to walk in the fruit of the Spirit.

APRIL 14

*Then the Lord said to Moses, "Behold, I will rain
bread from heaven for you. And the people shall go
out and gather a certain quota every day, that I may
test them, whether they will walk in My law or not."*
—Exodus 16:4

Many times we are quick to blame others or the devil for our circumstances, but it is the Lord who is allowing the situation to happen in order to test us. He wants to see how we will react, to see if we will return to our old ways, or to see if we have passed the test and are ready to move onto the next one. For the Israelites, God was testing them to see if they believed that He would provide for their needs. He rained manna down from heaven for them to gather but they were allowed only to gather as much as they would eat for that day. Some of them worried about what they would eat the next day and instead of trusting that God would provide for them, they gathered extra and kept it for the next morning. To their surprise, the extra manna that they had saved was no longer edible. It was full of worms (Exodus 16:20). They had failed the test.

Are you being tested right now? Is there something the Lord has been asking you to surrender? Tell yourself enough is enough and surrender it to the Lord. He will give you the strength and discipline to pass the test.

APRIL 15

For all the promises of God in Him are Yes,
and in Him Amen, to the glory of God through us.
—2 Corinthians 1:20

The Word of God is powerful, piercing the very depths of your soul and spirit (Hebrews 4:12). It brings life into your heart and causes you to change your ways and thinking. It reveals the true condition of your heart—where it is now and where it needs to be. The sharpness of the Word penetrates deep into your soul and profoundly influences your life.

God's Word teaches you about the God we serve. It reveals to you the promises that God makes to His people and teaches you how to pray. When you pray the Word, you are proclaiming the promises that God has for you. When you pray the Word, it allows His Word to sink deep into your heart and gives you strength and new hope. The Word teaches you God's will for your life and His promises to care for you. Praying the Word gives you confidence that you are praying God's will and not your own. Your mouth is made like a sharp sword when you proclaim the Word of God (Isaiah 49:2). Use it to pierce and conquer the enemy during your battles.

As you read the Word, you may find a verse that speaks to your heart. When that happens, write it in a book of promises. Then proclaim that promise in your prayer time and throughout the day. When you read the Word of God, do not rush through the words, but take the time to savor the spiritual food. Allow it time to digest into your heart and soul. Believe that the promises you speak are powerful and will come to pass. Expect and receive those promises. For all the promises of God are Yes and Amen.

APRIL 16

*Now the serpent was more cunning than any beast of the
field which the Lord God had made. And he said to the
woman, "Has God indeed said, 'You shall not eat of
every tree of the garden?" Then the serpent said to the
woman, "You will not surely die. For God knows that
in the day you eat of it your eyes will be opened, and you
will be like God, knowing good and evil."*
—Genesis 3:1, 4–5

Satan is the father of lies (John 8:44) and comes to kill, steal and
destroy (John 10:10). By his cunning ways, he will twist God's
words to make them sound like the real thing or cause you to
question what you really heard from God. He succeeded in planting a seed of doubt into Eve. Next, Satan poisoned her mind into
thinking that God was withholding from her. If she ate from the
tree of knowledge of good and evil, she would become like God—
knowing good from evil. Just a few words from Satan caused Eve
to focus on something she knew was against God's wishes.

Be aware of the cunning ways that Satan will use to con you
into temptation. Once you start to entertain a thought that you
know is displeasing to God, you have allowed the enemy to come
into an open door of your heart. He will say anything to you to
cause you to fall into sin. Eve entertained the thought of eating
the apple and then started to lust for it, seeing the beauty of it and
how good it would taste. She justified to herself why it was alright
to eat it. In the end, it destroyed the close relationship God had
with Adam and Eve and they were kicked out of the garden of
Eden (Genesis 3:22–24). Do not accept and allow the lies of Satan
to destroy your relationship with God. When temptation comes,
resist it. Set your heart and mind on God and not on the cunning, justifying words of Satan. Then praise God for your victory
of overcoming the enemy once again.

APRIL 17

Now therefore, thus says the Lord of hosts: "Consider
your ways! "You have sown much, and bring in little;
you eat, but do not have enough; you drink, but you
are not filled with drink; you clothe yourselves, but no
one is warm; and he who earns wages, earns wages to
put into a bag with holes." Thus says the Lord of
hosts: "Consider your ways!

—Haggai 1:5–7

Haggai had a message from God that he was to deliver to the people of God. Twice the Lord said, "Consider your ways!" Haggai tells them that they have planted much, but gather little; that they eat and drink but are never full; that they clothe themselves, but they are never warm enough; and they earn wages, but put them into a bag with holes. The people have lavished their own homes while allowing the house of the Lord to be in ruins (Haggai 1:9). God warns them that all their efforts have been in vain and that the neglect of the temple has resulted in His judgment on them (Haggai 1:9–11).

Do you consider your ways? Do you give careful thought to the things you do to determine if they align with what God wants for your life? It is so easy to assume that you do. But it's time that you have some serious self-examinations before the Lord. You need to stop long enough from your busy schedules to evaluate your life in light of God's Word. You need to daily examine yourself, with the help of God's Word to make sure you are headed in the right direction. If you don't set a high standard and strive to live as God wants you to live, you will soon find yourself going astray. God wants to reveal His ways to you so that you can walk in His paths. When your ways are in alignment to God's ways, you will experience His power and have peace in your heart. Consider now, from this day forward, your ways!

APRIL 18

*"For every tree is known by its own fruit. For men
do not gather figs from thorns, nor do they gather
grapes from a bramble bush. A good man out of the
good treasure of his heart brings forth good; and an evil
man out of the evil treasure of his heart brings forth evil.
For out of the abundance of the heart his mouth speaks."*

—Luke 6:44–45

The Bible is a love letter from God telling us how to live our lives. We all produce fruit, but what kind of fruit are we yielding? If we go about our daily lives without examining ourselves, how do we really know what we are made of? The Bible tells us to consider our ways (Haggai 1:7), examine our ways (Lamentations 3:40), guard our mouths (Proverbs 13:3), and set our hearts and our souls to seek the Lord (1 Chronicles 22:19). We really don't realize how vital it is to do these things, but they will determine the kind of fruit we will produce in our lives.

Your life is like a bowl of cherries. You have good fruit inside of you, but if you are not careful, the fruit may start to rot. Daily examine yourself and pick out any fruit that has become rotten so that the rest of your good produce does not decay. What kind of fruit are you producing? How would your coworkers or friends describe you? Better yet, how would the Lord describe you? Take the time to ask Him to reveal the good and rotten fruit. Then be willing to toss out that which is rotten.

APRIL 19

Then He touched their eyes, saying,
"According to your faith let it be to you."
—Matthew 9:29

What is the level of your faith? Do you believe that you will reach the destiny that God has for you? Do you believe that God will take away that stronghold that keeps you in bondage? Are you in a crisis right now? Do you believe that God is in the midst of that crisis? Throughout scripture we read about the many promises of God. These promises are for you and me, but they are all dependent upon our faith. It takes faith to move the mountains that are before us. God promises to move those mountains, but only if we believe (Matthew 17:20). The more we believe in His promises, the greater our faith will grow. Are you faced with a task you have never done before? Have faith in God that you can do all things through Christ which gives you the strength and the wisdom to do so (Philippians 4:13). According to your faith be it unto you.

Do not be afraid to put this truth to the test even now. Faith focuses on the promises from God and not on the obstacles in front of you. Faith is the substance of things hoped for, the evidence of things not seen (Hebrews 11:1). Israel was in a drought and Elijah prayed for rain. He told Ahab to go up and look toward the sea. He went up and looked and he said "There was nothing." Seven times Elijah said "Go again!" Then it came to pass on the seventh time, there was a cloud as small as a man's hand arising out of the sea. Then the heavy rains came (1 Kings 18:41–45). God is a rewarder to those who believe in Him and diligently seek after Him (Hebrews 11:6). I say to you, go up and look toward your sea and see what you see. If you see nothing, go again and again until it comes to pass that you see a cloud of hope as small as a man's hand. When you do, know that your victory has come.

APRIL 20

So Moses returned to the Lord and said, "Lord, why
have You brought trouble on this people? Why is it
You have sent me? For since I came to Pharaoh to
speak in Your name, he has done evil to this people;
neither have You delivered Your people at all."

—Exodus 5:22–23

Even though Moses was walking in obedience, the outcome of his circumstance was not what he had expected. Instead they were just the opposite. Pharaoh made the conditions even harder for the Israelites. So Moses questioned God, "Lord, why have You brought trouble on this people? Why is it You have sent me?" He questioned whether God had made a mistake in sending Him and actually blamed God for the hardship the Israelites were facing. Had Moses not lost hope, He would not have questioned God. He would have told the Israelites, hang in there, God is faithful.

But even so, God was faithful to His covenant. The Lord told Moses, now you shall see what I will do to Pharaoh. I am the Lord. I have remembered My covenant. I am the Lord and I will bring you out from under the burdens of the Egyptians. I will rescue you from their bondage, and I will redeem you with an outstretched arm (Exodus 6:1–6). And the Lord did as He promised.

If you are in a situation now and you are questioning whether God has made a mistake, remember who God is and that He does not make mistakes. Give God time to finish your story. When you feel oppressed, it is difficult for you to believe in the promises that God has proclaimed to you. Discouragement will come, but continue to have trust in God. Discouragement is a choice. Choose not to be discouraged and hold onto your faith. Hear the Lord tell you—"Now you shall see what I will do. I am the Lord. I will bring you out from under your burdens. I will rescue you from your bondage and I will redeem you with an outstretched arm." Then watch the Lord do as He promised to you.

APRIL 21

But when Pharaoh saw that there was relief, he hardened his heart and did not heed them, as the Lord had said.

—Exodus 8:15

Pharaoh refused to obey God, but when the hardship was more than he could bear, he promised to obey God. But once Pharaoh received some relief, he forgot about his promise, he rebelled, and returned to his old ways. His heart had hardened once again to the things of God.

There are many Pharaoh's of today, people who promise God that they will turn from their ways and follow Him if only He will heal them of their fatal disease or get them out of their predicament. Although God honors His word, many turn their backs on Him, returning to their old ways of living, and forget how the Lord has rescued them.

Three times in Hebrews we are warned, "Today, if you hear His voice, do not harden your hearts" (Hebrews 3:7, 3:15, and 4:7). You may ask yourself, what causes my heart to be hardened? In Hebrews 3:13, scripture tells us that our hearts are hardened through the deceitfulness of sin. The enemy has a cunning way of causing you to be deceived by your sins, making you believe that something you know in your heart is wrong in the eyes of God is really not that bad. Because of your fleshly desires, you become numb to that sin and harden your heart to what is the truth.

God speaks to you in many ways, through His Word, through other people, through dreams and visions, and through thoughts that He brings to you. Be sensitive to hearing His voice and not hardening your heart when He is trying to speak to you. Rebelling against God will have consequences. Choose to surrender to the voice of God. The rewards of obedience will last much longer than the temporary gratifications from the pleasures of the flesh. Today, if you hear His voice, do not harden your heart!

APRIL 22

"But indeed for this purpose I have raised you
up, that I may show My power in you, and
that My name may be declared in all the earth."
—Exodus 9:16

It is God who decides to make His goodness pass before you and exercise His right to pour out His mercy as He sees fit (Exodus 33:19). In some cases, He chooses not to do so. This was the case with Pharaoh. He hardened his heart to the things of God (Exodus 8:15, 32, 9:34). Pharaoh thought that he did not have to heed to the voice of God. He expressed his attitude in Exodus 5:2, "Who is the Lord, that I should obey His voice to let Israel go? I do not know the Lord, nor will I let Israel go." So God showed Pharaoh who He was and that He rules with great power.

It is not that Pharaoh was beyond the help of God's mercy, but God simply chose to withhold His mercy and left him to his own wickedness. God is Soveign and rules with great power and always has a purpose for why He does or does not do things. He will move heaven and earth for His will to be fulfilled. We are all a part of His plan and He has a purpose for each and every one of us. You cannot possess the attitude that Pharaoh had and test God's mercy. Do not harden your heart as in rebellion. Willingly heed to the Lord's voice. The Lord wants to show His power in you. Whatever your calling is, God will perfect you and raise you up that His name may be glorified.

APRIL 23

I cry out to the Lord with my voice; with my voice to the Lord I make my supplication. I cried out to You, O Lord: I said, "You are my refuge, my portion in the land of the living."
—Psalm 142:1, 5

The Lord is our refuge and strength. He is our help in times of trouble and despair. Each of us are important to God and He cares about every detail of our lives. When you cry out to Him, He listens with a sincere heart. He takes every word you say to Him very seriously.

When you go before God, you do not have to worry about whether you are saying elaborate prayers or whether you are saying the right thing. God looks at your heart and knows what you are feeling (Luke 16:15). He knows the secrets of your heart (Psalm 44:21). You do not have to put on a front. Just be yourself and let God know how you are feeling. Pour out your complaint before Him and declare before Him your trouble (Psalm 142:2). God listens to every cry in your heart (Genesis 30:17, 22).

God is the best friend you will ever have (John 15:15). He will never turn His back on you. He will never stab you in the back or put you down. He is the lifter of your soul. He is faithful and true to His promises (Deuteronomy 7:9). Do you need someone to talk to today? Do you need someone who will listen with an open heart? Do you need a friend who will stand by you no matter what you are dealing with, someone who has a listening ear? God is that person. Talk to God—He is a good listener and wants to be your best friend.

APRIL 24

*I love the Lord, because He has heard
my voice and my supplications.*

—Psalm 116:1

David said that he loved the Lord because He heard his voice and his prayers for mercy. Each of our voices is unique and God knows every one of them. Cry out to God in a crowd of people and He will be able to distinguish your voice from all others. How amazing it is to know that He hears and knows our voices. Every prayer we pray, He hears and moves on our behalf.

Others may not listen to you, but God hears every word you speak. God says that when you call upon Him and go and pray to Him, He will listen to you (Jeremiah 29:12). Others may not pay attention to your needs but God knows every detail of your life. Your life is a journey. Sometimes you come to a crossroad and don't know which way to go. When you seek the Lord, He will guide you to the right path to follow.

Are you weak? God is mighty and can move mountains. When you have no faith left, God is faithful and true to you even when you don't deserve it. God has great plans for you. When you are down, discouraged or wonder what the future holds for you—look up, believe, and trust in God. He has great plans for you, plans to give you a future and a hope (Jeremiah 29:11).

APRIL 25

Therefore humble yourselves under the mighty hand
of God, that He may exalt you in due time, casting
all your care upon Him, for He cares for you.
—1 Peter 5:6–7

Think back to yesterday. What was on your mind? Did you have worries or cares? Did you give them to the Lord, or did you struggle and try to work them out on your own? Regardless of your concern or worry, God wants you to bring everything to Him and trust Him to take care of you.

You need to take Jesus at His Word. When He says I am the Deliverer (2 Kings 17:39), allow Him to free you from a stronghold. When He says I am your Provider (Genesis 22:8), stop worrying and believe that your needs will be met. When He says I am the Forgiver (Psalm 99:8), accept His forgiveness, forgive yourself and unload your guilt. When He says I am your Guide (Psalm 48:14), commit your way to the Lord, trust in Him, and He shall bring it to pass (Psalm 37:5). When He says I am your Caregiver (Deuteronomy 11:11–14), obey His commandments, love and serve Him with all your heart and soul, and allow Him to care for your needs.

When you give Him a worry, a stronghold, or a fear, don't take it back. No matter what the situation may look like remember that God's thoughts and ways are higher than yours (Isaiah 55:9). God will do what His Word promises, so hold onto that hope and promise. Cast your cares upon Him today and allow God to be God. He cares for you, and in due time He will exalt you (1 Peter 5:6).

APRIL 26

"And the King will answer and say to them, 'Assuredly,
I say to you, inasmuch as you did it to one of the least
of these My brethren, you did it to Me.'"
—Matthew 25:40

God blesses us so that we may be a blessing to others. You choose how you will respond to others. Greatness in the kingdom of Heaven is measured by small acts of kindness: giving someone some food, a drink, a place to sleep, some clothing or a visit (Matthew 25:35–36). When you bless others, you are blessing Christ and when you ignore others, you are ignoring Christ.

You are a disciple of Jesus Christ and you are to love others and serve the least of your brothers with compassion. You don't think about the consequences of turning your back on someone in need but Jesus is clear about the consequences of your actions. "Then the King will turn to those on the left and say, 'Away with you, you cursed ones, into the eternal fire prepared for the devil and his demons. For I was hungry, and you didn't feed me. I was thirsty, and you didn't give me a drink. I was a stranger, and you didn't invite me into your home. I was naked, and you didn't give me clothing. I was sick and in prison, and you didn't visit me.' "Then they will reply, 'Lord, when did we ever see you hungry or thirsty or a stranger or naked or sick or in prison, and not help you?' "And he will answer, 'I tell you the truth, when you refused to help the least of these my brothers and sisters, you were refusing to help me.' "And they will go away into eternal punishment, but the righteous will go into eternal life" (Matthew 25:41–46, NLT).

When you fail to do good, the sin of omission—failing to notice the many opportunities for showing kindness to others—will have severe consequences. You are Jesus's hands and feet here on this earth to be a blessing to all those you come in contact with. Consciously remind yourself of this truth and to put it into practice each day. Who are you going to bless today?

APRIL 27

"He who believes in Me, as the Scriptures has said,
out of his heart will flow rivers of living waters."
But this He spoke concerning the Spirit, whom those
believing in Him would receive, for the Holy Spirit
was not yet given, because Jesus was not yet glorified.
—John 7:38–39

Life is always a give and take. Before one can enjoy the benefits of a gift or something purchased, either he or the giver must pay the purchase price. There is always a cost involved. In these scriptures, believers are promised the gift of the Holy Spirit. They had not yet received the gift because the price had not been paid. In order for the Holy Spirit to come, Jesus had to pay the ultimate price, He had to die. On the cross Jesus said to the Father, "Into thy hands I commit My Spirit" (Luke 23:46). Jesus willingly gave of Himself, knowing that after He died and was glorified, He would send the Holy Spirit to be our Helper, to be the Living Water that would satisfy our spiritual thirst. The promises of God are free for you to receive, but remember that Christ paid the ultimate price for your free gifts.

Life is always a give and take. Jesus gave His life that you might take of His Spirit. In order to receive it, you must take it and accept it. In John 14:16–17 Jesus said, "And I will pray the Father, and He will give you a Helper that He may abide with you forever. The Spirit of Truth, whom the world cannot receive because it neither sees Him nor knows Him, but you know Him." The gift of the Holy Spirit is given to those who believe in the Lord Jesus Christ. It is a lifetime gift that will not rot, decay, or lose value. It is a gift that will change your life forever. Have you received the gift of the Holy Spirit? If not, pray to the Father, and He will give you a Helper that will abide in your forever.

APRIL 28

If you keep My commandments, you will
abide in My love, just as I have kept My
Father's commandments and abide in His love.

—John 15:10

There is a relationship between love and obedience. The deeper you love the Lord, the more you want to keep His commandments. The more you keep His commandments, the more you abide in His love. God is love, and if you abide in Him, you abide in love. In your relationship with Christ, love is everything. When you love someone, you go out of your way to please that person. I can remember when I was growing up, I always wanted to please my mother. I believed that if I pleased her, she would then love me. Some people view their relationship with God like this. But it is totally different. You do not have to do anything to gain God's love, for God is love, and He loves you unconditionally. You obey God not to gain His love, but you do it because you love Him. It is your love for Him that causes you to want to obey.

It is only through the grace of God and this love relationship that you are able to avoid sin. In Ezekiel 36:27, God says that He will put His Spirit in you so that you will follow His laws and be careful to obey His instructions. It is the Holy Spirit who gives you a new heart and fills you with His Spirit to cause you to walk joyfully and willingly in His ways and keep His commandments. Is the Holy Spirit dwelling in you and are you abiding in the Father's love? Are you keeping the commandments of the Lord? Pray that you will continually abide in His love. Heavenly Father, allow the Holy Spirit to dwell within me to cause me to walk joyfully and willingly in Your ways and to keep Your commandments. Allow me to continually abide in Your love. In Jesus's name I pray.

APRIL 29

But if you indeed obey His voice and do all that I speak,
then I will be an enemy to your enemies and an adversary
to your adversaries. For My angel will go before you…
—Exodus 23:22–23

If there is one thing in life that you do not want, it would be for God to be your enemy. Think about the havoc, chaos and destruction that could happen to you. On the other hand, if there is one thing in life that you do want, it would be for God to be your advocate. No matter what you would have to defend, God would be there to uphold you. Jesus tells us that even when you are brought before governors and Kings for His sake, to not worry about how or what we should speak for He will give us the very words we need in that hour. He has promised that it will not be you who speaks, but the Spirit of our Father who speaks in you (Matthew 10:18–20).

God promises to be an enemy to your enemies and an adversary to your adversaries. This should empower you to know that you never face your battles alone—the Lord sends His angels before you for protection against the spiritual enemies and every life situation that you encounter. God tells you to be sober and be vigilant because your adversary the devil walks about like a roaring lion, seeking whom he may devour (1 Peter 5:8). If God is an adversary to your adversaries, then God will be an adversary to the devil on your behalf. You are never alone. In order for you to be guaranteed this protection, obey Him. If today you hear His voice, harden not your heart (Hebrews 4:7). Oh, the rewards that accompany obedience! Allow God to be your adversary—obey His voice.

APRIL 30

"The secret things belong to the Lord our God, but those things which are revealed belong to us and to our children forever, that we may do all the words of this law."
—Deuteronomy 29:29

There are many things that the Lord holds secret to His heart and reveals them to us only when we are ready to receive them. Some secrets are revealed only to those who have a deep, intimate relationship with Him. Think about the things that you hold secret in your heart. Do you share them with just anybody? The obvious answer is no. Do you share it with all your friends? Probably not. More than likely your deepest secrets are discovered only to those with whom you share a deep trusting relationship.

God has already revealed things to each of us and they are promised to us and our children forever. Has God revealed something to you that has not come to pass yet? Claim it now, it is yours. It belongs to you and your children. Receive it in faith. As you read scripture and you see a promise from God, claim it and receive it in faith. God loves to reveal these secret nuggets to you as you devote time to read His Word.

Do you desire to know the secret things of God? I do and I'm sure you do as well The only way that these things will be revealed to us is by having an intimate relationship with Jesus. He longs to fellowship with you and to share those secrets to you, but you have to put the time and effort into building that relationship with Him. Got time? Got time for Jesus? As you spend time with Jesus, you will hear the whisper of His voice as He shares a secret word with you.

MAY 1

"Until now you have asked nothing in My name.
Ask, and you will receive, that your joy may be full."
—John 16:24

This scripture and many others challenge us to ask God for specific things we want. God wants to give you the desires of your heart and see you blessed and happy. When you ask, always ask in faith. God will respond to your request. Sometimes you may not see the answer right away, but believe that God is working things out on your behalf. The Bible tells us we do not have, because we do not ask (James 4:2).

The Lord appeared to Solomon in a dream and said "Ask! What shall I give you?" (1 Kings 3:5). Solomon asked and he received what he asked for and much more (1 Kings 3:13). Why? Because his heart was right with God. Solomon loved the Lord, walked before Him in truth, in righteousness, and in uprightness of heart. God blessed him as a result of his lifestyle. Blessings come when you are faithful to God. After Solomon had finished building the Temple of God, the Lord appeared to him a second time and said to him, "I have heard your prayer and your petition. I have set this Temple apart to be holy—this place you have built where my name will be honored forever. I will always watch over it, for it is dear to my heart" (1 Kings 9:3). Solomon asked in faith and the Lord gave him the desires of his heart.

Jesus is continually with you. Are you seizing the moment and yelling out to Him, asking in faith? What is on your heart today? Whatever it may be, ask God in faith. He will respond in a way that meets your needs and brings glory to His name.

MAY 2

Blessed be the God and Father of our Lord Jesus
Christ, the Father of mercies and God of all comfort,
who comforts us in all our tribulation, that we may be
able to comfort those who are in any trouble, with the
comfort with which we ourselves are comforted by God.
—2 Corinthians 1:3–4

When you are faced with trials and tribulations, you can be sure that God, the Father of mercies and the God of comfort, will come to your aid when you cry out to Him. Everyone wants to see miracles and divine healing, but are we willing to go through the trial so that the miracle or healing can take place? Jesus was willing. Through the suffering He endured, and by His resurrection from the dead, we all have a Heavenly inheritance of eternal life with Jesus waiting for us. This promise is for all who receive Jesus as their personal Savior. What hope and comfort this should bring when you have to face death one day.

Often you are unable to understand or relate to someone's pain unless you've walked in their shoes. Do not look at your circumstances as "Woe is me." Instead, view them as a means for God to touch your life as well as the lives of others around you. Be willing to face whatever may come your way so that the Lord will use your circumstance to bring comfort to another.

Witnessing what God has done in your life brings hope and comfort to others who are going through the same situation. When others see what God has done for you, it will build hope and faith in their spirits that God will do the same for them. The next time you are faced with a tribulation, remember that the Father of mercies and the God of all comfort will be your strength and comfort so that you will be able to give to another the same comfort God has given to you.

MAY 3

Then Jesus answered and said to her, "O woman,
great is your faith! Let it be to you as you desire."
And her daughter was healed from that very hour.
—Matthew 15:28

There are many healings and miracles waiting to happen. Our world is full of wickedness, oppression, sickness, and trouble. The Lord is counting on you to lead the suffering to the fountain of life in Christ Jesus. Many make their requests known to the Lord, but they do not have the faith to believe that God will work in their behalf. Jesus told the woman that her faith was great and her request was granted. She had let her wish be known to the Lord believing in faith that He was able to meet that need. When you experience a trauma, it is hard to hold the faith. But when you turn to the Lord in corporate prayer and speak life into the situation, healings and miracles happen.

Where is your faith today? Do you believe in the miracles and the promises of God? Are you ready to put your faith into action? Be a pillar of strength to someone who is facing a battle. Fight the good fight with them by praying in faith for their miracle. Jesus honors and responds to our faith. Many people approached Jesus out of faith to be healed. A leader of a synagogue came and knelt before Jesus. He told Jesus that his daughter has just died, but that her life would be restored if Jesus would only lay His hand on her. So Jesus and his disciples went with him, and as they did, a woman who had suffered for twelve years with constant bleeding came up behind him. She touched the fringe of his robe, for she thought that if she could just touch his robe, that she would be healed. Jesus turned around, and when he saw her he said, "Daughter, be encouraged! Your faith has made you well." And the woman was healed at that moment (Matthew 9:18–22, NLT). Allow your faith to be the reason why you or someone else becomes well.

MAY 4

*Oh, the depth of the riches both of wisdom and
knowledge of God! How unsearchable are His
judgments and His ways past finding out.*
—Romans 11:33

Our God is incomprehensible. As hard as you may try, you will never completely understand God's ways or why He does the things He does. His greatness, power, wisdom, and knowledge are incomprehensible. His holiness, mercy, and love are inconceivable. His ways are unsearchable. We think you know a lot about God but we know very little about Him. As the heavens are higher than the earth, so God's thoughts and ways are infinitely higher than yours (Isaiah 55:9). Oh the depth of the riches of His wisdom and knowledge. His excellence in power and judgment and His ways are beyond finding out.

And yet in the fullness of His power and glory, He has one thing in mind—to fellowship with you and me. Even God is not satisfied with riches and power. He wants more, He wants us. If you would only come to grasp the fullness of His love and the desire to be one with you. Although His ways are unsearchable, that does not mean that you should stop looking. Desire to know more about Him. Desire to find the depths of His riches, both of wisdom and knowledge. Desire to know the depths of His love for you. Desire Him!

MAY 5

And the Word became flesh and dwelt among us, and we
behold His glory, the glory as of the only begotten of the
Father, full of grace and truth. For the law was given through
Moses, but grace and truth came through Jesus Christ.
—John 1:14, 17

At the beginning of the gospel of John, it is written "In the beginning was the Word, and the Word was with God, and the Word was God" (John 1:1). Jesus was more than a great teacher or prophet, He was God. The Word became flesh and dwelt among the people to behold His glory—the Glory of God. Whatever Jesus said or did, He did it with grace and in truth.

The only way to get to know Truth is to have a personal relationship with Jesus. Rules and laws will never give you answers to the deep questions you hold in your heart. Religion is about rules and laws and having the right answers. There are a lot of smart people who are able to say many right things, but their hearts are far from God. Sharing your life with Jesus will be far more illuminating than any answer to rules.

The ways and means in which the Lord wants to communicate with you is limitless. You just have to believe that God desires a relationship with you and He will use any means He can to get your attention. King Nebuchadnezzar experienced this first hand. God gave him a dream and Daniel was able to describe the dream and interpret it. The king responded, "Truly your God is the God of gods, the Lord of kings, and a revealer of secrets, since you could reveal this secret" (Daniel 2:30–47). God will speak to you through dreams, visions, music, and other people, but He especially speaks to you through His Word. More and more will be revealed to you in the Bible as you build your faith, trust and relationship with Jesus. The Word of God is not a set of rules, but rather it is a relationship with God. Spend time in the Word and see your relationship with Jesus grow.

MAY 6

"O my God, incline Your ear and hear; open Your eyes and
see our desolations, and the city which is called by Your name;
for we do not present our supplications before You because of
our righteous deeds, but because of Your great mercies."
—Daniel 9:18

Just look around, read the newspapers, or watch a little television, and you will see that this world is in dire need of the Lord's hand. God's ear is not too deaf that He cannot hear, nor is His arm too short to touch those in need (Isaiah 59:1). God sees everything that is going on in this world. Daniel saw the conditions of this world and he did something about it. He humbled himself, sought God and cried out to Him with sorrowful repentance, and asked for God's mercy.

God's Word gives us a hope and a solution regarding our nation's woes. "If My people who are called by My name will humble themselves, and pray and seek My face, and turn from their wicked ways, then I will hear from heaven, and will forgive their sin and heal their land" (2 Chronicles 7:14). First we must humble ourselves and acknowledge that without God, we can do nothing. Second, we must pray. Pray the Word, pray about the conditions of this nation, pray for our government and those in authority over us that God may give them wisdom and direction for this nation. Pray for Israel that God will protect her from the threats of attack. There are so many needs that we can pray about. Third, we must seek His face, listen for His voice, and obey what God tells us to do. Lastly, we must turn from our wicked ways.

The Word of God makes it clear what pleases and displeases Him. God makes it obvious how we should live our lives. We must turn from our sinfulness and obey the Word of God. If we do these things, then God will hear our cries from heaven, He will forgive us of our sins, and heal our land. The world is in desperate need of God's intervention and healing. Let us go before our Maker, humble ourselves, and seek God for mercy.

MAY 7

My sheep hear My voice, and I know them,
and they follow Me. And I give them eternal
life, and they shall never perish; neither shall
anyone snatch them out of My hand.
—John 10:27–28

These verses always remind me of a time when I was at a park just spending some quiet time away from everyone. I was watching some geese and the Lord began to speak to me through them. I watched how the flock stayed together. There was one that was leading the whole flock. Wherever the leader went, the rest of the geese followed. The leader came to a road that was heavily traveled by people visiting the park. The leader stopped, stretched its neck high, looked to the left and then looked to the right. Seeing that there was no traffic, he began to cross the road. The other geese proceeded to follow the leader. None of the other geese looked to see if there was traffic coming on either side. They just followed their leader. Had it not been for the mercy of the drivers, the geese would have had their lives cut short.

Then the Lord spoke to me saying that this is how people are acting today. They are aimlessly following after a leader, never questioning their actions or checking to see if they could be in danger. It is important to know who we are following. There are many false prophets deceiving many people who will ultimately lose their lives and perish if they do not realize that they are following the wrong leader. Jesus said, "My sheep hear My voice, and I know them, and they follow Me." The only way to know His voice and follow Him is by spending time with Jesus. The more we know about Him and hear Him speak to us, the easier it is to recognize the counterfeit prophets. We are all His sheep. He has a destiny for each of us, but we must be led by Jesus. Who are you following? Are you following His voice?

MAY 8

So it was, when I heard these words, that I sat down and
wept, and mourned for many days; I was fasting and praying
before the God of heaven. "Please let Your ear be attentive
and Your eyes open, that You may hear the prayer of Your
servant which I pray before You now, day and night, for the
children of Israel Your servants, and confess the sins of the
children of Israel which we have sinned against You.
Both my father's house and I have sinned."
—Nehemiah 1:4, 6

It's not about me. It's about Him—seeing God in action. Often our prayers are about me, me, me—praying for our own needs, while there are others with greater needs and on whom our prayers should be focused. Many things happen in life over which we have no control. Instead of gossiping about people, hold them up in prayer.

Nehemiah not only prayed for his people, he wept, mourned and fasted for them. He acknowledged to God their sinfulness and corrupt action against Him. Nehemiah reminded the Lord of the word He had given to Moses, that if they returned to Him and kept His commands, He would hear their prayer (Nehemiah 1:6–9). Prayer becomes powerful when God's people fear Him, confess their sinfulness, and pray for the needs of others.

In Galatians 6:2 we are told to bear one another's burdens. How do you bear one another's burdens? Pray for them and let them know that you genuinely care about them. Stop the rumors and be a part of the solution instead of adding to the problem. Take the needs of others to God in prayer. Be willing to mourn and fast for the corrupt things you see in this world. Be a Nehemiah who prays, weeps, mourns and fasts for the condition of this nation.

Ask God to place someone on your heart today. As you pray and see God move, not only is the other person blessed, but you are as well, knowing that your prayers have been answered.

MAY 9

For since the beginning of the world men have not heard
nor perceived by the ear, nor has seen any God besides you,
who acts for the one who waits for Him. But now, O lord,
You are our Father; we are the clay, and You are our
potter; and all we are the work of Your hand.
—Isaiah 64:4, 8

God acts on behalf of those who wait on Him. The problem is that we become too anxious and move ahead of God's timing. We lose our patience, our temper, our tongues and God's perfect plan. Like a one-thousand-piece puzzle, some things take time and God has to place all the pieces together before we see the whole picture. If we try to put ourselves in a position where we're not supposed to be, not only will we be out of place from where the Lord wants us to be, but someone else may be left standing confused, hurt, or not sure where they belong. When we move ahead before God's timing, we may even become lost. And one lost piece in a jigsaw puzzle can ruin the entire picture.

Are you willing to let God be the potter of your life and be the works of His hands? Are you willing to let God be the potter of others' lives and not interfere with the Master's plan for their lives? We are all vessels of the Potter's hand and He should be the one who molds and shapes us. Do not be the one who causes another to be lost by the words you speak. Do not interfere with the works of the Potter's hand but allow Him the time and method He chooses to shape and form all His children. Allow God to work in His timing not only in your life, but in the lives of those around you, so that we all may be a part of the big picture.

MAY 10

*"Look at the birds of the air, for they neither sow
nor reap nor gather into barns; yet your heavenly
Father feeds them. Are you not of more value than
they? So why do you worry about clothing? Consider
the lilies of the field, how they grow: they neither toil
nor spin; and yet I say to you that even Solomon in
all his glory was not arrayed like one of these."*
—Matthew 6:26, 28–29

Do you believe that God will provide for all your needs? Then why do you worry so much? God not only wants you to believe that He will provide for you but He also wants you to trust Him to do it. You need to let go of your earthly cares and put your trust in Him. Jesus told the crowd, "Do not worry about your life, what you will eat or what you will drink; nor about your body, what you will put on" (Matthew 6:25). He repeats these same words again in Matthew 6:31. Worry, worry, worry. There will always be something to worry about. That is our human nature but it should not be the case.

Worry causes distractions; it preoccupies your mind with thoughts that cause anxiety, stress and pressure. Jesus tells us that we can stop worrying because He is mindful of our daily needs. Nature and animals do not worry about their tomorrows. God provides for them, and you are more valuable to God then they are. The best way to break the power of worry is to refuse to think about tomorrow. Jesus tells the crowd, "Therefore do not worry about tomorrow for tomorrow will worry about its own things." Instead, seek first the kingdom of God and His righteousness and all these things shall be added to you" (Matthew 6:33–34). Most anxious thoughts are related to the future and not about today. You need to give God your tomorrows. Live each day to the fullest with faith, believing your tomorrows are already taken care of.

MAY 11

*"Who is more important, the one who sits at
the table or the one who serves? The one who
sits at the table, of course. But not here! For
I am among you as one who serves."*
—Luke 22:27, NLT

Many people do not think that what they do is important or really matters, but to the Lord, everything matters. The disciples were arguing about who was the greatest and Jesus asked them this question, "Who is more important, the one sitting at the table or the one serving?" In Jesus's day, washing of feet was a task that was always given to the lowest of lowest servants. Jesus humbled Himself to that degree, being one of the lowest of lowest servants (John 13:5). He did it to show His disciples how much He loved them. I also think He did it to demonstrate that no matter what you are called to do, servanthood is important to the Lord.

We are all a part of the Master's plan and each of us is important to Him. Because you are important to Him, everything you do is important to Him. Jesus calls you to be His servants. It's the little things in life that really matter. Never underestimate how God can start something big, with one small action, to change a life. Every time you reach out and touch a heart, a person changes… the world changes. Every encouraging word spoken to another, changes a life…changes the world. Every time you forgive, a life changes…the world changes. Every act of love, changes a life… changes the world. Every act of kindness, whether seen or unseen, changes a life…changes the world.

Everything you say or do does matter and touches lives. No matter how small or how big it may seem, you are changing a life and thus changing the world. Do not think that what you do is not important, for everything matters to the Lord.

MAY 12

That Christ may dwell in your hearts through faith;
that you, being rooted and grounded in love, may be able
to comprehend with all the saints what is the width and
length and depth and height— to know the love of
Christ which passes knowledge; that you may be filled
with all the fullness of God.

—Ephesians 3:17–19

It is only through the power of the Holy Spirit that our inner man is strengthened (Ephesians 3:16). When you allow Christ to dwell in your heart, He becomes the foundation which enables you to become rooted and grounded in love. My husband and I planted a dogwood tree last year. The tree was small and could easily bend when a strong wind blew. We supported the tree on three sides with cords that were staked to the ground. This allowed the tree to gain strength over the next year while it grew stronger and the roots grew deeper into the ground. Over the weekend, we removed the stakes, for the tree was well grounded and no longer needed them for support.

Like the tree, you need to be rooted and grounded in the love of Christ that you might be filled with all the fullness of God. Storms will come your way, and if you are not grounded in His love, the storms of life will easily uproot you. Whether you are young or mature in the Spirit, you need to stake yourself into the solid foundation of Jesus Christ so that He can ground you securely in the truth of His unconditional love. It is in the abiding love of Christ that you are able to endure all things. He will provide you the ability to stand firm, giving strength to your inner man to live triumphantly.

MAY 13

But may the God of all grace, who called us to His
eternal glory by Christ Jesus, after you have suffered a
while, perfect, establish, strengthen, and settle you.
—1 Peter 5:10

God is the God of all grace. Grace is God's love in action on your behalf. It is His forgiveness, acceptance, wisdom, strength, and His favor that empowers you to do that which you are called to do. If you put your hope and trust in Him, you will accomplish all that you set your mind to do. God must be the source of your hope and trust. The God of all grace must be the source of your strength, for it is He who will perfect and establish you (Psalm 138:8). God is your strength and power, and He will make your way perfect (2 Samuel 22:33).

God will begin to work out His purposes in your life and continue to work through you until His works are completed. You are His hands in action touching lives all around you. Every day, humbly place yourself in His hands, confessing your helplessness, and yielding yourself to receive from Him the fulfillment of His promises. It is God who performs all things for you and through you. The Lord will make you abound in all the work of your hand (Deuteronomy 30:9). Be confident of this very thing, that He who has begun a good work in you will complete it until the day when Jesus Christ returns (Philippians 1:6). May the God of all grace make you perfect in every good work. May He perfect, establish, strengthen, and place you on a firm foundation.

MAY 14

Now He who establishes us with you in Christ and
has anointed us is God, who also has sealed us and
given us the Spirit in our hearts as a guarantee.
—2 Corinthians 1:21–22

I have read this scripture many times, but two words really jump out and speak to me today: sealed and guarantee. It is God who establishes us and anoints us to do the things we do. It is God who perfects us through the workings of the Holy Spirit in our lives. He establishes us and then seals all that He has accomplished in us.

Webster's dictionary defines seal: to fasten with to prevent tampering; to close or make secure against access, leakage, or passage. This means that what God has done in our lives is a done-deal, sealed, and no one including Satan can tamper, loosen, or steal that which the Lord has sealed. Our salvation is a sealed deal and God has put His Spirit in our hearts as a guarantee.

God Almighty guarantees us that He will work in us that which is pleasing in His sight through Christ Jesus by the power of the Holy Spirit. We are called to a life in which faith in the almighty power of God is our only hope. Through Christ we have obtained our inheritance. We are sealed. He has identified us as His own, guaranteeing that we will be saved on the day of redemption (Ephesians 4:30). Believe that what God has sealed in your life, is sealed and secured forever.

MAY 15

*You will keep him in perfect peace, whose mind
is stayed on You, because he trusts in You.*

—Isaiah 26:3

God wants you to trust in Him so that your heart is filled with His peace. He is your Counselor, Mighty God, Everlasting Father, and the Prince of Peace (Isaiah 9:6). You are filled with His Spirit, and if the Holy Spirit dwells in you, then you should have the peace of God within you as well. But that is not always the case. When conflicts come your way, instead of talking things over with your Counselor and getting His wisdom for the situation, you are too busy trying to resolve the issues on your own. Instead of trusting in Almighty God who has the power to conquer and destroy, you try to change things in your own strength, and then worry because you are not winning the battle.

What robs your peace? Is it finances, your job or problems at home? Maybe it's your health or issues with friends or family? Determine what robs your peace and then give it to the Lord. The best way to find peace is to spend some time with the Lord and let Him know your troubles. There is a peace that surpasses all understanding. We can obtain that peace only by being in the presence of the Lord (Philippians 4:7). His peace is sufficient for anything we may face. He will keep you in perfect peace if your mind is focused on Him.

MAY 16

*"So I sought for a man among them who would make a
wall, and stand in the gap before Me on behalf of the
land, that I should not destroy it; but I found no one."*
—Ezekiel 22:30

The Lord sought for only one man to stand in the gap but
found no one. That's a scary thought—to think that there was not
a single person who would stand in the gap for the Lord. We are
the instruments of His hands and God is looking for godly men
and women who will step forward, stand in the gap, and restore
righteousness in our nation.

Had it not been for Moses, God would have destroyed His
people (Psalm 106:23). The Lord was displeased when he found
that there was no justice for the evil and iniquity and was amazed
to see that no one intervened to help the oppressed (Isaiah 59:16).
The Lord hears each and every prayer and stands ready to grant
mercy to those for whom you pray. You may not be called to save
an entire nation, but God is calling upon His faithful ones to stand
in the gap. In Moses's day, one man made a difference. Will you
be the person who makes the difference in your family, workplace,
and community? Will you be one who intercedes before the Lord
on behalf of another so that the Lord will turn away His wrath?

MAY 17

"But you shall receive power when the Holy Spirit has come upon you; and you shall be witnessed to Me in Jerusalem, and in all Judea and Samaria, and to the end of the earth."
—Acts 1:8

The great work of bringing the knowledge of Christ to every creature has been entrusted to the church. Many do not feel it is their responsibility, nor do they consider the consequences of their neglect. God calls each of us to be His witnesses, His ambassadors in this world, continually testifying of His wonderful love and His power to redeem. We are to introduce people, who don't yet know Jesus, to the love and grace of God available to them in Christ. Our life and actions should be a living proof and witness of what Jesus can do.

When Jesus chose His apostles, they were ordinary people like you and me. They had no special gifts or training, yet Jesus chose them. You do not need special gifts or eloquent words to be a witness for Christ. You just need the love of Christ to be so full in your life that you can't help but witness for Him. Jesus empowered you with His Holy Spirit in order to do what He did.

We are commissioned to go into the world and preach the gospel to every creature (Mark 16:15). Are you about the Father's business? Share the joy of what you know with others. Be a witness for Jesus. Let the Father's love be revealed to every soul you come into contact with. There are many hurting people. They need to know that no problem is too great for Jesus to solve, no wound is too deep that Jesus can't heal, and no mountain is too big that Jesus can't remove. Be a light to those around you and testify of the mighty works of Jesus. Walk in fellowship with Jesus Christ so that He can reveal Himself through you.

MAY 18

Sow for yourselves righteousness; Reap in mercy; break
up your fallow ground, for it is time to seek the Lord, till
he comes and rains righteousness on you.

—Hosea 10:12

Now that spring is here, everyone is busy working in gardens. There is much work to be done: prepare the soil, dig up weeds, scatter seeds, plant shrubs, water and fertilize the newly planted seeds or shrubs, and protect the plants from frost. As time passes and summer arrives, we are able to enjoy the bountiful crops and the beauty of our labor. Springtime is a time that should remind you to look at the internal garden within you. Continually plow up the broken ground in your heart to prepare the soil for good seed to grow. Unattended fields yield weeds and hard ground, becoming unproductive and useless.

Lord, I break up the fallow ground of my heart so that it is ready to receive seeds that will bear much fruit. I dig up roots of wickedness. I uproot tradition that hinders the Holy Spirit from working in my life. I uproot pride and cultivate humility in my heart. Wash away the seeds of doubt, discouragement, and fear before they have a chance to take root in my heart. I pull out every weed before they have time to choke out the tender shoots.

Lord, I tend to my garden and the gardens of others. I scatter compliments and plant affirmations. I nurture new spiritual growth in each of us. I cultivate seeds of love and compassion. I sow courage and strength within us. Lord, I water our gardens with kindness and fertilize them with prayer and positive words in hope of a bountiful harvest. I keep watch over my heart and over my spiritual life. I will not allow sin to germinate in the soil of my heart. Break up the hard places in my life and rain righteousness upon me. I thank You Lord for the beautiful harvest You are preparing in me.

MAY 19

And when Jesus went out He saw a great multitude; and
He moved with compassion for them, and healed their sick.
—Matthew 14:14

Jesus moved with compassion. He saw the many needs of the people that were brought to Him and he met those needs (Matthew 4:24). It did not matter the type of illness or the character of the persons needing healed, Jesus moved with compassion and healed them all. I am sure there were many who disbelieve in Jesus, many who were unworthy of receiving healing, many who were criminals, and many who were underserving of a touch from the Lord; and yet, Jesus healed them. Why do you think He did so? Could it be that the same power Jesus had to heal also gave Him the power to perceive their potential? Jesus was not looking at their past or their present condition when He touched and healed them. He was looking at their future.

Does it mean that every person He touched gave their lives to Christ and used their miracle for good? Undoubtedly there were some who did not. Perhaps they all eventually took their renewed health for granted and reverted to their evil ways. But that did not stop Jesus from touching them. Like Jesus, you need to be His hands and His feet, reaching out to others with compassion, understanding, and love. You need to touch the lives of others as Jesus would have touched them, giving them hope and a new future. Look beyond the past and the present of a person and see the potential that is in them. Help them to reach that potential. Be the hands and feet that Jesus is calling upon in His people.

MAY 20

*"Believe Me that I am in the Father and the Father
in Me, or else believe Me for the sake of the works
themselves. At that day you will know that I am
in My Father, and you in Me, and I in you."*
—John 14:11, 20

Although Jesus walked on earth as man, He lived in the Father and the Father lived in Him. Everything He did was what the Father did in Him. This is how we should picture our lives. If we are filled with the Holy Spirit, then Christ lives in us. We must live our lives in faith that we are in Christ. As the Father worked in Christ, so Christ will work in us if we yield ourselves to His power.

The secret to this mystery is to daily abide in Christ, allowing Him to fill you with wisdom, knowledge, and understanding. He will equip you with the materials you need to advance His kingdom. Jesus said, "And that day you will know that I am in My Father, and you in Me and I in you." What day was He referring to? He was referring to the day when the Holy Spirit fills your heart.

If you are not filled with His Spirit, ask the Lord to fill you with His Spirit right now. If you are filled with His Spirit, may the Lord touch you with a new awareness that you are in Christ, and that Christ works through you, and that you can do all things through Him. The Holy Spirit will equip you to do the works of Jesus. The very works that you do will bear witness of Christ in you (John 5:36).

MAY 21

*The truthful lip shall be established forever, but a lying
tongue is but for a moment. Lying lips are an abomination
to the Lord, but those who deal truthfully are His delight.*
—Proverbs 12:19, 22

God hates lying; it is an abomination to the Lord. He delights
in truth and you please Him when you tell the truth. Sometimes
truth hurts, but truth must be told. Your words are powerful and
they must be spoken in truth and in love. When you speak truth
but not in love, it can have a negative affect and bring discouragement, anger, and harm to others. But truth spoken in love can
positively change a person's life forever.

Also be willing to accept truth that is spoken to you. Many
times you are deceived by the enemy and it is not until the Lord
or another person points it out to you that you see your sinful
ways. Sometimes you walk in blindness until someone else reveals
to you that you have not used wisdom in some area of your life.
People who speak truth in love are there to help another, not to
bring them down. Accept truth and allow it to help you grow and
mature.

There are many reasons why people lie. Many lie to cover
their tracks in order to keep themselves from getting into trouble.
Others lie to hide their true feelings. Some lie to follow their own
fleshly desires or to get out of doing something they do not want
to do. No matter what excuse one may use, God hates a lying
spirit. It stirs up the same heavenly anger as adultery, drunken-
ness, and murder (1 Corinthians 6:9–10). Dishonesty is contrary
to the character of God. Next time, think twice before telling that
"white" lie. Ask the Lord to reveal to you if there were any times
this past week that you have not spoken in truth. Then confess
your sins to God, ask for forgiveness, and strive to live a life that is
pleasing to God.

MAY 22

And He said to them, "Why are you troubled?
And why do doubts arise in your hearts."
—Luke 24:38

Two weapons Satan uses to cause you to question God are fear and doubt. Doubt and uncertainty lead to fear. If you don't get these emotions under control, they will cause you to question God's ability to work things out in your life. Many times you struggle with emotions that are not valid because you jump to conclusions before God has time to work on your behalf. Other times you doubt because God did not answer the way you expected Him to. When you doubt, in a sense you are telling God, "I don't trust You. I don't believe You have my best interest at heart."

When doubt or fear begins to creep into your heart—feed it the Word of God—I will trust in the Lord at all times and I will not lean on my understanding for I know God's ways are better than my own (Isaiah 55:8–9). I commit my ways to the Lord, I trust in Him, and He shall bring it to pass (Psalm 37:5). God's perfect love casts out all fear (1 John 4:18). It is the Lord that goes before me. He will be with me, He will not fail me nor forsake me, I will not fear nor be dismayed (Deuteronomy 31:8). Every battle I face, is not mine, but the Lord's, and He will fight my battles (2 Chronicles 20:15).

Let the Lord be the strength of your life in all circumstances regardless of what you see. God has given you a spirit of power and love and a sound mind (2 Timothy 1:7). Use these weapons to fight Satan in his own tracks and you will be victorious in every battle you face. Though you walk in the flesh, you do not war according to the flesh for the weapons of your warfare are not carnal but mighty in God for pulling down strongholds (2 Corinthians 10:3–4). With God on your side, you are more than a conqueror through Christ (Romans 8:37).

MAY 23

For the weapons of our warfare are not carnal but
mighty in God for pulling down strongholds, casting
down arguments and every high thing that exalts
itself against the knowledge of God, bringing every
thought into captivity to the obedience of Christ.
—2 Corinthians 10:4–5

The mind is our greatest battlefield because that is where you say things about yourself and others that no one else can hear. It is a place where Satan can come in and influence your thoughts, which in turn influence your actions. You are a threat to Satan, so he will try to put doubt, fear, confusion and other unhealthy spirits into your mind to make you less confident in who you are in Christ. You have the power within you, through Christ, to bring every thought captive and to pull down the strongholds Satan tries to plant in your mind.

You need to renew your mind daily through His Word. Philippians 4:8 tells us what things we should meditate on: whatever things are true, whatever things are noble, whatever things are just, whatever things are pure, whatever things are lovely, whatever things are of good report, if there is any virtue or anything praiseworthy—meditate on these things. If your thoughts are not true, honest, just, pure, lovely, of good report, or praiseworthy, do not allow those thoughts to take root in your mind and heart. It is up to you to guard your mind. Meditate on God's Word. Know who you are in Christ, and speak the truth of God's Word into your heart when your mind becomes a battlefield.

MAY 24

And in the process of time it came to pass that Cain brought an offering of the fruit of the ground to the Lord. Abel also brought of the firstborn of his flock and of their fat. And the Lord respected Abel and his offering, but He did not respect Cain and his offering. And Cain was very angry, and his countenance fell. So the Lord said to Cain, "Why are you angry? And why has your countenance fallen? If you do well, will you not be accepted? And if you do not do well, sin lies at the door. And its desire is for you, but you should rule over it."
—Genesis 4:3–7

What really got Cain in trouble was his attitude. He became angry that his offering was not accepted and he allowed that anger to cause him to eventually kill his brother (Genesis 4:8). God warned Cain that sin was knocking at the door and it desired to rule him, but if Cain wanted to, he could rule over the anger. You choose what kind of day you are going to have by your attitude and the way you look at things. Here are some positive attitudes written by others:

- If you don't get everything you want, think of the things you don't get that you don't want.
- It's not what they take away from you that counts. It's what you do with what you have left.
- If you don't like something, change it; if you can't change it, change the way you think about it.
- A positive attitude may not solve all your problems, but it will annoy enough people to make it worth the effort.
- Every thought is a seed. If you plant crab apples, don't count on harvesting Golden Delicious.
- Blessed is he who expects nothing, for he shall never be disappointed.
- Enjoy the little things, for one day you may look back and realize they were the big things.

So what kind of day are you choosing to have today? Look for the positive in every situation.

MAY 25

*Then great multitudes came to Him, having with them
the lame, blind, mute, maimed, and many others; and
they laid them down at Jesus' feet, and He healed them.
So the multitude marveled when they saw the mute
speaking, the maimed made whole, the lame walking,
and the blind seeing; and they glorified the God of Israel.*
—Matthew 15:30–31

God is in the healing business. He wants to see all His children made whole. Many believe that the signs, wonders, and miracles that Jesus performed are not for today and are marveled when they hear of them happening. What He does for one, He can do for all.

This past Friday we witnessed God's miracle power at our church service. A lady from our church had fallen down some stairs and had broken five bones around her ankle and the toe bones across the front of her foot. She was in a lot of pain and could not put pressure on her foot. She was supposed to wear a cast for 6 weeks and then go through two months of physical therapy. People prayed in faith believing that God could and would heal her. God showed up and performed the miracle. She took off the walking boot and was able to walk on her foot with very little discomfort. She could actually feel the bones going back into place as the people prayed. Sunday she came to service wearing high heels. To God we give the Glory! Thanks be to God for His mercy, His love, and His miracle.

I told my husband about the miracle and his reaction was "no way, no way." He had a hard time believing that God showed up and performed the miracle. He said that we see it all the time on television only to find out later that it was all fake. He was marveled at what he heard. God is real and He desires to see all His people whole. This is one of many miracles to happen. Have faith and believe that what He does for one, He will do for you as well. Believe and expect your miracle. To God be the Glory!

MAY 26

And the Lord God commanded the man, saying,
"Of every tree of the garden you may freely eat; but of the
tree of the knowledge of good and evil you shall not eat,
for in the day that you eat of it you shall surely die."
—Genesis 2:16–17

How do you determine whether something is good or evil? When something happens, are you confident in your ability to discern the difference? Some things you initially think are good turn out to be horribly destructive and other things you think are evil turn out for your good. Adam and Eve thought in their hearts that eating the apple from the tree of knowledge of good and evil was a good thing, but in the end, it was very destructive. For their disobedience, the Lord sent them out of the garden of Eden (Genesis 3:22–23)

How many times have you been like Adam and Eve, where the Lord has told you one thing, but through your own reasoning, you have decided to do something else because you felt it was the better thing to do? You play God in your independence, creating your own list of good and evil to suit your desires. Who are you to become your own judge and determine what is right and wrong? In the end, like Adam and Eve, you will see the destructiveness of your choices.

When you choose to follow your own paths, you are choosing a life apart from God. Your independence will only separate you from God, your source of life. When you look inward toward your own intellect for determining what is good and evil, spiritual death will come knocking at your door. Give up your right to determine what is good and evil on your own terms and choose to allow the Lord to make all decisions. A wise believer takes the time to listen with his spiritual ears to hear what the Spirit says is good and what is evil and then follows the voice of the Spirit. Be a wise believer.

MAY 27

"For what will it profit a man if he gains the whole
world, and loses his own soul? Or what will a man give
in exchange for his soul? For whoever is ashamed of Me
and My words in this adulterous and sinful generation,
of him the Son of Man also will be ashamed when He
comes in the glory of His Father with the holy angels."
—Mark 8:36–38

Mark 8:34–38 is a passage where Jesus is calling us to take up our cross and follow Him. Verse 37 asks the question, "What will a man give in exchange for his soul?" When I read this passage, I usually pair this verse with the previous one, "For what will it profit a man if he gains the whole world and loses his own soul?" But today, the Lord had me pair the verse with the one that follows it. Immediately the question came to my mind, "Are you willing to exchange your soul because you are ashamed or afraid to speak about the Lord?" Woo, that hit me hard.

How many times have you betrayed Jesus not because of words you have spoken but because of your silence? Never pass up an opportunity to uphold Jesus, to testify of His great works, and to speak of His love and mercy. By words, a man may sin against God, but by silence, you rob God of His Glory. You never know who will be touched by your witness. Never be ashamed of the Gospel of Jesus Christ, for it is the power of God to offer salvation for everyone who believes (Romans 1:16).

Are you testifying of the works of Jesus to others? Do you testify of His works just to other Christians or do you share the love of Jesus to perfect strangers? What's holding you back? Look for opportunities to share with others what the Lord has done for you and what He wants to do for all of His children. Don't allow your silence to rob God of His Glory. When you testify of Jesus before men, He will witness for you before the Father. If you are ashamed of Him before men, He will be ashamed of you when He stands before the Father on your behalf.

MAY 28

*"Take My yoke upon you and learn from Me, for I am
gentle and lowly in heart, and you will find rest for your
souls. For My yoke is easy and My burden is light."*
—Matthew 11:29–30

All of us need rest, and Jesus promised to give us rest when we turn to Him. Jesus knows our hearts, our burdens, our weariness and He will lift every burden from us if we give them to Him. He will relieve our souls of much stress if we will just learn to lay every care in His hand. Jesus said that he who abides in Him ought to walk just as He walked (1 John 2:6). Jesus walked in obedience. He was compassionate, gentle, and lowly in heart. He found rest for His soul by constantly going to the Father in prayer, seeking the Father's wisdom and guidance, and laying all His burdens in the Father's hands.

You tend to cling to your miseries or troubles and think that you can resolve them yourself. God wants you to give them to Him so that He can work them out for you. Jesus said to learn from Him. When He touched people, He moved with compassion and love (Matthew 14:14). He did not condemn but was gentle to those He touched. Jesus is waiting for you to come to Him so that He can nurture you and give you rest. Jesus found time to go to the Father to find rest. Do the same.

Jesus said, "My yoke is easy and My burden light." The yoke you carry is only as heavy as you allow it to be. The more you give to Jesus, the lighter the load will be. The burdens you carry are really His, they belong to Him. When you choose to own them, then weariness and heaviness come. When you allow Him to have them, the burden is light. Are you weary and heavy laden? Cast your cares upon the Lord and He will give you rest (1 Peter 5:7).

MAY 29

Happy is the man who finds wisdom,
and the man who gains understanding.
—Proverbs 3:13

What makes you happy? Are you a person who is generally happy for the most part or do you find yourself struggling to find joy in your life? Happiness is a choice. you choose to think and do things that will make you happy. Actions do matter. It's not just what you believe that brings happiness but your thoughts and actions play a major part as well. Unhappy people tend to think negatively all the time. They can rarely see the positive in any given situation.

The happiest people are those who pursue intimacy and personal growth with the Lord. Happy people don't judge themselves according to man's standards but they know who they are in Christ and measure themselves through the Word of God. Happy people know their strengths and use them. They tend to think positively and do not let their circumstances get the best of them. Happy people always find good in every situation because they get their understanding from the Lord.

You are to be a good steward of what God gives you and be willing to share with others so that they may be blessed with wisdom, understanding, and the joy of the Lord. When you see someone down and out, try to bring out the best in them and let them know that they are a conqueror. Try to encourage them to see the good in their situation and that God will see them through. Remind them that the joy of the Lord is their strength (Nehemiah 8:10) and to not allow Satan to rob them of that joy. You are atmosphere changers. Spread some joy, happiness and the love of the Father to those around you.

MAY 30

Death and life are in the power of the tongue
and those who love it will eat its fruit.
—Proverbs 18:21

The words you speak are so powerful. They can bring life to a person or they can crucify them to death. People do not realize the power of a spoken word and how negative words spoken can bring curses upon a person. You speak so often never thinking about what was spoken and then wonder why you feel so miserable. A friend's husband used to tell others that he wanted to live long enough to see his two daughters get married. They were young at the time but he said this through the years. Two weeks after his second daughter's wedding, he was diagnosed with cancer and died less than five months later. you really need to be careful with the words you speak.

If negative words have that power, just think of the power you possess when you speak positively to yourself and others. The words you speak are a heart issue and if you are a negative person, then that is where you need to start. Scripture tells us that out of the abundance of the heart the mouth speaks (Matthew 12:34) There is an old saying, "We are what we eat." What words are you feeding yourself with? If you set your heart to continually offer praise to God, the fruit of your lips will be that of praise and encouragement to others (Hebrews 13:15).

Other people eat from the fruit of your lips. Death and life are in the power of the tongue and those who love it will eat its fruit. What fruit are you offering today? Purpose in your heart to offer good nutritious fruit with lots of vitamins to get people through the day.

MAY 31

"Behold, I am with you and will keep you wherever you go,
and will bring you back to this land; for I will not leave
you until I have done what I have spoken to you."
—Genesis 28:15

No matter where we are, whether on this land or in a foreign country fighting for our freedom, God is always with us. We all pray that our American soldiers will return home safely, but freedom is not always free. Many courageous men and women have paid the ultimate price to protect our freedom and our rights of life, liberty, and pursuit of happiness. To them we owe a debt of gratitude and we say, "Thank you." May the Lord richly bless you.

On this Memorial Day, remember to keep our veterans in prayer and honor them for the many sacrifices that they have given to make our nation more secure. Thank veterans for their service and dedication. When you are at a restaurant and there are service men or women there, buy their meals as a sign of gratitude. Reach out to the veteran's family members to see if their needs are being met. Many have lost substantial finances due to a loved one serving. Pray for the families of those who have lost loved ones. Greater love has no one that this, than to lay down one's life for his country (John 15:13).

JUNE 1

*"Behold, I send the Promise of My Father upon
you; but tarry in the city of Jerusalem until
you are endured with power from on high"*
—Luke 24:49

What was the "promise" that Jesus had sent to His disciples? The apostles had come to know Jesus intimately. They had seen Him in action. They saw His mighty works, the miracles and healings, and were taught by Jesus daily. They witnessed the power from on High in Jesus's life. Could it be that they believed in the words Jesus spoke, "Most assuredly, I say to you, he who believes in Me, the works that I do he will do also; and greater works than these he will do, because I go to My Father" (John 14:12)? Could it be that they had high expectation that this was about to happen to them?

Joyfully they went to Jerusalem. They prayed, believed, and yielded themselves to the mighty power of Jesus Christ. And then the "promise" came. Jesus breathed on them and they received the Holy Spirit—the power from on High to do greater works than those which Jesus did (John 20:22). It is the indwelling power of the Holy Spirit working through them, that enables them to do the works of the Father.

The "promise" was not only for the disciples but for all believers. Jesus told His followers in Luke 11:13 to ask for the Holy Spirit and the Heavenly Father will give it to them. All who believe are to ask and expect God to fill them with His Spirit and to be empowered with the power of Christ. It is this supernatural power within that will cause you to do greater works than even Jesus did.

Jesus, You said that for those who believe, even greater works than these will he do. Lord I believe, breathe on me and let the Breath of God empower me to do even greater works than what you did.

JUNE 2

Even so the tongue is a little member and boasts great
things. See how great a forest a little fire kindles.
—James 3:5

Do you find it strange that God would entrust you with the most powerful weapon on this earth. Few forces have as much power as the words that pass through your lips. Your tongue has the potential to be used for good or evil, to build up or tear down, to empower or devour, to heal or to hurt, to bless or to curse. You are in control of whether you make or break a person.

Your words can spark a child to accomplish great feats, encourage a spouse to conquer the world, ignite a friend's dream into a flame, or encourage a believer to run the race. Your words can make or break a marriage, sew together or tear apart a relationship, build or bury a dream, or draw a lost soul to Jesus Christ.

A knife in a surgeon's hand brings healing or life. A knife in a murder's hand brings death and destruction. You choose whether you will be a surgeon or a murderer with the words you speak. The tongue is difficult to control, especially when your emotions kick in. One of the greatest spiritual disciplines is to bring your tongue under the submission of the Holy Spirit.

You are shaped by the words from those around you. It is the cry of one's heart to be loved and accepted and sometimes a simple word of encouragement can make all the difference. When you have been criticized most of your life, it is hard to not criticize others. But if you ask the Holy Spirit to tame your tongue and guide you in the words to speak, you can discipline your tongue to speak life and not death to others. Think before You speak. Will the words I speak ignite the fire in another's heart or will it extinguish their flames? You will be either person who brings out the best in others or the worst. Death and life are in the power of the tongue (Proverbs 18:21). Choose to bring life to others.

JUNE 3

Moreover the law entered that the offense might abound.
But where sin abounded, grace abounded much more,
—Romans 5:20

As we mature in our Christian walk, our beliefs and views about God begin to change. We come to realize how much our Heavenly Father really loves and cares about us, and that there is nothing we can do that will ever stop Him from loving us. We begin to hold onto the promises of God. We let go of the condemnation Satan tries to guilt us with as he whispers in our ear, "Remember when you did this...remember when you did that." His scheme of clothing us with unworthiness, guilt, and shame no longer wears us down, for we have clothed ourselves with royalty garments from the King.

Many look at the Bible as a book of do's and don'ts, but really the Bible is a love book from the Father. The purpose of the laws was not to condemn us of our sins, but to make obvious the sin in our lives and the need for redemption. We all struggle with sin, but where sin abounds, grace abounds much more. What a promise and relief to know that we do not have to live in condemnation for our actions and words (Romans 8:1). No matter what we have done in our lives, His grace was there for us to embrace. His grace continues to be here for us to embrace today.

When Satan tries to remind you of all the things you've done wrong in your life, remind him that although you may have sinned, God's grace abounded more. Tell Satan that the Lord not only forgave you of your sins, but he forgot them as well (Hebrews 8:12). The Lord refuses to keep a list of our wrongs, and we should not keep a list either. Tell Satan that your sin was washed with the blood of Jesus and is remembered no more. Today's scripture is one of the many promises of God with which we need to remind ourselves when guilt, shame, and condemnation come knocking at our door.

JUNE 4

Have you not known? Have you not heard?
The everlasting God, the Lord, the Creator of
the ends of the earth, neither faints nor is weary.
His understanding is unsearchable. He gives
power to the weak, and to those who have no might
He increases strength. Even the youths shall faint
and be weary, and the young men shall utterly fall.
—Isaiah 40:28–30

Have you ever wondered about how much power and strength the Lord has? To think that He created the heavens and earth in six days. Look at the billions of people whose needs are met by Him every day. It makes me exhausted thinking about it. And yet our Creator never faints nor gets weary. His understanding is unsearchable. He continually gives, gives, and gives. He provides power to the weak, and to those who have no might He gives added strength. What a mighty God we serve.

Are you tired and weary? Do you feel like giving up? Do you feel like you've given all you can give and you cannot give any more? God does not want you to be burned out. Surrender everything to the Lord. His hands are large enough to hold anything you need Him to handle. Do not depend on your own strength but depend on His. Wait on the Lord and He will renew your strength (Isaiah 40:31). Only God has the power to bring all matters to their proper ending. When you try to work things out on our own, you interfere with the solutions He wants to bring forth.

Do you trust God? He loves you, and because of His great love, He wants to take care of you. Give Him all your worries and rest in His arms. Rejoice in His rest and see your strength renewed. The joy of the Lord is your strength (Nehemiah 8:10). The more joy you have, the stronger you will be. Rejoice and be glad in all circumstances, for that is where you will find strength and power for whatever comes your way.

JUNE 5

For I am persuaded that neither death nor life, nor angels nor principalities, nor powers, not things present not things to come, nor height nor depth, nor any other created thing, shall be able to separate us from the love of God which is in Christ Jesus our Lord.
—Romans 8:38–39

Once we accept God's love through faith in Jesus, nothing can ever separate us from that love. If that is true, then why are there so many unhappy Christians? Why do many feel so separated from God? One reason that comes to my mind when I ask myself this question is that people are not willing to let go of their past. Our past is something that holds many back. Forget about your past failures, your past disappointments, and your past shortcomings, and give them to the Lord. Start afresh today. Don't let the things from your past hold you back from your destiny for today. Press forward. Say to your heart—nothing will separate me from the love of God which is in Christ Jesus.

Fear is another obstacle that separates us from the love of God. When we sin, instead of going to the throne of grace to obtain mercy, many run away from it fearing God. Fear is not from God. Satan will use it to draw you away from God. Do not allow fear to separate you from the love of God. You have a High Priest who understands your weaknesses. He was in all points tempted as you are, yet he did not sin (Hebrews 4:15). He knows your weaknesses; He knows you are mortal. He knows your sinfulness. It was because of the Father's love that Jesus died for your sins. You are to go boldly before the throne of grace to receive the Lord's mercy and find grace to help you when you need it most (Hebrews 4:16). Say to your heart—nothing will separate me from the love of God which is in Christ Jesus.

JUNE 6

Beware, brethren, lest there be in any of you an evil
heart of unbelief in departing from the living God;
but exhort one another daily, while it is called "Today,"
lest any of you be hardened through the deceitfulness of sin.
—Hebrews 3:12–13

There are many Bible verses warning us about deception. Apostle Paul warns us not be deceived because we can't live in sin and not suffer the consequences (Galatians 6:7–8). We are warned about false prophets arising among us who will secretly bring destructive heresies (2 Peter 2:1) and will disguise themselves as apostles of Christ (2 Corinthians 11:13). Satan uses deception to trap believers. The reason Satan tries to deceive you, is to get you to believe something that is simply not true. Deception is a lie about the true reality of something. Once deception sets in, it becomes a stronghold in your mind causing you to incorrectly think about something. Satan will use deception to cause you to doubt the truth of God's Word.

The lies of the devil always have a ring of truth to them. Look at how he deceived Eve in the garden of Eden (Genesis 3:1–24) and tried to deceive Jesus before He began His ministry (Matthew 4:1–11). Satan will take advantage of the circumstances around you and flavor his words until they are almost the truth. The best counterfeit is as close to the authentic thing as possible. It is so easy to deceive yourself when you start to entertain the lies of the enemy.

One way to avoid being deceived is by reading the Word on a daily basis. The scriptures tell us that there is no deceit found in the words Jesus spoke (1 Peter 2:22). His words are authentic—they are genuine—they are truth. When Satan tries to deceive you, do not receive the counterfeit. Instead go to the authentic Word of God and believe the genuine truth of His words. Then exhort one another daily with the authentic Word of God so that your heart will not be hardened against God through deception.

JUNE 7

I will both lie down in peace, and sleep; for
You alone, O Lord, make me dwell in safety.
—Psalm 4:8

Wouldn't it be nice to not have a care in the world and be at peace all the time? Few if any experience this and yet it is very obtainable if you put your trust in God. So how do you maintain a sense of peace when trials come? The answer is found in having a close abiding relationship with Jesus. He is the Source who gives rest and peace. When the misery of you striving on your own is greater than the pride which drives the striving, then you will turn to the One who holds all comfort and security. The peace the world gives is only temporary, and the sooner you learn this and quit striving on your own, the faster you will obtain His peace.

You are not equipped to handle your problems, only God can do that. Find courage, hope and strength in Him and in His Word. Paul tells us that we are not to be anxious about anything; instead, we are to pray about everything telling God what we need and thanking Him for all He has done for us. Then we will experience the peace of God which surpasses all understanding. His peace will guard our hearts and minds as we live in Christ Jesus (Philippians 4:6–7).

You do not have to know the whys or the how. You do not have to know the when or the outcomes of your situations. You just have to lay them all down. Take the burdens from your shoulders and give them to Jesus. When you do, you will be able to lie down in peace and sleep, for it is through Christ that you will have found the grace, mercy, forgiveness, hope, peace, and everlasting security. Dwell in the shelter of the Most High and you will find rest in the shadow of the Almighty. The Lord is your refuge, your fortress, your God. Trust in Him (Psalm 91:1–2).

JUNE 8

Father, I desire that they also whom You gave Me may be with Me where I am, that they may behold My glory which You have given Me; for You loved Me before the foundation of the world.
—John 17:24

Before the foundation of the world was created, God had us in mind. He knew that man would fail Him, that man would hurt Him, and that man would sin against Him. That did not stop Him from creating man because He loved us so much. And out of that love for us, before the foundation was created, God had already prepared our plan of redemption.

His plan was going to be based upon a covenant. And even though man could not keep that covenant due to our sinful nature, He determined that He would become man so that He could fulfill the covenant for us. God chose to restore mankind through an unbreakable eternal covenant. God Himself would fulfill the terms through the cross, the shedding of His blood and giving of His own life for the redemption of our sins. For God made Christ, who never sinned, to be the offering for our sin, so that we could be made right with God through Christ (2 Corinthians 5:21).

Jesus as man's representation fulfilled all the law and prophets as man without sin. If He had yielded to the temptations and Satan, it would have nullified the covenant, we would never have been able to have fellowship with the Father, and we would have been lost forever. What would motivate Jesus to risk everything? It was His ultimate perfect love for us. When Jesus committed His Spirit and gave His life on the cross, the blood flowed, the exchange was made and the covenant was sealed. Jesus laid the foundation for our redemption (1 Corinthians 3:11). This eternal covenant is unbreakable. He fulfilled the terms of the covenant. Our salvation is in Jesus Christ and no other name. It is impossible to be lost forever unless you deny the Son. Focus on the promises that have been fulfilled. Can you see the splendor of His love, the fullness of who He is? He gave Himself to you. Does He have all of you?

JUNE 9

In My Father's house are many mansions; if it were not so,
I would have told you. I go to prepare a place for you. And if
I go and prepare a place for you, I will come again and receive
you to Myself; that where I am, there you may be also.

—John 14:2–3

Some of us own our homes while others have not yet purchased their dream house. For those who have already purchased their homes or for those who are dreaming of purchasing their home in the future, think of the excitement you felt or will feel moving into a place you can call your own. Some may have had a lot of hassle to go through: the bank loan did not go through the first time, delays in the building of your home, bad weather, some remodeling or cleaning needed done. But the day finally came or will come that you get to call your house your home. The excitement, relief, and joy living in your new home becomes reality.

Although we call our house our home, it is not our permanent home, for the Lord is preparing a mansion for us to live in eternality. I've never lived in a mansion, but I can only imagine the size and glamour of the rooms that the Lord has prepared for us who know Jesus as our personal Savior. There will be no hassles like we may have faced with our own homes, nor will there be any payments. The payment was already made at Calvary thanks to Jesus.

Imagine what that place will be like; the peace, the beauty, the splendor, the love, the adoration for our Father. And when it is our time to go to our heavenly reward, Jesus Himself will come and receive us. It is beyond our imagination. Although we may try, no one has ever imagined what God has prepared for those who love Him: to be with Jesus face-to-face forever and ever.

JUNE 10

And the Angel of the Lord appeared to him, and said to him, "The Lord is with you, you mighty man of valor!" Gideon said to Him, "O my lord, if the Lord is with us, why then has all this happened to us? And where are all His miracles which our fathers told us about, saying, 'Did not the Lord bring us up from Egypt?' But now the Lord has forsaken us and delivered us into the hands of the Midianites."
—Judges 6:12–13

How do you hold up when pressured? It's easy to stay positive when things are going well. But when adversity comes, you find out what you are really made of. When adversity struck Gideon, he saw himself and his people as weak and unworthy. He questioned where God was in the midst of his battle. Immediately the Lord encouraged Gideon to go with the strength he had and rescue Israel from the Midianites for He was sending him. Gideon responded with an extremely low self-esteem telling the Lord that his clan was the weakest of the whole tribe and that he was the least in his entire family. Again the Lord encouraged Gideon telling him He would be with him and He will destroy the Midianites. Gideon still questioned God and wanted a sign to prove that the Lord was speaking to him (Judges 6:14–18).

The Lord told Gideon that He would save Israel, but Gideon couldn't see it. He was relying on his own strength and not the Lord's. Gideon was looking at his weak army and not the power of God. Listen to what the Lord is telling you. When the Lord calls you strong, don't declare you are weak. When the Lord says I will be with you, don't try to fight the battle on your own. When you are faced with life's difficulties, you have to remember that the battle is not yours, but the Lord's (2 Chronicles 20:15). When the Lord is on your side, there is no comparison between the mighty hand of the God and that of mankind. When you rely on the Lord, you have unlimited power and wisdom. Allow the Lord to be in the midst of your battle.

JUNE 11

"If anyone has ears to hear, let him hear." Then He said to them, "Take heed what you hear. With the same measure you use, it will be measured to you; and to you who hear, more will be given"
—Mark 4:23–24

How much the Lord reveals to you really depends on what you do with the truth that has already been spoken to you. When you listen to sermons, teachings, the Word of God, or the voice of the Lord, listen with a sincere heart so that the truth spoken to you can penetrate deep within your heart. You have to follow Truth with passion and conviction, allowing the Lord to uproot justification, rationalization, compromise, and rebellion.

We all want to grow, and we have prayed for truth to be revealed to us. God has revealed His truth to you in many ways. You have a wealth of knowledge stored up inside of you. It is one thing to have that knowledge, but it is another to practice what you have been taught. You are to train and discipline yourself to walk in the Spirit of Truth. The closer you listen, the more understanding and revelation you will be given.

Father, I thank you for Your Truth, for You are Truth. I open my ears to hear what the Spirit of Truth is speaking. I will not allow the truths that are revealed to me to sit idle, but will allow the Spirit of Truth to germinate them deep into the cores of my being. I desire to please You and to do Your will. Reveal the truths that have been spoken to me which I have failed to apply to me life. Stir up a passion within me to apply those truths. Uproot words that have been spoken to me that are dishonest and have caused me to walk in deception. I break the curse of those lies in Jesus's name. Spirit of Truth, set me free.

JUNE 12

Whereas you do not know what will happen tomorrow.
For what is your life? It is even a vapor that appears for
a little time and then vanishes away.

—James 4:14

What are you hearing the Lord telling you to do today? Seize the day, seize the hour, and seize the moment. The Israelites failed to do this. They hardened their hearts in rebellion and tested God, trying Him even though they saw the works of His hand. For forty years the Lord was grieved with them. The Lord said they were a people who went astray in their hearts and did not know His ways (Psalm 95:8–10). Today, if you hear His voice, do not harden your hearts as in rebellion (Hebrews 3:15). You may not have forty years to get right with God like the Israelites did. You are to make the most of what time you do have on this earth and heed to the voice of the Lord.

No one knows what tomorrow will bring. Listen with your heart and hear what the Lord is asking you to do, then do it. Do not put off until tomorrow what can be done today. Seize the opportunities that God gives you today, for tomorrow may be too late. What is a life? It is even a vapor that appears for a little time and then vanishes away. As quickly as a vapor vanishes, that is how quick your life can be taken away from you. You are not guaranteed tomorrow, so make the most of today. Instead of testing the Lord in rebellion, you ought to say, "If the Lord wills, we shall live and do this or that" (James 4:15). Lord I will to do your will. Reveal any rebellion that is hidden in my heart as I strive to hear your voice and obey.

JUNE 13

I can do all things through
Christ who strengthens me.
—Philippians 4:13

God has given each of us a measure of faith. It is up to us to develop it. You grow in faith by exercising it, by trusting God in every aspect of your life. When you completely submit every area of your life to God, you are telling God—I can't God, but You can. When you do not submit an area of your life to God and try to work it out on your own, you are telling God—I don't need You God, I can handle this on my own. Which are you telling God?

The more you surrender to God and watch Him work things out in your life, the greater your faith builds. Faith is saying to God—I believe You will. Do you want your faith to grow? What area of your life are you struggling with this very moment? Surrender it to God. Believe in your miracle Stand in faith with God and do not partner with the lies of Satan. Continue steadfastly in prayer. Pray about your situation and don't lose heart (Luke 18:1). Be strong and courageous. Believe that you can do all things through Christ (Philippians 4:13). Speak those things into existence which are unseen (2 Corinthians 4:18). Watch God move on your behalf and let faith arise in you.

JUNE 14

Let no one deceive you by any means; for that Day will not come unless the falling away comes first, and the man of sin is revealed, the son of perdition. The coming of the lawless one is according to the working of Satan, with all power, signs, and lying wonders, and with all unrighteous deception among those who perish, because they did not receive the love of truth, that they might be saved.
—2 Thessalonians 2:3, 9–10

Sharpen your spiritual discernment, because the time is coming when the majority of the church will abandon sound doctrine and will embrace whatever doctrine fits their lifestyle or seems popular at the moment. Anchor your faith in the Word of God and His truth, and not in churches, or following after those who perform signs and wonders. Paul warns us that Satan is performing compelling signs and lying wonders, counterfeiting many of God's works, luring many into deception and false doctrine. If you do not know God's Word, you could be lured and deceived as well. It's hard to recognize a counterfeit unless you know the real. Do not be fooled in these last days. Study the original so that you will recognize the counterfeit.

Many will believe the lie because they do not believe the truth. People will believe something. That is why it is so important that you do not run after signs, wonders, and miracles. You are to stand firm. You are to hold onto the teachings which you were taught, because God from the beginning chose you for salvation through sanctification by His Spirit and belief in the truth (2 Thessalonians 2:13–15). If you are being led by the Holy Spirit, you will never fall into deception. The Holy Spirit will quicken your spirit to the lie. Hold fast to the Truth. As you place your faith in God's truth and exercise discernment that comes from the Holy Spirit, you will be able to recognize and affirm true signs and wonders done for the glory of God.

JUNE 15

Search me, O God, and know my heart;
try me, and know my anxieties.
—Psalm 139:23

My husband is retired and has the pleasure of being able to sleep in. In the evening before a work day, I will choose the clothes that I am going to wear to work and have everything laid out for the next day. When I get ready for work in the mornings, I use a dim light coming from the bathroom so that I don't awaken him with a bright light. I get dressed, close the bedroom door, and then head for the kitchen.

Many mornings I don't examine what I have put on, but trust that everything matches and coordinates together. One day, while I was at work, I reached down to pick something off the floor and realized that my socks did not match. One was black and the other was navy. The dim light coming from the bathroom had deceived me into thinking that both of the socks were black, but the truth was revealed when the socks were exposed under the bright florescent lights.

Many times you become accustomed to your ways and believe you are doing the right things until you expose yourself to the Light. Unless you ask the Lord to examine your heart, you may not realize that your heart is the wrong shade and does not match your true color. If you allow the Lord to examine your heart, He will expose the darkness in you and make your crooked paths straight. Had I examined myself in a bright light, instead of the dim bathroom light, I would have been able to correct the mistake before I left for work. If you don't examine yourself in private and allow the Lord to reveal the true condition of your heart before you leave for work, then be prepared for them to be exposed in public where others can see what is hidden in your heart. Make sure you are properly dressed, both on the inside and outside. Before leaving your home, examine yourself in His light and make sure the true color of your heart matches what you are wearing on the outside.

JUNE 16

Moreover David said, "The Lord, who delivered me from the paw of the lion and from the paw of the bear, He will deliver me from the hand of this Philistine." And Saul said to David, "Go, and the Lord be with you!" Then David said to the Philistine, "You come to me with a sword, with a spear, and with a javelin. But I come to you in the name of the Lord of hosts, the God of the armies of Israel whom you have defiled."
—1 Samuel 17:37, 45

David was a man of courage. His courage was not rooted in his own strength but was rooted in the Sovereign Lord. He knew that His God was the God of the armies and would deliver Goliath into his hands. David recognized that his success lay in the hands of God and he acknowledged that he would be victorious because of it (1 Samuel 17:46).

Never go into battle entertaining thoughts of defeat; you will lose every time. David recalled what the Lord had done for him in the past, delivering him from the lion and the bear. He expected the same sort of help and faithfulness of God in this battle as well. Never go into battle alone. David recognized this and knew who to call on to help in the fight. Who do you call on when you are faced with a battle?

Never go into battle afraid. Fear conquers and destroys you instead of Satan. Do not allow inner fears or outward appearances to cause you to become afraid. Our challenges may be great, but God is greater than any circumstance. Face your enemies head-on standing on the promises of God. When you go to battle, be strong and courageous. Believe that the battle is the Lord's and He will give you victory over the enemy (2 Chronicles 20:15). Confront your opponent with confidence that you will succeed. Believe that this day the Lord will deliver your Goliath into your hand.

JUNE 17

"For the Lord will not forsake His people, for His great name's sake, because it has pleased the Lord to make you His people."
—1 Samuel 12:22

Throughout the Bible, we see the Lord reaching out to His people, comforting them, healing them, reassuring them and revealing Himself to them. In this Scripture we find the promise from God that He will never forsake us. When you feel like everyone else has abandoned you, be reassured that God has not forsaken you but is right there with you.

Jesus knew what it was like to be lonely. At the very hour that He needed someone the most, they abandoned Him. Just feel the anguish He must have experienced that very moment, knowing that He was about to be tortured, ridiculed and put to death and that His closest friends were not available to give Him comfort. And yet, Jesus did not focus on what He did not have, but on what He had. He went to the Father for His comfort (John 16:32). Jesus knew how to be comforted even when faced with abandonment.

Sometimes the Lord will allow none of your friends to be available because He wants you to go to Him for comfort, wisdom or guidance. When you are faced with loneliness, the first thing you need to do is turn your focus away from what you don't have and draw your attention to what you do have. No matter what you are facing today, you are never alone; Jesus is right there with you. Draw near to Him and He will draw near to you (James 4:8).

JUNE 18

He makes me to lie down in green pastures; He leads me
beside the still waters. He restores my soul; He leads me
in the paths of righteousness for His name's sake.
—Psalm 23:2–3

Are your tired and drained? Do you feel like you have no energy to do anything? Do you wake up in the morning tired before you even start your day? Then it's time to break away and spend some time with the Lord. He is the only one who can restore your soul. How? By being in His presence, even if it's only for five minutes, ten minutes or an hour. Many strive to obtain comfort and rest apart from God, but those means will never restore your soul. Have you ever taken time to sit or lie down in a green pasture or beside a still water stream? If you haven't, try it. You will find tranquility there as nature really speaks to you. This is the peaceful relationship that God wants with you.

Jesus knows what you need before you even ask and He delights in meeting those needs. He knows the physically, emotional, and spiritual fatigue that wears you down. Sometimes you just need to get away from your usual environments where there are many distractions and go to a still quiet place. Make the time to lie down in green pastures or beside a still water. It is the Lord that is leading you to do so. The Great Shepherd is there waiting for you so He may bring peace to your heart and soul. He is waiting there to give you guidance and wisdom. Expect that Jesus will care for you. Rest in His presence knowing that He will refresh you, comfort you, nourish you and give you strength.

JUNE 19

"Therefore do not worry about tomorrow,
for tomorrow will worry about its own things.
Sufficient for the day is its own trouble."
—Matthew 6:34

All of us have worried about one thing or another. Where did that worry get us? Did it help us resolve the situation or did it compound matters? Worry and anxiety boil down to one issue—our lack of trust in God. No matter how fast your mind races or how hard you try to reason things out, there will be circumstances in your life over which you have no control. Things will not always go your way. The sooner you learn to cast your cares upon the Lord and leave them there, the sooner you will find rest.

Just because things do not go your way doesn't mean that God does not have your best interest at heart. In the midst of your battles, the Lord is watching to see how you will react, to see if you will call upon Him and trust in Him. Is something laying heavily on your heart today? Give that care to the Lord, trust in Him, and He will give you rest (Matthew 11:28). It is one thing to know that God cares about you and wants you to cast your cares upon Him (1 Peter 5:7), but knowing and believing are two different things. Do you believe that God cares about you and He will give you rest in the midst of your storm? If not, pray as the father prayed when Jesus said to him, "If you can believe, all things are possible to him who believes." Immediately the father of the child cried out and said with tears, "Lord, I believe; help my unbelief!" (Mark 9:23–24). Pray that prayer over and over again until your heart believes it. Believe in the One who will give you rest. Believe that all things are possible through Christ!

JUNE 20

"But the hour is coming, and now is, when the true worshipers
will worship the Father in spirit and truth; for the Father
is seeking such to worship Him. God is Spirit, and those
who worship Him must worship in spirit and truth."
— John 4:23–24

Everything you do is a form of worship. Even your daily tasks are a form of worship when you give honor to God for giving you strength, enabling you to get things done. How do you know if the way you worship pleases God? The answer is to look at your heart. God always looks at the heart of the worshipper. If your worship is to draw attention to oneself or to be seen by men, then your worship will be in vain. But if your worship is solely to glorify the Lord, acknowledging who He is, and giving honor to Him, then your worship brings delight to God.

Nothing escapes the loving and Soveign eyes of the Lord. Observe in Mark 12:43–44 how Jesus watched a poor widow put into the collection what amounted to be just one cent. He called His disciples to Himself and said, "I tell you the truth, this poor widow has given more than all the others who are making contributions. For they gave a tiny part of their surplus, but she, poor as she is, has given everything she had to live on." The Lord didn't care about the amount. What was important to Him was the heart of the giver. Whether you are praising, giving thanks, singing, praying or giving financial blessings, the issue always comes down to motivation. If the motivation behind what you're doing is not right, the Lord will not be impressed. Instead, seek the Lord, ask for forgiveness, and ask Him to change your heart so your motivation will be right. Worship the Father in spirit and truth. In all you do, do it unto the Lord.

JUNE 21

"Will a man rob God? Yet you have robbed Me! But you
say, 'In what why have we robbed You?' In tithes and offerings."
"Bring all the tithes into the storehouse, that there may be food
in My house, and try Me now in this," says the Lord of hosts,
"If I will not open for you the windows of heaven and pour out for
you such blessing that there will not be room enough to receive it."
—Malachi 3:8, 10

This last promise in the Old Testament tells us how abundant the blessings will be. God promises us that if we are faithful to Him, that He will open up the windows of heaven and pour out a blessing that there shall be no room to receive it. We can never out give God. Giving to God is the first step toward financial freedom. If you don't give to God, not only in tithes, but in offerings as well, then you are robbing God. Your money, your time, and your resources are really God's. It was never yours from the beginning (1 Chronicles 29:14). Giving always results in increase. His promises have been tried and proven. Personally I have seen the rewards of my obedience. I know the Lord has restored to me beyond what I could ever imagine.

God invites you to try Him, to prove His promises, to test His truth. He not only invites you, He challenges you: Give me a tenth of your income and see what I will do for you. God does not need your money, He simply wants you to discover the rewards of obedience. Giving to God is the prerequisite for enjoying true financial freedom. Have you taken the challenge of bringing your tithes and offerings into the storehouse? If not, what holds you back? Make a special offering this week and see if God will not open up the doors of heaven for you. Do you need a financial break, a healing, or a miracle in the storms of your life? Test God and see if He is not true to His word. The rewards from tithing and offerings are knocking at your door.

JUNE 22

He who dwells in the secret place of the Most High shall abide
under the shadow of the Almighty. I will say of the Lord, "He
is my refuge and my fortress; My God, in Him I will trust."
—Psalm 91:1–2

Have you ever watched infants in the arms of their parents? The contentment and peace they feel knowing that they are in the tender arms of their parents is apparent. A few minutes earlier, they may have been screaming, crying, and wanting refuge from the calamity in their lives; now they're in the tender arms of a loved one. As infants are secure in their parents' arms, so the Lord wants you to experience the same peace when you abide under the shadow of His wings. When calamities happen in your life, where do you take refuge? The word refuge means a shelter, a protection, a fortress, a hope, or a place of trust.

In Isaiah 25:4, God is described as a refuge from the storm and a shade from the heat. God can be whoever you want Him to be. He is your strength when you are weak. He is your hope when you feel as though life is falling apart. He is your light in the midst of your darkness. He is your Healer when you are stricken with an illness or disease. He is your peace and refuge in the midst of your storms.

Where do you find hope when you receive a bad medical report? Where do you find comfort when the world around you seems to be crashing in? Abide under the shadow of the Lord's wings and you will find refuge until the calamities have passed by.

JUNE 23

*Let no corrupt word proceed out of your mouth, but what
is good for necessary edification, that it may impart grace to
the hearers. And be kind to one another, tenderhearted,
forgiving one another, even as God in Christ forgave you.*
—Ephesians 4:29, 32

M any times you allow your emotions to do your talking. You are frustrated and speak words of frustration; you are hurt and speak words that end up hurting or offending others. When you become frustrated or hurt, seek the Lord immediately so that your emotions do not become who you are or what you speak.

When you talk, do not say harmful things, but say what people need—words that will help others become stronger and encouraged. Before you speak, you need to ask yourself, "Will what I say edify others to help them become stronger or will it put them down?" When you lift someone up, it lifts you up too. Do not withhold encouragement to those who are discouraged or oppressed. Your words might be what makes or breaks a person.

Let people know that they are loved and forgiven and that God loves them. Forgiving others is fundamental to having one's own prayer for forgiveness answered (Matthew 6:14, 15). Be quick to make amends even when it is not your fault. A little kindness goes a long way, especially when someone is not expecting it. Impart grace to the hearers and grace will be imparted to you.

JUNE 24

For we are His workmanship, created in
Christ Jesus for good works, which God prepared
beforehand that we should walk in them.
—Ephesians 2:10

God works through different people in different ways, but in the end, He achieves His purpose through us all (1 Corinthians 12:6). You are His workmanship created in Christ Jesus for good works. Every believer receives spiritual gifts, not merely to encourage and build one's own faith, but to teach and build up the faith of all God's children.

God does not call you to be perfect in everything you do. But He does expect you to step out in faith and obedience to do that which He has prepared beforehand for you to do. And when you do, He will perfect you along the way. If you wait until everything is perfected, you may be waiting for a long time and nothing will ever be accomplished.

Never compare yourself with others, for we all have a diversity of activities that must be accomplished and those activities are not achieved the same way. Some may face disappointments or failure along the way, but every failure, every frustration, every disappointment, and every accomplishment has a purpose. All things work together for good (Romans 8:28). God knows what you need, when you need it, and He will take care of the rest. When you examine yourself, see yourself as God perceives you. God rejoices over you (Isaiah 62:5) even though He knows you are not at your full potential yet. He sees and values your worth and the great promises that lies ahead of you. You are His workmanship, designed and created in Christ Jesus by God so you can do the good things he planned for you long ago. We are all a part of the Master's plan. Collectively we are His masterpiece, His work of art.

JUNE 25

For I desire mercy and not sacrifice, and the
knowledge of God more than burnt offerings.

—Hosea 6:6

God values a relationship with Him more than He desires your service and sacrifices for Him. He desires you to have a genuine heartfelt relationship with Him. God is concerned with the attitudes of the heart. As you pursue Jesus wholeheartedly, you will learn to walk in the characteristics of Christ. God desires mercy and not sacrifice. Jesus even quoted this desire to explain His reason for eating with tax collectors and sinners (Matthew 9:13) and to explain why His disciples were harvesting on the Sabbath (Matthew 12:7). He wants to reveal more of Himself to you each day. He greatly desires hearts on fire for Him. So how do you get to know God better? First have a desire in your heart to want to know Him more. If the desire is not there, you will not make the effort to spend time alone with God. When you go before the Lord, be honest with Him, confessing your sins, and asking for forgiveness. Understand your reliance on Him, He is your only source of comfort, wisdom, and power.

To better know God, become interested in what interests Him. Read His Word. By reading the Bible, you open your heart to Him. The Lord will then speak to you about His love, His mercy, His desires, and His ways. The more you understand God, the more you begin to apply His Word to your life. God is constantly inviting you to walk with Him, accept His invitations. Give the Lord total control of your decisions, your time, your talents, and your possessions. He knows what to do with them. Your knowledge of God will grow as you increasingly recognize His love for you. As you get to know God on deeper levels, your ability to trust and obey Him will increase and His grace and mercy will multiply in your life. What does the Lord require of us but to do justly, to love mercy, and to walk humbly with our God (Micah 6:8).

JUNE 26

Yes, we had the sentence of death in ourselves, that we should not trust in ourselves but in God who raises the dead, who delivered us from so great a death, and does deliver us; in whom we trust that He will still deliver us.
—2 Corinthians 1:9–10

When I look back at my life, I see the many mistakes that I have made. I thought I knew what was best for me, but in the end, it was not in my best interest. Sometimes God allows us to fall into deep valleys and allows us to make mistakes in order to show us that we are never really in control, but that He is always in control and knows how to rescue us from impossible situations. We should never regret the things that we have done. Instead, we should use the mistakes as opportunities to grow, to realize how vulnerable we are and how much we really need to depend on God.

No matter what you are faced with because of where you have allowed yourself to go, God is always there to help you get out of the mess that you have gotten yourself into. To help avoid some of these messes, you need to seek God daily and allow Him to order your day, to give you guidance, direction, and wisdom to make the correct choices.

The Lord says cursed is the man who trusts in man and makes flesh his strength, whose heart departs from the Lord but blessed is the man who trusts in the Lord, and whose hope is the Lord (Jeremiah 17:5, 7). Be blessed and not cursed. Do not trust in your own wisdom and strength but trust in God's wisdom to guide you through the pathway of life. His strength to carry you along the way. When you go to God and trust that He has heard your prayers, there will be inner peace knowing that God is in control and guiding your day. Trust in God and not in yourself and allow God to deliver you from whatever you may be facing today.

JUNE 27

Now thanks be to God who always leads us in triumph in Christ, and through us diffuses the fragrance of His knowledge in every place. For we are to God the fragrance of Christ among those who are being saved and among those who are perishing.
—2 Corinthians 2:14–15

Did you realize that what you say and do leaves an aroma in the atmosphere around you? In the physical realm, the fragrance of perfume has a way of lingering even after a person has left the room. There are times when my husband will get into my car and ask who has been riding with me. The fragrance from the person still lingered where she had been sitting. Some people wear the same perfume every day and you can distinguish who is nearby, without seeing them, just by the aroma that is in the air.

In a spiritual realm, your attitudes, gestures, deeds, and spoken words diffuse a fragrance into the atmosphere and will linger long after you have left the room. What fragrance are you leaving? Are you leaving the fragrance of Christ? Are you leaving the fragrance of His knowledge in every place? I diffuse oils, and there are times when I choose a certain oil because of the aroma it disperses. Do people want to be around you because of the aroma you are dispersing? In meetings at work, I can almost always anticipate how the meeting will go based on the people attending the meeting. Some people tend to come to meetings with the same attitudes and their aroma lingers in the air long before the meeting has even started.

I love the smell of freshly baked brownies or bread, especially when they first come out of the oven. The aroma overwhelms my taste buds and my mind tells me "I must have a piece." When we have been basking in the presence of the Lord, the aroma of His presence should touch the taste buds of others to the point that they are saying "I must have what they have."

JUNE 28

But you are a chosen generation, a royal priesthood,
a holy nation, His own special people, that you may
proclaim the praises of Him who called you out of
darkness into His marvelous light.

—1 Peter 2:9

How do you see yourself? Do you see yourself as royal and handpicked by God? Do you see yourself as one of God's children? How you see yourself, and how you think God sees you, will have a dramatic impact on your destiny in life. You were handpicked by God. Imagine yourself standing in a crowd of millions of people and God stretches out his arm and points His finger at you and says, "I choose you." How does that make you feel? Makes you feel special, doesn't it? You are special, I am special, we all are special and loved by God. We are the apple of His eye (Zechariah 2:8).

We are royal priests—we have royal blood in us and flowing through us. We are owned by God, He possesses us, and no one can take us away from Him. Allow God to possess you. He will open your eyes in order to turn you from darkness to light and from the power of Satan to God. Then you will receive forgiveness for your sins and an inheritance among those who are sanctified by faith in Him (Acts 26:18). For it is God who commanded light to shine out of darkness, who has made this light shine in your heart so you could know the glory of God that is seen in the face of Jesus Christ (2 Corinthians 4:6).

See yourself as God sees you, and not how you think He sees you. God calls you chosen, royal, holy, and special so that you might begin to act like who you really are. Believe in who God says you are. Do what God says you can do and become who God says you are. The only person who holds you back is you. Let go of yourself and let God be God in you.

JUNE 29

In that day it shall be said to Jerusalem: "Do not fear;
Zion, let not your hands be weak. The Lord your God
in your midst, the Mighty One, will save; He will rejoice
over you with gladness, He will quiet you with His love,
He will rejoice over you with singing."
—Zephaniah 3:16–17

None of us really know the depth of how much the Lord loves us. Zephaniah 3:17 tells us that the Lord is in our midst, rejoicing over us. God rejoices over you even though He knows that you are still a work in progress and have not fully become all that He has planned for you. He delights over you just where you are in your walk with Him.

The Lord is in your midst rejoicing over you, cheering you onto victory. He is there to strengthen and encourage you. He has a special song He sings over each of us. Hear the melody in your heart right now as He sings over you, quieting your heart with His love. you are never alone and when you take your eyes off your circumstances and fix your eyes on Jesus, you will see life differently. Instead of thinking negatively, ask the Holy Spirit to teach you to think over the problem with the mind of Christ, using pure thoughts that will bring honor and glory to Jesus.

Although you may walk in disappointment and not really understand what is going on, God knows what lies ahead. He has seen the finished portrait. He knows that through Christ you will succeed and be victorious. Being victorious does not mean that you will never suffer or feel pain. Jesus endured both and yet He did not give up. He knew that in order to complete His mission, He would have to endure to the end. He did just that because He wanted to accomplish the Father's will more than anything else. In order to complete your mission, you have to endure to the end. We all can walk in victory because Jesus was our example and His Holy Spirit lives in us. Draw on His strength and keep reminding yourself that the Lord is rejoicing over you with gladness as He cheers you on to victory.

JUNE 30

Do not love the world or the things in the world. If anyone
loves the world, the love of the Father is not in Him. For all
that is in the world—the lust of the flesh, the lust of the eyes,
and the pride of life—is not of the Father but is of the world.
                                                    —1 John 2:15–16

God tells us that we are not to love the world or the things in
this world. Two real struggles of this world are lust and pride. The
lust of the flesh which seeks after its own self-pleasing desires, and
the lust of the eyes which sees and seeks the glory of this world,
started in the garden of Eden. When Eve saw that the tree was
good for food, that it was pleasant to her eyes, and a tree desir-
able to make her wise, she took of its fruit and ate. She also gave
the apple to her husband Adam and he partook of the fruit with
Eve (Genesis 3:6). Just because someone agrees with you does not
make your actions right. Adam and Eve's pride and their lust for
pleasant things of the world caused sin to destroy the close fellowship they had with God.

The world is no different today. Lust and pride still have a
terrible influence over Christians who do not know that in Christ,
the victory over sin has been won. Most Christians are either too
ignorant of the snares of the enemy or they feel too powerless to
conquer them. But if Christ conquered sin on the cross and His
Spirit lives in us, then we too can conquer sin if we allow the power
of the Holy Spirit to rule in our lives.

God wants you to fully yield to Him with no thought of
personal gain or ambition. If you wish for anything, wish for more
of His presence. If you long for anything, long for more of His
love and righteousness. Live your life today in the power of the
Holy Spirit with confidence knowing that you have victory over
the world and all its lusts. Put your trust in the mighty power of
God who lives in you.

JULY 1

And they went out and preached everywhere,
the Lord working with them and confirming
the word through the accompanying signs.
—Mark 16:20

M any times people don't witness the works of the Lord because they are afraid that if they pray for healing or a miracle for a person that it may not come to pass. But we have to remember that it is not we who are responsible for bringing the signs and miracles, it is the Lord. Before there can be a reaction on God's part, there has to be an action on our part. Our responsibility is to preach, to teach, to pray, to witness, and to obey God's commands, and He will confirm His word through accompanying signs. If something does not come to pass when we pray, then there is more to the picture in the eyes of the Lord than what we can see. He knows what is best in each situation.

When God confirms the Word, He makes it firm, He establishes it, He secures it into place. The miracles that accompanied the disciples' preaching confirmed to the people that the messengers were telling the truth, that God was backing up their messages with supernatural powers and phenomena. We are God's disciples too and these same signs will follow those who believe (Mark 16:17).

Your mouth is an open vessel for the river of God's grace to flow through. It is to be used to bring healing and hope to those God has placed in your daily paths. You are to be faithful, delivering God's Word. He will surely bless it and confirm it with accompanying signs and miracles. Be an open vessel to the Lord and watch God's river of grace flow into peoples' lives.

JULY 2

"Or how can you say to your brother, 'Let me remove the speck from your eye'; and look, a plank is in your own eye? Hypocrite! First remove the plank from your own eye, and then you will see clearly to remove the speck from your brother's eye."

—Matthew 7:4–5

Jesus does not forbid criticism, opinions, or condemnation of wrongdoing. What He does forbid is the spirit of faultfinding that causes one to overlook his own shortcomings while judging in regards to the sins of others. We have all fallen into this trap from time to time. When we do, we are as guilty of sin as the person we are judging.

Most of us wouldn't consider selfish ambitions in the same category as someone stealing, murdering, committing adultery or being drunk, but sin is sin. They are all works of the flesh and those who practice such things will not inherit the kingdom of God (Galatians 5:19). Most of us don't think twice about the words we speak under our breath but are quick to judge a harsh word spoken by someone else. Sin is sin. Most of us don't examine the cloak that is covering our hearts but we are quick to criticize the outward appearance of another. Sin is sin. We do not think twice of robbing God of our time, resources, tithes or offerings but will judge another for stealing something that belongs to another. Sin is sin. Many are the planks in our eyes.

When we do these things, God calls us hypocrites and asks us to first remove the plank from our own eyes before removing the speck from our brothers eyes. When we find ourselves faultfinding another, we need to set aside some time and take a close examination of our lives. Allow the Lord to magnify your life, your motives, your attitude, and your heart and see what plank He reveals in your own life that needs to be removed.

JULY 3

Bear one another's burdens,
and so fulfill the law of Christ.

—Galatians 6:2

None of us know what we may face tomorrow. One day we are living a life of joy and peace and are able to take on the whole world. The next day we are faced with a burden too heavy for one to carry alone: the loss of a friend or loved one, the termination of a job, a daughter pregnant out of wedlock, a son high on drugs, or a bad report from the doctors. We were not meant to carry our burdens alone. We are to help each other carry our burdens.

Everyone needs friends who are true and who will offer support. Friends have a way of knowing that something is not right. A true friend often recognizes what the other person needs without even asking. Words have a lasting impact. You never know how a small act of kindness or a few words of encouragement will touch someone's heart for many years to come.

You are to treat others the way you would like to be treated. Comfort the fainthearted, uphold the weak and be patient with all (1 Thessalonians 5:14). Picture yourself in the same situation as your friend. What would you like someone to do for you? What would you like someone to say to you? Consider the words you would like to hear, and chances are others would probably like to hear them too. Make a list of words that you would like to hear, and then use those same words to bless others. Fulfill the law of Christ by bearing another's burden.

JULY 4

There is therefore now no condemnation to those who are
in Christ Jesus, who do not walk according to the flesh,
but according to the Spirit. For the law of the Spirit of life in
Christ Jesus has made me free from the law of sin and death.
—Romans 8:1–2

There is freedom and liberty when you give your life to Jesus. You have been given freedom from guilt and condemnation when you walk according to the Spirit. You are made right with God by placing your faith in Jesus Christ. And this is true for everyone who believes, no matter who we are. Everyone has sinned. We have all fallen short of God's standards. Yet God, in His grace, freely makes us right in His sight. He did this through Christ Jesus when He freed us from the penalty for our sins. For God presented Jesus as the sacrifice for sin. People are made right with God when they believe that Jesus sacrificed His life, shedding His blood. God did this to demonstrate His righteousness, for He himself is fair and just, and He makes sinners right in his sight when they believe in Jesus (Romans 3:21–26). What love He bestows upon us!

When you walk in the Spirit, you are set free from the bondage of walking according to the flesh, following the sinful desires of your old life. To walk in the Spirit, you follow the desires of the Holy Spirit, to live in a way that pleases God. Because of salvation by faith through Jesus Christ, Christians are free from God's banishing judgment. But not all people have this freedom. There are many who are still held in bondage and captivity to sin and judgment because they have not given their lives to Jesus. If they only knew the rewards of surrendering their life to God then they would do it immediately.

This Independence Day, remember to pray for all unbelievers, that they may be able to find freedom and liberty for their souls through Christ Jesus. Also remember to pray for those serving in the armed forces who are fighting that we may have freedom from our enemies. May God's life, liberty, and pursuit of happiness fall upon each and every person.

JULY 5

"If anyone comes to Me and does not hate his
father and mother, wife and children, brothers
and sisters, yes, and his own life also, he cannot
be My disciple. And whoever does not bear his
cross and come after Me cannot be My disciple.
So likewise, whoever of you does not forsake all
that he has cannot be My disciple."
—Luke 14: 26–27, 33

In these verses, three times Christ repeated the words that without doing this, "you cannot be My disciple." There is a price to pay to be a follower of Christ and many are not willing to pay that price. They would rather do their own thing than to surrender all to Jesus. Jesus calls us to be more loyal to Him than to any human being. Do not compromise your walk for anyone. Recognize and anticipate that your personal discipleship and commitment to Jesus can result in division and rejection from loved ones. Being a disciple of Jesus Christ includes surrendering yourself to the Lord and forsaking all selfish personal ambitions. The phrase "do not forsake" is not instructing you to totally abandon your belongings but to prioritize them.

Why does God put such a high demand on us? It's because the sinful nature we have inherited from Adam is so wicked and evil. The hating of your own life will make you willing to bear the cross and carry within you the death sentence to your evil nature. Not until you hate this life with a deadly hate will you be ready to give up the old nature of sin. God wants your total commitment. Forsake all. In the path of following Jesus, coming to know Him and loving Him more, you will be willing to sacrifice all, including self, to make room for Him. When you become conscious of what it means to know Christ and to love Him above all else, then what once appeared too difficult to accomplish, becomes quite easy to do. The cost and rewards of being one of His disciples are truly worth it all.

JULY 6

*It is good to give thanks to the Lord, and to
sing praises to Your name, O Most High; to
declare Your lovingkindness in the morning,
and Your faithfulness every night.*

—Psalm 92:1–2

The Lord calls us into fellowship with Him throughout our day. He loves to hear our praises, for it brings honor to His name. Singing is one form of lifting up your praises to the Lord. Even if you feel you cannot carry a tune, the Lord loves the sound of your voice. Singing also lifts up one's spirit when feeling low. Delight yourself in the Lord with song and praise (Psalm 69:30). He will put a new song in your mouth (Psalm 40:3).

Declarations are another form of worship. When you make declarations, you are springing forth God into action for something to happen on your behalf. Throughout the day, declare scriptures of the promises God has spoken to you as well as scriptures of the characteristics of God. He is faithful, and when you make declarations of God's faithfulness, it not only stirs up faith within you, but also causes the Holy Spirit to quicken to the things you pray. Declare who you are in Christ every day and it will empower you to believe that you are who Christ says you are. You are what the Word says and not what you feel. Truth is truth, God's Word is Truth—declare who God is until it empowers you to believe who God is and who you are in Christ.

You are blessed and you need to express your thankfulness to the Lord. Do not take the things that the Lord does for you for granted. Do not take His love and the many blessings He showers upon you for granted. Let Him know how thankful you are. Declare His lovingkindness in the morning and His faithfulness every night. Give thanks to the Lord and sing praises to His name. Honor the Lord and He will manifest Himself to you.

JULY 7

Now may the God of peace who brought up our Lord
Jesus rom the dead, that great Shepherd of the sheep,
through the blood of the everlasting covenant, make you
complete in every good work to do His will, working in
you what is well pleasing in His sight, through Jesus
Christ, to whom be glory forever and ever.
—Hebrews 13:20–21

The God who raised Jesus from the dead is the same God who is working in you and through you to complete every good work and to accomplish His will in your life. It is not by your own strength, but it is by His strength working in you that you are enabled to do anything worthwhile. To make you complete means that God will make the necessary adjustments and repairs, equip, train, and disciple you to accomplish His will and purpose. It is God who works in you, giving you the desire and power to do what pleases Him (Philippians 2:13). If you will only surrender to the works of His hands! It is only then that you will experience the peace which the God of peace has for you.

Are you experiencing God's peace? Are you allowing the Lord to work in you what is well pleasing in His sight, or do you try to accomplish things in your own strength? Are you allowing the great Shepherd to make you complete? Surrender your day to Him. Rely on His strength. Jesus, the great Shepherd, is the Overseer of your soul (1 Peter 2:25). Find peace in your soul knowing that the God who raised Jesus from the dead is working in you and through you. What more could we ask!?

JULY 8

*"But My people would not heed My voice, and Israel
would have none of Me. Oh, that My people would
listen to Me, that Israel would walk in My ways!"*
—Psalm 81:11, 13

Hear the cry of your Heavenly Father. He longs for you to have fellowship with Him, so He may speak to you and you may listen to Him. If people took the time to know the Lord, they would find that He is a God of love, a God who cares about every detail of their lives. Nothing is more urgent, more necessary, and more rewarding than hearing what God has to say to you. Many are so willing to listen to people, but never take the time to listen to what God has to say. God is capable and willing to talk to each of us, if we allow Him. God does not play favorites. He doesn't speak to one person and ignore another. Each of us is precious in His eyes and He longs to fellowship with all of us. God is serious about His relationship with you. He expects you to respond to His voice, adhere to His Word, and make changes in your life that draws you close to Him.

Think over this past week, and recall a conversation you had with a friend. Can you remember where you were, the words spoken, and the attitude you felt in your heart? Now think over this past week and recall what you read in God's Word and what He spoke to you regarding that Word. Are you able to remember the place, the conversation, how you felt, and how God responded? Many can recall conversations with friends but few can remember conversations with God.

God is there for you. He wants to speak life into you. Sometimes He will nurture you with His love. Sometimes He will challenge you to change your thinking or get rid of an unhealthy feeling or opinion. Other times He will give you wisdom. Whatever the Lord does speak, it is a means for you to change in some way and to give you peace, strength, and joy. Take the time to listen to God. It is the most important thing you can do.

JULY 9

Commit your actions to the Lord,
and your plans will succeed.
—Proverbs 16:3, NLT

Recently my friend and I had the pleasure of taking her three grandchildren to Valley Worlds of Fun. Because the youngest boy was too small to rid the bumper cars by himself, I rode with him. I pressed on the gas pedal and helped him steer the car. Although I was trying to help him, I could not direct the car in the right direction because his little hands grasped the wheel so tightly. So I just let him have control and waited for the car to crash into the side of the track. To his understanding, he was doing what he thought was best to direct the path of the car.

Many times we think and act like this little boy. Instead of allowing God to direct our paths, we proceed on our journeys in our own power and strength. God knows what the outcome will be, but allows us to continue to go off course because our hands are so tightly grasped around doing things our own way. Who's doing the steering on the journey you are on right now? Are your hands so tightly wrapped on the steering wheel that God can't do the guiding? If you want God to direct your paths, be willing to let go of the steering wheel and allow God full control of where you go and how you get there.

Letting go and giving God full control is not always easy to do, especially when your life is in chaos. But when you do, it shows God that you trust in Him and are not leaning on your own understanding. God really does care, and when you acknowledge Him, He will direct your paths. Trust in the Lord with all your heart.

JULY 10

But those who desire to be rich fall into temptation and a snare,
and into many foolish and harmful lusts which drown men in
destruction and perdition. Command those who are rich in this
present age not to be haughty, nor to trust in uncertain riches
but in the living God, who gives us richly all things to enjoy.
—1 Timothy 6:9, 17

It is the Lord who richly gives us all things to enjoy. When we become blessed with riches, we can easily fall into many temptations, especially the love of money and striving to remain rich. We are warned in 1 Timothy 6:10 that the love of money is a root of all kinds of evil and some people have even strayed from their faith in their greediness. Jesus told a parable of a rich man whose yield was so plentiful that he would tear down his barns and build bigger ones to hold all the crops. Then the pride in his heart told him to take it easy, to eat, drink, and be merry for he had plenty for many years to come. The Lord called him a "fool," for that very night his soul would be taken and then who would get everything he had worked for. We are fools if we store up earthly wealth for ourselves but not have a rich relationship with God (Luke 12:13–21).

We are reminded that there is only one source of true security and that is in your living God. When you see God as your sole provider, your heart is content. There is no more striving, for you know that God will supply all your needs out of His goodness. One of Satan's schemes is to redirect your focus on what you don't have, bringing discontent to you. When the enemy tries to shift your focus, draw your eyes back to all that God has blessed you with. Hold onto the promises of God that He shall give you the desires of your heart (Psalm 37:4).

JULY 11

*I will praise You, for I am fearfully and wonderfully
made; marvelous are Your works, and that my soul
knows very well. How precious also are Your thoughts
to me, O God! How great is the sum of them!*
—Psalm 139:14, 17

Psalm 139 provides you with the insight into the Father's knowledge and His abundant love for you, just the way you are. He knows how you are made, your strengths and your weaknesses, and your sinful nature. Nothing is hidden from Him. He knows your innermost hurts, fears and disappointments, yet He longs for intimacy with you. Oh, how great are God's riches and wisdom and knowledge. How impossible it is for you to understand his decisions and his ways (Romans 11:33).

Read Psalm 139 in its entirety, and you will come to understand God's perfect knowledge of man. There is so much you take for granted in your everyday life, but when you sit down and meditate on the Word of God, you come to realize how much God loves you and longs for a personal relationship with you. The Lord understands your thoughts. There is nowhere you can go to flee from His presence. His Spirit is always there. It is His right hand that holds you up. He is the one that fearfully and wonderfully made you. His thoughts toward you are precious and are as countless as the sands at the ocean. No matter what you do, He loves you.

Allow the truth in this Psalm to comfort you and give you hope. Realize that God knows you intimately and wants you to know Him intimately. He loves you more than you can ever imagine and is present with you in every place and in every situation. Allow the Word to transform, heal, and lead you into a deeper relationship with your loving Lord.

JULY 12

"Most assuredly, I say to you, unless a grain of wheat falls into the ground and dies, it remains alone; but if it dies, it produces much grain. He who loves his life will lose it, and he who hates his life in this world will keep it for eternal life."
—John 12:24–25

Many people deceive themselves because they seek to be alive in God before they are dead to their own natures. Just as a grain of wheat can't produce a crop without dying first, your dying to self must occur in order for you to have spiritual growth. I love to garden, and each year I start the season off by planting seeds in pods. In the darkness of their grave, they are at the mercy of my hands, trusting me to care for them so that they may raise up to be healthy plants. Had these seeds never been planted, they would have remained alone, never to produce a crop of their own.

When Jesus was on the cross, He gave up His spirit into the power of death. "Father, into thy hands I commit My spirit" (Luke 23:46). He gave up all control and sank into the darkness and death of the grave, surrendering Himself completely into the Father's hands, trusting Him to raise Him up again. Like Jesus, surrender your spirit to God without knowing how your new life will turn out, yet willing to put to death your old carnal ways and to absolutely trust in God to raise you up into your new life.

Do you want to be used by God? Do you want to produce much fruit in your life? Do you want to make a difference in the advancement of the kingdom of God? Be the grain of wheat that falls into the ground and dies. Be willing to surrender yourself completely into the Father's hand, trusting Him in the darkest hours, while He nurtures you into your new life.

JULY 13

Behold, I give you the authority to trample on
serpents and scorpions, and over all the power of the
enemy, and nothing shall by any means hurt you.
—Luke 10:19

Serpents and scorpions are symbols of spiritual enemies and demonic powers which Jesus has given followers power and authority to trample upon. Never lose heart when confronted with disappointment and never fear when confronted with a scheme from the enemy. The Lord controls all that touches you. Romans 16:20 tells us that the God of peace will crush Satan under our feet shortly.

To crush means to trample upon, break in pieces, shatter, bruise, grind down, or smash. This is what the Lord is doing to Satan. Visualize the destruction God is bringing upon Satan. The Lord has given you this same authority to trample upon demonic powers and spiritual enemies when they attack you (Psalm 91:13).

When you are faced with a roaring lion or a cobra, roar louder and bite harder. The enemy only has as much power over you as you allow him to have. Give him an inch and he'll take a mile. Take authority over the spiritual enemy. Symbolically crush it, break it into pieces, shatter it, grind it, or smash it. Do whatever it takes to demolish it. Visualize yourself destroying it so that it no longer has control over you and you are walking in victory. Remember—nothing shall by any means hurt you.

JULY 14

*Jesus said to them, "My food is to do the will
of Him who sent Me, and to finish His work."*
—John 4:34

Doing the will of the Father was the food that sustained Jesus. He learned at an early age to hear God's voice and He pleased the Father by depending on His Spirit to do exactly what the Lord asked Him to do. He lived to do the will of the Father. At the end of His earthly ministry, He could say "I have glorified You on the earth. I have finished the work which You have given Me to do" (John 17:4). And on the cross, He could truly say "It is finished" (John 19:30). His finished work secured the victory over Satan.

Doing the will of the Father must be the food that sustains you. Learn to hear God's voice and please the Father by depending on His Spirit to do exactly what the Lord asks you to do. Have the mindset of Christ, to think, say, and do what Christ would do. Literally "Put on Christ." In doing so, you will make no provision for the flesh and its lusts (Romans 13:14) but instead will do the will of God in all things, great and small, and finish His work.

Live to do the will of the Father. Let the beauty of Jesus be seen in you. Let the compassion of Jesus flow through you. Let the words of Jesus speak through you. Let the peace of Jesus rest upon you. And may the love of Christ abide in you. May your response be the same as Jesus'—My food is to do the will of our Father and finish His work. When you do, you too will be able to say, "I have glorified You on the earth. I have finished the work which you have given me to do."

JULY 15

For what man knows the things of a man except the spirit
of the man which is in him? Even so no one knows the things
of God except the Spirit of God. Now we have received, not
the spirit of the world, but the Spirit who is from God, that we
might know the things that have been freely given to us by God.
—1 Corinthians 2:11–12

I used to be a computer programmer. A software program would respond to information based upon the commands I had written. The outcome of the application may not have produced the correct results, but based upon the commands the software program was given, the application responded just as it had been programmed. Until the results were compared to a source of truth, no one would know the results were inaccurate.

Your spirit responds similarly to the way that a computer responds. From the time of birth, God has programmed His moral code into the hearts of every person. Early on you know right from wrong. But over time, you reprogram your own moral code of how you should live. Based upon the commands written, you think your way of living is correct. But until you compare the results to the source of truth, you will never know that you are walking in sin.

When you become a Christian, the Spirit of God falls upon you and lives in you. A change begins to occur within your spirit, for the Spirit of God begins to do an overhaul on the code that was written in your heart. The Holy Spirit begins to renew your mind to more specific and complete truths. You begin to see that some of the things that you thought were morally right were not, and a shift begins to occur in your spirit. As the process continues, your mind and heart tune into the moral code of the Holy Spirit. Daily you program things into your mind. Be certain that the moral code you have written is accurate and lines up with the moral code of God. Compare the results of your code to the Word of God to insure that all programming is from the Spirit of God and not from the spirit of man.

JULY 16

(As it is written, "I have made you a father of many nations") in the presence of Him whom he believed—God who gives life to the dead and calls those things which do not exist as though they did. He did not waver at the promise of God through unbelief, but was strengthened in faith, giving glory to God, and being fully convinced that what He had promised He was able to perform.
—Romans 4:17, 20–21

God never promises you anything He cannot deliver. Put your faith in God and trust in Him regardless of how your situation looks. Faith is the substance of things hoped for and the evidence of things not seen (Hebrews 11:1). Faith recognizes the problem, gives it to God, acknowledges Him in the midst of that problem, and declares His truth and promise on the matter. Faith does not deny the situation at hand but declares that God is greater than that obstacle. Faith does not deny that a sickness is in the body, but declares that by His stripes I am healed. Faith does not deny financial need, but acknowledges Jesus's ability to meet those needs. Faith does not deny you are a sinner, but puts your trust in Jesus for salvation and receives God's free gift of eternal life.

Whatever God shows you, whatever God speaks to your heart, take hold of it in faith. Call those things that are not as if they are. All the promises of God are yours. See them, believe them, allow faith to come in, and claim them. They are yours. When God gives you a revelation, believe it and do not waiver at the promise of God through unbelief.

You can always tell if a person believes a promise or not just by listening to them speak. One reason you don't see more miracles is because of unbelief. Cultivate an atmosphere of faith in your own heart. Claim victory before you even see the results. Lord, forgive me when I have walked in unbelief, skepticism or doubt. Cleanse me now from these spirits. Wash me, cleanse me, and fill me with fresh faith, great faith, faith to move mountains.

JULY 17

Then He said, "Go out, and stand on the mountain
before the Lord." And behold, the Lord passed by, and a
great and strong wind tore into the mountains and broke
the rocks in pieces before the Lord, but the Lord was not in the
wind; and after the wind an earthquake, but the Lord was not
in the earthquake; and after the earthquake a fire, but the Lord
was not in the fire; and after the fire a still small voice.
—1 Kings 19:11–12

Many people expect God to speak to them in some tangible way or they don't feel God is speaking. It is rare that God speaks to people in a loud audible voice. In order to hear that still small voice, you have to quiet yourself in complete silence. Many people are uncomfortable with silence, but it is in the silence that you are able to hear that still small voice of God.

Quietness is essential to listening and hearing. If you are too busy to sit in silence in His presence, if you are too occupied with thoughts and concerns about your life, if you have filled your mind hour after hour with chatter and worldly music, then you are going to have difficulty truly listening to that still small voice of God. How many times has someone spoken to you and you don't hear a word they have said because your mind was too occupied with something else? I know I have done it. It's easy to do. That's what happens to you many times when God is trying to speak to you. God is talking but you're really not listening.

Set aside times to wait upon the Lord in silence. You have to train yourself to sit quietly. When your mind begins to drift, meditate on one characteristic of God and focus on that characteristic. Ask the Lord to turn off the cares and worries of this world for a few minutes so that you can listen to Him. Ask the Lord to speak to you. Then sit quietly and listen to what the Lord speaks to your heart.

JULY 18

Give me understanding, and I shall keep Your law;
Indeed, I shall observe it with my whole heart.
I have more understanding than all my teachers,
For Your testimonies are my meditation.
—Psalm 119:34, 99

"To understand" means to become wise through the thinking process that occurs when one observes, ponders, reasons, learns, and reaches a conclusion. The psalmist understood that true wisdom must come by meditating on the Word of God. He asked God to not only teach him the ways of His laws, but to give him understanding about those laws so that he could observe them with his whole heart (Psalm 119:33–34). The psalmist understood that if he kept his eyes looking at worthless things, it would lead to covetousness. Therefore, he asked God to turn his eyes from worthless things, and to incline his heart according to His word, to fulfill His promises to His servant who was devoted to fearing Him (Psalm 119:36–38).

The psalmist loved God's word. It was his meditation all day long (Psalm 119:97). Dwelling on it made him wiser than all his enemies and gave him more understanding than all his teachers (Psalm 119:98–99). Dwelling on God's Word and allowing God to speak to your heart is a great way to allow His truths to take root in your heart. You are to read scripture, observe it, ponder on the words spoken, reason and learn from them. You are to allow God to help you reach the proper conclusion. As you read the Word, ask the Lord to speak to you and to give you a clear understanding of what you have read. Then observe, with your whole heart, what you have just learned.

JULY 19

And we know that all things work together for good to those who love God, to those who are the called according to His purpose.
—Romans 8:28

God promises us that all things work together for good to those who love Him. You have to remember that what the enemy meant for evil, God will turn it into good. You are in this world but not of it. You will face trials and tribulations, but instead of allowing them to knock you down and overcome you, allow Christ to help you overcome the situation and become victorious. The battle you are facing today is not over until God says it's over and you have victory. It is not over until you win.

Many get so discouraged when faced with tribulations. Instead of looking at the situation at hand, build your faith and see God working in it. Choose to embrace triumph in Christ even though victory may not be in sight yet. See that faith and actions work together and by your actions, faith will be made complete (James 2:22). Rejoice in every little breakthrough until the victory has been won. You can allow your trials to be a stumbling block, or you permit them to be a stepping stone to building your faith in Christ. Remember, the greater the trial, the greater the testimony. Allow God to write your testimonies for you and allow faith to be made perfect in you.

JULY 20

"And I have filled him with the Spirit of God,
in wisdom and in understanding, and in the
knowledge, and in all manner of workmanship."
—Exodus 31:3

Have you ever worried about how God views your life? Do you worry that He sees all the flaws and mistakes and loves you less because of them? Do you worry that you will not be used by God because you feel that you do not have the skills of someone else? Fear not and do not worry. God knows everything about you and loves you completely just the way you are.

Just as a carpenter knows every mistake in their building project, God knows every flaw in you. A flaw in a house does not lower the overall value of the masterpiece and usually goes undetected by those who are not experienced in the trade. Likewise, the flaws in each of us do not lower the value that the Lord places on us. You are His workmanship, His masterpiece, and you are valuable in His eyes. God does not look at your flaws. Instead, He looks at your entire being and sees a person of worth and of great promise.

Although you are not perfect, God rejoices over you. You are His workmanship, created in the image of Christ, to do His works (Ephesians 2:10). These works were prepared by God before you were given the assignments. Therefore, God has already given you the tools needed to perform the skills with accuracy. No matter what the assignment may be, God has filled you with His Spirit, His wisdom, His understanding and His knowledge to fulfill that which He has called you to do. God will use each of us for His purpose. If He had wanted other people to do the task he assigned to you, He would have asked them. But He has chosen you for such a time as this. Give yourself the time needed to perfect yourself in the tools that God has placed in your hands, and allow Him to complete the workmanship in you.

JULY 21

Then David danced before the Lord with all his might;
and David was wearing a linen ephod. So David and
all the house of Israel brought up the ark of the Lord
with shouting and with the sound of the trumpet.
—2 Samuel 6:14–15

King David was bringing the ark of God to the City of David. He would sacrifice oxen and sheep along the way. Then King David danced before the Lord with all his might. While he was dancing, Saul's daughter, Michal, who was also King David's wife, looked through a window and saw him leaping and whirling before the Lord and she despised him in her heart (2 Samuel 6:16).

When King David returned home to bless his family, Michal came out to meet him, and with disgust in her voice, proceeded to tell King David that his actions had been very undignified for a king. He retorted to Michal that he had been dancing before the Lord in appreciation and celebration of all the Lord had done for him. Michal's thoughts toward her husband did not stop King David from devoting himself wholeheartedly to the Lord. The Lord honored King David's worship but was displeased with Michal's response. As a result, the Lord shut her womb, causing her to remain childless throughout her entire life (2 Samuel 6:20–23).

Everyone has different ways of worshiping the Lord. You should never be a stumbling block to another's style of worship. Don't let your attitude toward someone else's worship cause the womb of your dreams to be shut. Never let anyone, even a family member, discourage you from your form of devotion to the Lord. King David loved the Lord with all his heart, soul and strength. He responded not only to life's circumstances, but also to celebrations of victory, with a heart of worship. Respond to life's challenges with a heart of worship; dance before the Lord with all your heart, soul, and might and see your problems whirl away.

JULY 22

Trust in the lord with all your heart, and lean
not on your own understanding; In all your ways
acknowledge Him and He shall direct your paths.
—Proverbs 3:5–6

I cannot begin to imagine living my life without the Lord, and yet there are millions of people who do. The many trials and tribulations I have faced make me wonder, "If it had not been for the Lord, where would I be?" Solomon knew that only a fool tries to solve life's problems without God's help. Eventually people will reach a point in their life where there is nowhere else to turn but to God.

Do not lean on your own understanding but to trust in God. Being a Christian does not mean that you will not be faced with everyday life challenges. Trials will come in all shapes and sizes. Some will be expected, others will catch you off guard. Some tests will require you to endure to the end, while others may end before they even start. Some challenges may require you to make the right decision immediately, while others allow you ample time to decide.

Regardless of the shape and size of your trials, you are to acknowledge God in all your ways, seek Him for wisdom, and He will direct your paths. That means trusting Him with all your heart that He will make the right decisions for you. As kids grow older, they think they know it all and want to make their own decisions without the guidance from their parents. Many times we Christians are like kids. We think we know all the answers to life's problems and don't need or want to seek advice from our Heavenly Father.

God always has a purpose behind every trial you face. In order for that purpose to be fulfilled, turn to Him for the answer. If you seek your own wisdom, you may come up with a solution, but it may not be God's intended plan of action and you may bypass the lesson to be learned. Acknowledge God in all your ways and allow Him to direct your paths.

JULY 23

Therefore, brethren, having boldness to enter the Holiest by the blood of Jesus, by a new and living way which He consecrated for us, through the veil, that is His flesh, and having a High Priest over the house of God, let us draw near with a true heart in full assurance of faith, having our hearts sprinkled from an evil conscience and our bodies washed with pure water.
—Hebrews 10:19–22

In the temple there was a veil between the Holy Place and the Holiest of Holies. It was behind this veil that the high priest entered alone once a year. The veil symbolized the sinful human nature. When Christ died, this veil was torn in two (Matthew 27:51). God provided a new living way of entering God's presence through the torn veil of His flesh. We can now boldly enter heaven's Most Holy Place because of the blood of Jesus.

Many Christians cannot attain close fellowship with God because they have not circumcised their hearts and yielded their flesh to the Lord. They desire to enter into the Holiest of Holies, yet allow the flesh with the affections and lusts to rule over them. You cannot expect a full abiding fellowship with God except through the torn veil of your flesh, through a circumcised heart, and through a life with the flesh crucified with Christ.

When you yield yourself unto God and draw near to Him with a sincere heart, you can boldly go into His presence, without hesitation, in full assurance and in faith that He is there to welcome you. God provided this new living way of entering God's presence because He wanted fellowship with His people. Do you desire to be closer to God? Reflect on what He has done for you. The veil has been cut so that you may boldly enter into the very presence of God. During your devotional time with the Lord, visualize the veil being cut in half and you walking into the Holiest of Holies. God is waiting to meet you there.

JULY 24

Therefore we also, since we are surrounded by so great a
cloud of witnesses, let us lay aside every weight, and the sin
which so easily ensnares us, and let us run with endurance
the race that is set before us, looking unto Jesus, the author
and finisher of our faith, who for the joy that was set before
Him endured the cross, despising the shame, and has sat
down at the right hand of the throne of God.
—Hebrews 12:1–2

When running a race, a person's eyes and heart's desire are always set upon the goal and the prize. Runners train hard with one goal in mind, and that is winning the race. You are in a race, an eternal race, and you are to keep your eyes focused upon Jesus, the one who has already won His race and is waiting for you to finish yours. You do not have to worry about winning the race, you just have to keep your eyes focused on Jesus and finish it.

To focus means to give your undivided attention, looking away from distractions in order to fix your gaze on one object, that being Jesus. If you ever travel in an Amish community, you will notice plenty of horses and buggies on the roads. The horses have blinders on the sides of their heads so that they can see only what is ahead of them and not be distracted by things on either side.

There are many things that can weigh you down, ensnare you, distract you and get you off course if you do not wear blinders and keep your eyes focused on the race and the prize. Jesus did not allow Himself to be distracted. His eyes were not focused on the shame, rejection, humiliation and pain. His eyes were focused on finishing the race, at any cost, and looking forward to the prize—sharing eternity with us. Are you going through some rough times? Do not allow the circumstances to distract you. Look at nothing but Jesus, the one who began and will complete your faith.

JULY 25

*By this we know love, because He laid down His life
for us. And we also ought to lay down our lives for
the brethren. But whoever has this world's goods, and
sees his brother in need, and shuts up his heart from
him, how does the love of God abide in Him?*
—1 John 3:16–17

You were born to love and be loved. Jesus's love for us is what compelled Him to lay down His life for us. That same compelling love dwells within each believer. It is only the love of Christ possessing your heart that will enable you to love others. It is only your faith in Christ that enables you to accept His great command to lay down your life for others. A soldier is willing to die for his fellow comrade. In the defense of fire, are you willing to die for your comrade in Christ? Are you willing to defend your brother when he is being attacked, threatened, or beaten up? Are you willing to stand in the gap for him when he has no strength left inside of him to continue fighting?

The greatest attack against you is the words spoken by others and the thoughts that follow. Defend your brethren when someone is speaking against them or be courageous enough to walk away from the gossip and chatter. You are to a live godly life and the love of God in your life will be evident by the way you treat others.

The greatest need a person has is to be loved. If you close your heart from him when he needs defended, when he needs a friend, or when he needs uplifted, how does the love of God abide in you? You are not simply to talk about love but you are to demonstrate that love by giving to and caring for those in need physically, emotionally, and spiritually. You are to live and love as Christ did. Lay down your life for your brethren today.

JULY 26

And from Jesus Christ, the faithful witness, the
firstborn from the dead, and the ruler over the kings
of the earth. To Him who loved us and washed us
from our sins in His own blood, and has made us
kings and priests to His God and Father, to Him
be glory and dominion forever and ever. Amen.
—Revelation 1:5–6

Do you really know how much the Lord loves you? Have you really pondered over this everlasting love? He willingly washed away your sins with His own blood. Is this not proof enough of His love for you and that He will never leave you or reject you? He gave up His life for a cause—to prove His love for us. So how do you experience that agape love deep within your soul?

Talk to God often. Whatever is upon your heart, talk to Him about it. Ask Him to help you to experience the depths of His love for you. The more you spend time with Him, the more you will feel His love. Our Father loves us so much that he calls us his children, and that is what we are! But the people who belong to this world don't recognize that we are God's children because they don't know Him (1 John 3:1). Believe what He says about you, that you are a son of God and you are royalty. He paid a great ransom for us.

Jesus Christ is the King of Kings, He has made us kings under His Lordship. He has delegated His power and authority to us so we may take dominion on the earth (Luke 9:1). He will strengthen us through His Spirit to reign as kings over sin. This involves faithfully witnessing the love of Christ, the Victor over sin, to those who have not experienced the love of Christ in their lives. As kings, we are to confront the powers of darkness, prepare for and engage in spiritual warfare, do the works of the Father, and give praise to whom praise is due. Yes, to Him who has loved us, has washed us from our sins in His blood, and has made us kings and priests—to Him be the glory and dominion forever and ever. Amen.

JULY 27

"But I say to you, love your enemies, bless those who
curse you, do good to those who hate you, and pray
for those who spitefully use you and persecute you."
—Matthew 5:44

In many of Jesus's teachings, He emphasized the importance of how to build and maintain right relationships with God and others. Your personal interaction with God should produce in you the characteristics of Christ that build and sustain all other relationships. Jesus told us to love our enemies, bless those who curse us, do good to those who hate us, and pray for those who spitefully use and persecute us. Jesus knew what the world would be like and the attitudes of people whom you would come into contact with. But He taught us that we should love by choice and not by our circumstances.

The eight words Jesus spoke on the cross, "For they do not know what they do" (Luke 23:34), revealed the mind of Christ and demonstrate to us how we should view the wrongful actions of others. Three words in this same verse express Christ's love, "Father forgive them." Jesus prayed for His enemies. In the hour of His suffering and shame, He poured out His love in prayer for them. Do you have this characteristic of Christ in you?

How do you react to your circumstances? Do you act in love or do you react to your circumstances? You can't control what other people say or do, but you can control how you react. Allow the Holy Spirit to control you and guide you in your response to the situation. As a believer, prove that the mind of Christ is your mind and that His love is what guides you in your relationship, with the world around you.

JULY 28

*"A little while longer and the world will
see Me no more, but you will see Me.
Because I live, you will live also."*
—Matthew 28:20

Often we don't realize what we have until it is taken away or is gone from us. We take so many things for granted: our health, our possessions, the essentials of life, family and friends, and sometimes even God. If you are a parent, you have spent many years raising your children, providing for them, teaching them, and giving them wise counsel. Then one day your children, now adults, leave the comfort of their home to start new journeys in their lives. You wonder what life is going to be like without them in your home, but realize that you must let them go.

I can only imagine the brokenness the disciples felt when Jesus spoke of leaving them. They could not think of living without Him. To comfort the disciples, Christ gave them the promise of the Holy Spirit (John 14:16–17), with the assurance that they would have His presence in a far more intimate sense than they ever had known while He was on earth. Before leaving them Jesus gave them the great commission to go and make disciples of all the nations, baptizing them, and teaching them to obey all the commandments He had given them. Then He gave them this assurance: I am always with you, even to the end of the world (Matthew 28:19–20).

It is so important to cherish the moments you spend with friends, family, and loved ones. Unlike Christ, who reassures us that He is with us always, the special people in your life cannot make that promise. Value the people that God has placed in your life. Appreciate each moment you spend with them, for it may be the last time you are physically together. Make the most of each relationship. Have a positive lasting effect by making the most of each word spoken. Lastly, honor, value, and cherish your relationship with God. Don't take His love for granted. Cherish each moment spent with Him and watch your love grow not only for God but for others.

JULY 29

My brethren, count it all joy when you
fall into various trials, knowing that the
testing of your faith produces patience.

—James 1:2–3

We often hear that we should never pray for patience. We know that we need it, yet we shun or regret the process by which we learn it. We want healing, so we run to the doctors instead of seeking God and receiving our healing from Him. We cannot wait to lose weight properly, so we prefer the fad diets instead. People cannot wait for their wealth to grow, so they take the chance of winning the lottery or some other get-rich quick scheme.

There are many reasons why you must go through trials. If you direct your heart into the love of God, He will give you the strength and patience to wait upon Him. You learn patience only by going through your trials and tribulations. When you are faced with a situation that requires you to wait upon the Lord, keep these thoughts in mind to help you persevere: God is teaching me to trust His ways and His timing; God is building my faith and patience through waiting; I am depending on God and not on myself or others; God knows what I need and what is right for me, but I am not ready for it yet; I may not get what I want because it would have a negative effect on someone else; God desires me to look at my motivation to make sure it does not oppose His purpose; I am going to examine myself because God may be trying to get my attention to some hidden sin in my life; God is love and whatever the outcome of my trial, His love will sustain me.

In times of difficulty, learn to endure, to trust, and to keep holding on. When you endure, trust, and keep holding on without setting a deadline, then you have learned the quality of patience. For when your faith is tested, your patience has a chance to grow.

JULY 30

So He said, "I will certainly be with you. And this shall be a sign to you that I have sent you: When you have brought the people out of Egypt, you shall serve God on this mountain."

—Exodus 3:12

Every person is born with a measure of faith. Often you will hear someone say, "I don't have faith." But everyone has faith. The question is who or what do they put their faith in. Children put their faith in their parents. They go to bed and sleep soundly knowing that when they wake up, mom or dad will be there to meet their needs the next day. When children get hurt, they go crying to their parents because they know that mom or dad will help make the pain go away. When they are hungry they don't have to worry about what they will eat, they can already smell the luscious food cooking in the oven. Children are care free because they trust in their parents.

Like children, have great faith that your Heavenly Father will certainly be there for you too. Everything depends on faith. Accept Christ's words as divine reality and trust the Holy Spirit to reveal the truth of it each moment of every day. There is not a day in your life where you will awaken and find that God is not there for you. His blessed presence is with you each and every day to provide for your needs and to care for you. Awake each day with full assurance that "You are certainly with me Lord." If you believe that in your heart, you will have the same care free spirit as children.

JULY 31

And he commanded them, saying, "Thus you shall act
in the fear of the Lord, faithfully and with a loyal heart."
—2 Chronicles 19:9

God considers loyalty an important trait. To be loyal means that you are faithful and devoted to someone or something. God wants you to remain loyal to Him, as well as to the people He puts in your life. King David knew the importance of loyalty. He prayed that God would give his son a loyal heart to be obedient to Him (1 Chronicles 29:19). Above all else, King David wanted his son to be loyal to God.

Real loyalty is a choice and it starts within. Loyalty is a moral commitment which can only be made when you value a relationship with another. Loyalty comes from the heart and is motivated by love. Loyal friends come to the rescue of others. They defend the other person and refuse to listen to gossip. Being loyal means you won't talk about people behind their back. A loyal person speaks truth no matter what the cost. When asked a question, a loyal friend gives an honest opinion instead of just saying what the other person wants to hear. True loyalty is built upon relationships—being devoted to God and loving others. It is not based upon circumstances, convenience or deception. It is based upon a true love and respect for the other person.

Examine your relationship with God and others in your life and determine if you are loyal to them. Trust others until they give you a reason not to. Take time to look at the needs of your friends and be there for them when they are having difficulties. Ask the Holy Spirit to reveal areas in your life where you may have been disloyal to God or to your friends. Pray like David did and ask God to give you a loyal heart to keep His commandments and be faithful to Him.

AUGUST 1

Reproach has broken my heart, and I am full of
heaviness; I looked for someone to take pity, but
there was none; and for comforters, but I found none.
—Psalm 69:20

Where do you go to find comfort? If you are like most people, you will tend to go to family members and friends. Others turn to food, drugs, and/or alcohol for comfort or relief from their heaviness. But we all know, once the temporary pleasure wears off, the pain still remains. So what are you to do? King David went to people around Him but could not find peace. I believe that God allows you to experience rough times, when people aren't around, so that you depend on Him. When King David had no one else to turn to, he turned to God and there he found comfort.

King David knew that he was suffering and in pain and asked God to rescue Him by His saving power. In the midst of his heaviness, he praised God with a song and magnified His name with thanksgiving. King David knew that this would please God more than anything else (Psalm 69:29–31). It pleases God when you praise Him in the midst of your heaviness and sorrow. It is telling God that you are trusting in Him no matter what your circumstances may look like. The Lord hears the cries of the needy and does not despise His prisoners (Psalm 69:33).

God is a God of love. He is the sole Comforter and only He can take away the pain. When you experience turmoil, heaviness, pain, or a broken heart, reach out to God and you will find comfort and resolve for your situation. In the midst of your storm, praise God with a song and magnify His name with praise and thanksgiving. This will please God more than anything else.

AUGUST 2

*"Therefore whoever hears these sayings of Mine, and
does them, I will liken him to a wise man who built his
house on the rock: and the rain descended, the floods
came, and the winds blew and beat on that house;
and it did not fall, for it was founded on the rock."*
—Matthew 7:24–25

In this parable, Jesus is teaching us about the importance of being obedient and compares our obedience to a man building a house. When you listen to God's Word and obey it, you build a strong foundation for your life. It is not enough to just hear the message; apply it to your life as well. If you hear and obey the message of God, your life has a solid foundation to stand on. When the storms of life come, you will stand firm because you are built on the Word of God.

Put your full trust in the Rock, the Lord Jesus Christ. There is no other firm foundation to stand on. Many people are building their lives without any foundation or they are building their lives on what they think is best, following after carnal principles of this world. Their lives are calm and everything seems to be going well for them. They don't stop to think about the foundation they have built their lives upon. Little do they realize that when the storm does eventually come, their foundation will be tested, but it will be too late to do anything about it. Their lives will crumble and fall because they had no solid base to stand upon and they will be washed away (Matthew 7:26–27).

The wise man is the one who believes in Jesus Christ and is saved. He is the one who comes to Christ for salvation, who hears his instructions and obeys them. The wise man is the one who builds his life on Christian values. The foolish man is the one who rejects Christ and is lost. He is the one who hears Christ's instruction but fails to follow His teachings and chooses to be disobedient. The foolish man builds his life on carnal principles and on the world's standards. What foundation is your life built upon? Be sure your life is built on the solid foundation of knowing and trusting Jesus Christ.

AUGUST 3

He who loves purity of heart and has grace
on his lips, the king will be his friend.

—Proverbs 22:11

The heart of the matter is a matter of the heart. You have a choice everyday regarding the attitude you will embrace for the day. Bitterness, jealousy or resentment in your heart will produce reactions to those same feelings in your everyday responses. The only way to be free is to let go of offenses and refuse to keep score. Victory comes when you choose to not speak from the flesh. When you let go of the offense and speak with grace, the aroma of Christ is released.

You need to watch the unguarded moments of frustration, anger, jealousy or pain that your mouth tends to spew out. While the Holy Spirit gives you the power to change the words you speak, the desire to change begins in the heart. Toxins leave a foul odor and will eventually destroy the land which it occupies. Toxic emotions and attitudes left in your heart will eventually pollute your body and its surroundings. Bitter angry words release toxins into the air and cause destruction to hearts and souls. The ungodly don't think before speaking, because they don't care about the effects of their words.

The heart of the matter is a matter of the heart. What is your heart speaking today? Do you weigh your answers before speaking? Do you carefully plan your words, or do you pour out your thoughts without concern for their impact? The heart of the righteous thinks carefully before speaking, but the mouth of the wicked overflows with evil words (Proverbs 15:28). Words do matter. How you express those words matter even more. Be pure in heart and speak with grace and love.

AUGUST 4

But Jonah arose to flee to Tarshish from the
presence of the Lord. He went down to Joppa, and
found a ship going to Tarshish; so he paid the fare,
and went down into it, to go with them to Tarshish
from the presence of the Lord.
—Jonah 1:3

Jonah bought a ticket in an effort to flee from the presence of the Lord. He wanted to escape from an assignment given to Him by God. Jonah felt that if he went far enough away from God's presence, that God would no longer seek to use him. It is amazing what people will do to avoid an order from the Lord. Instead, God followed Jonah and brought a storm upon the sea. Jonah knew that his own disobedience had put the ship in danger, but he would rather die than return to land and obey God's command (Jonah 1:12).

You will be put into situations where the Lord will ask you to do things that you are not comfortable in doing. The longer you prolong obedience, the more turmoil you place upon yourself and possibly upon others. You may try to convince yourself that ignoring or taking a different approach will relieve you of the responsibility God has placed upon you. But God cannot be fooled. You cannot hide from His Spirit nor flee from His presence (Psalm 139:7). He will cause circumstances to arise that will bring you face-to-face with the decision to align yourself with Him and to do what He has asked.

Is there something in your life that the Lord has asked you to do that you have been putting off? Seek God and ask Him to develop in you the character you need to walk in His gifts and calling. Then put your mind to the task and do that which God has requested.

AUGUST 5

"For I have come down from heaven, not to do
My own will, but the will of Him who sent Me."
—John 6:38

This past Sunday in service, we were told a story of a gentleman whom the Lord asked to go to Africa to be a missionary. The man's wife became pregnant. Under pressure from other people, they decided to wait until after the pregnancy to go. The baby was born with some illness or condition which postponed their departure once again. They never did go to Africa, but continued to do the work of the Lord here in the States. His passion for Africa never left him and he donated to charities for that cause. One day, now much older, he was looking back on his life and was talking to the Lord. The Lord spoke to him, "But I did not ask you to do those things, I asked you to go to Africa."

I think about this story often. Unless you walk in obedience to the will of God, all of your other actions will be misdirected and unfruitful. The Lord will reveal His will to you, but be willing to align your spirit with the Holy Spirit to fulfill His plan in you. Do not let the influences of others, or your personal desires, to interfere with God's will. There are many times the Lord speaks to you. An unyielding spirit will not be able to hear the voice of the Lord but a yielded spirit knows it is being guided by God.

I do not want to be like the gentleman in the story. I do not want the Lord to say to me, "I didn't ask you to do those things, I asked you to___." In your quiet time with God, ask Him if He has ever asked you to do something that you have not yet done. Listen with your heart and then be willing to do the will of the Father. It is never too late to yield your spirit unto the Lord and to do the will of the Father.

AUGUST 6

"So shall My word be that goes forth from My mouth; It shall not return to Me void, but it shall accomplish what I please, and it shall prosper in the thing for which I sent it."
—Isaiah 55:11

The Word of God isn't just words printed on a page. The Word of God is substance, it is Truth and Life. If Christians would only grasp the power that words have. The course of your life depends upon how you speak. Your words shall not return void, they will accomplish that which has been spoken. When you see a blessing in the Bible, claim it, decree it for your life, speak it forth and it is yours. Plant seeds of healing in your body, declare seeds of salvation for your household, plant seeds of wealth in your bank account. Your words shall not return void if they line up with the Word of God.

When you proclaim the Word of God, you dispatch angels to perform the words you release. The more words you release, the more the angels will perform on your behalf. God's Word is truth and when you proclaim God's Word, angels heed to the voice of His Word. I don't know about you, but I want all the blessings from God that are rightfully mine. All the blessings that you read about in God's Word are yours, you just have to claim them. Proclaim the Word and have the strength of angels on your side. Whatever you speak, it shall not return void. Speak life and blessings into your life and the life of those around you.

AUGUST 7

*Therefore, if anyone is in Christ, he is a new creation; old
things have passed away; behold, all things have become new.*
—2 Corinthians 5:17

Understand who you are in Christ. When you gave your life
to Christ, you became a new creation. The Lord tells you to not
remember the former things, nor consider the things of old, for He
will do a new thing in you (Isaiah 43:18–19). He tells you to forget
about them for it is nothing compared to what He is going to do.
We are children of the living God and we must be taught, disci-
plined and trained. As you grow in the Lord, you begin to throw off
your old sinful nature and former way of life, which was corrupted
by lust and deception. Instead, you put on a new nature, created to
be like God, truly righteous and holy by allowing the Holy Spirit
to renew your thoughts and attitudes (Ephesians 4:22–24).

You will always have shortcomings and weaknesses to overcome. If you focus on these obstacles, you will never overcome
them. You have to embrace who you are in Christ and believe that
you are more than s conqueror through Christ (Romans 8:37). Do
you believe that? In Proverbs 23:7 we are told, "As he thinks in his
heart, so is he." If you believe that you are a conqueror, you will
become a conqueror in all things. Think powerfully the way God
thinks. Align your thoughts with God's Word. Whatever the Word
says you are, claim it, for that is who you are. Know who you are
in Christ! Declare who you are in Christ! Believe who you are in
Christ! And be who you are in Christ!

AUGUST 8

But this is the covenant that I will make with the
house of Israel after those days, says the Lord: I will
put My law in their minds, and write it on their hearts;
and I will be their God, and they shall be My people.
—Jeremiah 31:33

Most of us read God's Word daily. It is our daily bread for survival. God's Word is filled with power and love. God's Word is filled with substance. Many people know what the Word of God says but they never experience the full benefits of its substance. The key to crossing the bridge between knowing and experiencing is obedience. Obedience enables you to abide in His love and gives you the full experience of His presence.

God not only wants to put His Word into your mind but He wants to write it on the tablet of your heart. Why? So that you will not depart from it (Jeremiah 32:40). God's Word will be engrained in you forever. As you meditate on the scriptures, God will cause you to draw near to Him. The Lord will give you a heart to know Him, and to know that He is the Lord. We shall be His people, and He will be our God, for we shall return to Him with our whole heart (Jeremiah 24:7).

Many Christians do not experience the power of God in their lives because they do not fear and reverence the Lord. Words just roll off their lips without any real meaning or substance. It is the fear of the Lord that causes your heart to change. It is the fear of the Lord that causes you to surrender your will to do His will. It is the fear of the Lord that causes you to bow down before Him when you are in His Holy presence. Ask God to write His laws in your mind and in your heart and to teach you how to fear Him.

AUGUST 9

Blessed be the God and Father of our Lord
Jesus Christ, who has blessed us with every
spiritual blessing in the heavenly places in Christ.
—Ephesians 1:3

Because of Calvary and Jesus's finished work on the cross, every spiritual blessing in heavenly places is ours through Christ Jesus. You do not have to do anything to earn them for they have already been given to you. You just have to believe and have faith that they are yours. Just because you do not see the blessing does not mean that it's not there or that it's not yours. You just have to move in faith and receive your blessing. Faith comes from hearing, and hearing by the Word of God (Romans 10:17). When God reveals a promise to you through the written Word, claim it, and believe it in your heart, until the faith within you arises to establish the blessings. God would not have quickened your spirit to a promise if He did not intend to give it to you.

Look through Ephesians 1 to see the many spiritual blessings you have because of Christ. The only way to receive them is through faith. Your life matters. You were chosen before the foundation of the world (v. 4). In Christ you are holy and blameless (v. 4). You have Christ's unconditional love (v. 4). You have been adopted by Christ Himself (v. 5). Through Christ you are redeemed through His blood and have forgiveness of sins (v. 7). He makes known His will to you (v. 9). God has given you eternal inheritance with Him (v. 11). You are sealed with the Holy Spirit (v. 13). The exceeding greatness of His power that raised Christ from the dead resides in you. These are just a few of the spiritual blessings that are yours through Christ. Receive them in faith, they are yours.

AUGUST 10

Then the Lord appeared again in Shiloh.
For the Lord revealed Himself to Samuel
in Shiloh by the word of the Lord.

—1 Samuel 3:21

Everyone wants to hear from God but how do we distinguish between God's voice, the voice of the Satan, and the voice of our fleshly desires? Samuel did not yet know the Lord (1 Samuel 3:7), but He grew up to become a great prophet of the Lord. Samuel, therefore, had to learn to recognize God's voice. Frequently your preconceptions about God influence what you think you hear from Him. If you consider Him to be a loving God, you will be open to His love for you. If you consider Him to be a judgmental God, you will expect to hear words of condemnation. Go before the Lord without any preconceptions.

Your relationship with God influences how you hear Him. The Lord revealed Himself to Samuel by His word. Samuel had to spend time reading and meditating on the Word, and as he did, God began to speak to Him. God desires all of us to have that same type of relationship with Him. It is in that love relationship that you begin to learn more about God, His characteristics, desires, and deep love for you. It is in that love relationship that you begin to recognize His voice and hear God speak to you.

You have heard many thoughts and ideas offered to you as if they were gospel truth. These cause you to walk in sin and spiritual bondage. Test what you hear with the Word of God to see if it is from God (1 Thessalonians 5:21) and ask the Holy Spirit to give you understanding on what you have read. Be careful not to misinterpret the meaning of the scriptures. Your misunderstandings will lead to deception and cause you to walk in paths that you should not travel. God tells you to boldly go before the throne of grace (Hebrews 4:16). Go boldly before the Lord and ask Him if what you are hearing is coming from Him. He will confirm His Word to you. Ask Him for clarification when you are confused about what you heard.

AUGUST 11

But if we hope for what we do not see,
we eagerly wait for it with perseverance.
—Romans 8:25

What expectations do you have? Do you expect negative things to happen in the midst, of your trial, or do you silently wait on God alone for your expectation is in Him? I recently went before the Lord and asked for healing for a person. I had high expectations that the Lord was going to heal this individual. I thanked the Lord throughout the week believing and expecting this individual to be healed. Although I had high expectations that the healing was going to take place quickly, it didn't happen.

I know the enemy wanted me to become disappointed and lose hope in this situation, but I refused to let him rob me of my answer to prayer. I had high expectation of what the Lord could and would do. Hope deferred does not mean that God has not heard my cries and that He will not answer my prayers. There is a reason for the delay and I have to just trust God in His timing. I will never lose hope to His promise that says, "By My stripes you are healed" (Isaiah 53:5). If you don't expect the healing to happen, it won't. The seeds have been planted and God's healing power has been activated with the words spoken. His Word shall not return void, but shall prosper in the thing for which He sent it (Isaiah 55:11).

Healing for the person came, but not in the way I expected. The sufferings that she went through cannot be compared with the glory that she now shares with Christ. She was delivered from the bondage of corruption and joined God's children in glorious freedom from death and decay (Romans 8:18–21). She received her heavenly reward. Don't be discouraged when your hope is deferred. Hold onto that dream, that healing, or that promise from God that you are expecting. Eagerly wait on the timing of the Lord and give Him praise for the victory to come. Silently wait on the Lord, proclaim the Word of God and your expectation will be fulfilled.

AUGUST 12

Then he fell to the ground, and heard a voice saying to him, "Saul, Saul, why are you persecuting Me?" And he said, "Who are You, Lord?" Then the Lord said, "I am Jesus, whom you are persecuting. It is hard for you to kick against the goads." So he, trembling and astonished, said, "Lord, what do You want me to do?" Then the Lord said to him, "Arise and go into the city, and you will be told what you must do."
—Acts 9:4–6

Saul was a man who hated Christians and thought that he was doing God a favor by threatening and murdering them. The Lord was not able to get Saul's attention, so God visited him in a profound way that did get his attention. Saul was more than ready to listen to the One who sent a light from heaven that brought him crashing to the ground. Saul definitely received a wakeup call.

Notice that the Lord did not ask Saul why he was persecuting His people. He asked Saul why he was persecuting Him. Everything you do in life, whether for good or for evil, you do it unto the Lord. You have to remember this when you become angry, dissatisfied, unthankful or unloving. You have to remember this when you do acts of kindness unseen by man but seen by God. "Inasmuch as you did it to one of the least of these, you did it to me"…"Inasmuch as you did not do it to one of the least of these, you did not do it to me" (Matthew 25:34–45).

It took temporary blindness to get Saul's attention. When adversity comes your way, it may be a means by which God is trying to get your attention. Not all adversity comes from the Lord. Examine your ways carefully and seek His face. Ask the Lord, "Lord, what do you want me to do?" Listen intently to what He says and then do it.

AUGUST 13

For His anger is but for a moment, His favor is for life;
Weeping may endure for a night, but joy comes in the morning.
—Psalm 30:5

Distress of soul and grief of heart will only bring destruction to your body. Sorrow and weeping has its season for a moment but then force your soul to rise up and worship and adore the Lord. In the darkest hour of your day, you can allow the joy of the Lord to be your healer and strength.

A calendar year has its seasons. As you anticipate the beauty of a tulip or rose in the spring, their beauty would not be enhanced without the coldness of winter. The cold snowy days had their part in the many colors you see in the blossoms of spring. Springtime is a reminder that the joys of summer are coming.

Your life has its seasons too. You go through trials and storms that make you stronger and prepare you for the springtime blossoms. You will go through periods of bitter cold and wonder if springtime will ever get here. You will experience extreme drought periods and wonder if the Lord is hearing your prayers. Harsh rains and flooding may occur causing you to think you are going to drown in the storms of life. Don't become discouraged with the seasons of life. You will not drown, the Lord does hear your prayers, and springtime will arrive. There will come a morning when hope is reborn and life finds a new beginning. Take your sorrows and pain before the Lord and watch for the joy and sunrise to follow. He will wipe away all your tears. Weeping may endure for a night but joy comes in the morning.

AUGUST 14

To Timothy, a beloved son: Grace, mercy, and peace
from God the Father and Christ Jesus our Lord.
—2 Timothy 1:2

May God's grace, mercy, and peace be with you. Grace and mercy have similar meanings but they are not the same. Grace is God blessing you despite the fact that you do not deserve it. Grace is God's unmerited favor upon you. Mercy is the punishment God withholds from you that you do deserve. We have all sinned (Romans 3:23) and as a result of our sin, deserve death (Romans 6:23) and eternal judgment in the lake of fire (Revelation 20:12–15). But in His mercy, God gives you time to repent, to turn from your wayward ways, and return back to Him. Knowing that God's grace and mercy have been extended to you results in you feeling the Lord's peace.

God loves you and died for you that you might spend eternity with Him. It is through His mercies that you are not consumed in the lake of fire. It is by His grace that you are saved (Ephesians 2:5). For the wages of sin is death, but the gift of God is eternal life in Christ Jesus our Lord (Romans 6:23). His compassion never fails. God is faithful and does not change (Hebrews 13:8). Let this be your hope—The Lord's grace and mercy will always be there for you to embrace.

Accept God's mercy, grace, and the eternal life He offers through Jesus Christ. You can do nothing to change His love for you, it is unconditional and flows freely from His throne of grace. Therefore, go boldly to the throne of grace, that you may obtain mercy and find grace to help in time of need (Hebrews 4:16). Embrace His love. Embrace His mercy. For the faithful love of the Lord never ends and His mercies never cease (Lamentations 3:22). May grace, mercy, and peace from God the Father and Christ Jesus our Lord be with you.

AUGUST 15

It is better to trust in the Lord
than to put confidence in man.

—Psalm 118:8

We all have had our trust broken at one time or another. People are human and although you would like to trust everyone, even the best of friends can say one thing and do another. God knew that this would occur and warned us that it is better to trust in the Lord than to put our confidence in man or ourselves.

The Lord also warns us against self-confidence. Just when you think everything is going well, just when you think that temptation won't take over, just when you put all the confidence in your self-wisdom and self-strength, things begin to crumble. The Lord warns us to take heed, lest our hearts be deceived (Deuteronomy 11:16). The Lord warns you to take heed, lest you fall (1 Corinthians 10:12). No matter how good things are going for you, always go to the Lord for reassurance that you are in His will. This will enable you to have full confidence that your plans are in the will of God.

Where is your confidence? Is it in God or in man? The Lord gives a warning and a blessing regarding whom you trust. Cursed is the man who trusts in man and makes flesh his strength, whose heart departs from the Lord. For he shall be like a shrub in the desert and shall not see when good comes (Jeremiah 17:5–6). Blessed is the man who trusts in the Lord, and whose hope is in the Lord. For he shall be like a tree planted by the waters, which spreads out its roots by the river, and will not fear when heat comes; but its leaf will be green, and will not be anxious in the year of drought, nor will cease from yielding fruit (Jeremiah 17:7–8). The choice is yours. Choose to trust in the Lord and receive His blessings.

AUGUST 16

For You are my rock and my fortress; therefore,
for Your name's sake, lead me and guide me. My
times are in Your hand; deliver me from the hand
of my enemies, and from those who persecute me.

—Psalm 31:3, 15

When you put your trust in God, you are able to say, "lead me and guide me." Notice in the above scripture that time is plural. That means that "All my time is in Your hand." The psalmist trusted God so much that He allowed everything he did to be guided by God. Do you trust God enough for Him to have full access of all your time?

Time is everything. It is what makes man into who he is today. In the pursuit of all you have done, all your efforts and accomplishments, time was the underlying factor. It took time to get to where you are today. Your communion with God has one underlying factor too—that you spend sufficient time alone with God. The quality of your intimacy with God lies in how much time you spend with God.

Time is so valuable and it seems to go by so quickly. Much time is spent on things of less importance and little time is spent on things that mean the most in life. If you had but one day or one week to live, how would you spend that time? You need to live each day as if it were your last and spend the time doing things that are important. Doing the will of the Father is one of the most important things you can do with your time. Start your day by asking God what He would have you to do that day. Yield yourself wholly unto God and tell Him, "My times are in thy hand."

AUGUST 17

But let him ask in faith, with no doubting, for he who doubts
is like a wave of the sea driven and tossed by the wind.
—James 1:6

The one truth Christ insisted that we must have is the necessity of faith and its unlimited possibilities. And yet this is the one truth that we come so short of—trusting God to fulfill in us all that He has promised. A person in faith does not settle with just some of the promises from God but seeks to claim every promise that God has made. He trusts the power of the Almighty God to work signs and wonders in his life. A person of faith makes the decision to take God at His word and claims the fulfillment of each promise and then looks to Him to accomplish them.

In Exodus, we read that God promised the Israelites the Promised Land (Exodus 3:8). But the Israelites could not enter into the Promise Land because of their disobedience and unbelief, even though the promise remained. The Lord's anger was aroused against them. Therefore, He made them wander in the wilderness forty years, until all the generation that had done evil in the sight of the Lord was gone (Numbers 32:13). There are many promises that the Lord has granted you that still remain because you have not claimed them or you have not believed God for the manifestation of those promises. God is waiting to fulfill all the promises He has for you. Is there a promise from God that you have not claimed yet? Claim it right now. Do not make the Lord have you wander for forty years and cause you to not enter into your promise because of unbelief.

A father went to Jesus for healing of his mute son. Jesus said to him, "If you can believe, all things are possible to him who believes." Immediately the father of the child cried out and said with tears, "Lord, I believe; help my unbelief!" (Mark 9:9–29) Is there unbelief or doubt in your heart that keeps you from receiving all that God has for you? Cry out, "Lord, I believe; help my unbelief!" God is pleased when you recognize your own inadequacy and seek His strength and encouragement. Ask Him to stir up the faith in you and then SIMPLY BELIEVE.

AUGUST 18

If a person sins and commits a trespass against the Lord by lying to his neighbor about what was delivered to him for safekeeping, or about a pledge, or about a robbery, or if he has extorted from his neighbor, or if he has found what was lost and lies concerning it, and swears falsely—in any one of these things that a man may do in which he sins: then it shall be, because he has sinned and is guilty, that he shall restore what he has stolen, or the thing which he has extorted, or what was delivered to him for safekeeping, or the lost thing which he found. or all that about which he has sworn falsely. He shall restore its full value, add one-fifth more to it, and give it to whomever it belongs, on the day of his trespass offering.
—Leviticus 6:2–5

Do not hide evil but bring it to the forefront, deal with it, and be set free from guilt. God commands you to deal with sin straightforwardly. Only through acknowledging sin and seeking forgiveness can you be set free from the powers of sin and guilt. You are to make restoration for sins you have committed against others whenever possible. This is a part of true repentance. The other part is to seek forgiveness and restoration from the Lord. When you confess your sin to God or to another person, try not to justify what you did. The Holy Spirit is convicting you of a sin that must be dealt with.

If you have wronged another person, you should not try to do deeds for that person as a substitute for repentance. Some people will try to be nice to a person when they have wronged them without dealing with the issue head on. When seeking to make amends, you need to deal with the issue face-to-face, admitting your wrongdoing, asking for forgiveness and then asking the person what they would consider fair payment or restitution for the hurt or injury you caused. Have you wronged another person? Ask God to give you the courage to speak with that person and bring restoration to the relationship. You need to be honest with yourself and deal with the internal issues that caused you to fall into sin. The best repayment may be a genuine change in your life.

AUGUST 19

But as many as received Him, to them He gave the right
to become children of God, to those who believe in His name.
—John 1:12

You are a child of the God Most High. It is through your faith in Jesus Christ that you believe that. Children have a lot of faith in their parents. They know that their basic needs are going to be met, and at times, their parents spoil them with things they ask for. Your Heavenly Father is no different. He likes to see you blessed and happy. There are so many treasures and gems that He has for you. As a parent, you would do anything to protect your children from danger and harm, sometimes being over protective. As a child of God, you are guaranteed of God's protection. His angels camp round about you and keep you in all your ways (Psalm 91:11).

Children trust in their parents. As a child of God, you have to trust in your Heavenly Father that He knows what is best for you. There is a bond between a parent and child. Parents love their children even when they have disobeyed or gone astray. God's love for you is everlasting. No matter what you do, He will always love you. You have to spend time with the Father to see how much He really does love you.

What does it mean to be loved? What does it mean to be loved by God? How do you express your love to your parents? How do you express your love to God? Meditate on these questions and allow God to speak to your heart about love. Then embrace the love of the Father and allow Him to pour out His love upon you.

AUGUST 20

*Then the Lord said to Joshua, "Stretch out the spear that is
in your hand toward Ai, for I will give it into your hand."
And Joshua stretched out the spear that was in his hand
toward the city. So those in ambush arose quickly out of their
place; they ran as soon as he had stretched out his hand, and
they entered the city and took it, and hurried to set the city on fire.*
—Joshua 8:18–19

B e quick to obey the Lord no matter what the cost. At times it
may seem foolish or out of character, but who are you to question
the voice of the Lord. Are you allowing the Lord to stretch forth
your hand? When Joshua allowed the Lord to use Him and he
stretched forth his hand, a city was taken over and destroyed with
fire.

The Lord will lead you in unexpected ways and may ask you
to do startling things, but He will never lead you astray. The Lord
did not force Joshua to obey. The Lord did not force Joshua to lift
up his hand. But when Joshua did, those in ambush arose quickly
and because of their obedience, they conquered the land. The Lord
does not force you to listen; you have to make that choice. There
will always be easier ways that may seem more reasonable, involve
less risk, or may be less painful, but your faith will not grow or
others may not be touched by choosing the easier route.

The Lord wants you to grow in faith and depend upon
Him as He stretches you and gives you opportunities to get out
of your comfort zone. Be sensitive to the Holy Spirit as He gives
you opportunities to grow. Obey the prompting of the Holy Spirit
and be obedient to His voice. Allow the Lord to stretch forth your
hand that He may do His works through you.

AUGUST 21

But whoever keeps His word, truly the love of
God is perfected in him. By this we know that we
are in Him. He who says he abides in Him ought
himself also to walk just as He walked.

—1 John 2:5–6

If you abide in Christ, then you are to walk just as Christ walked. How did Jesus walk? He walked with compassion and humility. Jesus did nothing of Himself but only did what He saw His Father do (John 5:19). Jesus went around doing the Father's business: healing the sick, setting people free from demons and boldly speaking into the lives of the unsaved. He met the needs of people and led them to the kingdom of God. His passion in life was to do the will of His Father (John 5:30). He was not afraid to speak truth. He walked in obedience, not because He had to, but because of His love for His Father.

Walking in obedience perfects the love of God in you. Walk in obedience because of your love for God, not because you're supposed to. The Lord makes His standard very clear to you. If my relationship to Him is that of love, I will do what He says. If I hesitate or if I disobey, then I love myself more than I love God and I have put myself in competition with God. When you are obedient, you show God that you love Him and have more faith in Him than you have in yourself. To obey God means that you relinquish what you want and choose what He asks.

God requires your obedience and places great importance on it. Throughout scripture you are told to abide in Him, "If you love Me, you will obey My commandments" (John 14:15). "Why do you call me 'Lord, Lord' and not do the things which I say?" (Luke 6:46). Many proclaim to have Jesus as their Lord but fall short of obedience. Jesus is telling you that you should not be calling Him Lord of your life if you are not doing the things He says to do. Choose to obey the Lord. Abide in His love and allow the love of God to abide in your heart. When your heart is filled with His love, obedience will follow.

AUGUST 22

Blessed is he whose transgression is forgiven, whose sin
is covered. I acknowledged my sin to You, and my iniquity
I have not hidden. I said, "I will confess my transgressions
to the Lord," and You forgave the iniquity of my sin.
—Psalm 32:1, 5

Psalm 32 could be titled "The Joy of Forgiveness." King David confessed his sin to God and restored his relationship with the Lord. Sin blocks your fellowship with the Lord and keeps you from experiencing God's goodness. King David could not enjoy the presence of the Lord as long as he had not repented of his sin. His unconfessed sin made him miserable. Once he confessed his sin, it cleared his heart spiritually and restored his relationship with the Lord.

The sooner you deal with sin, the sooner inner peace is restored. There are always consequences for your sin. Unconfessed sin not only eats at your heart, but separates you from God. If there is sin in your life, deal with it immediately. Do not try to justify it. Do not try to compromise truth because of your sin. Do not try to hide it, for the Bible is clear about what sin is. The Holy Spirit will convict you of your sin (John 16:8).

Seek God immediately when you have sinned. Ask Him to apply His forgiveness to your life and receive His mercy. Pray Psalm 51, asking God for His mercy according to His unfailing love and great compassion. Ask the Lord to blot out your transgressions and wash away your iniquity, to cleanse you, and create in you a pure heart. When you confess your sins, the Lord will renew a steadfast spirit within you and restore to you the joy of your salvation. Purpose in your heart to not sin again. God loves you and wants to enjoy your fellowship with Him.

AUGUST 23

And the devil said to Him, "If you are the Son of God, command this stone to become bread." But Jesus answered him, saying, "It is written, 'Man shall not live by bread alone, but by every Word of God.'"

—Luke 4:3–4

It is so important to know what is written in the Word of God. Jesus did not give in to the temptations of Satan because He knew what the Word said. If you do not know what the Word says, you can become sidetracked and be led astray without even realizing it. Jesus said that man cannot live by bread alone. If you take a look at the different loaves of bread in the supermarket, some look so much more appealing than others. Some even claim to be whole wheat and healthier for you. But if you take the time to read the ingredients, you will come to find out that what appeared to be good for you isn't so good after all. So many ingredients have been added to the contents, many of which you can't even pronounce, bringing harm to the body if consumed.

The enticing words that Satan uses may be appealing, but you need to take that bread and examine all the ingredients to make sure there have not been any impurities added to it. Just because someone says it's good and nutritious for you doesn't mean that it is. Just because it sounds appealing to the ears does not make it healthy. If you compare the ingredients to the Word of God, you will know whether it is healthy for you or not.

In His extreme hunger, Jesus refused to listen to the temptation of the Evil One. Yes, Jesus had the power to make bread to supply His hunger, but instead, He chose to have the Word of God sustain Him. Likewise, if you are to follow Christ, Regard the Word as a daily supplement and daily provision for your strength and well-being.

AUGUST 24

*Let this mind be in you which was also
in Christ Jesus, who, being in the form
of God, did not consider it robbery to be
equal with God, but made Himself of no
reputation, taking the form of a bondservant,
and coming in the likeness of men.*

—Philippians 2:5–7

Your thoughts influence your actions. So if you want to act like Christ, you have to think like Christ. How did Christ think? What was on His mind that should also be on yours? If you look at the life of Jesus, you will come to know what was on His mind. He was self-emptying, giving entirely of Himself. Christ relinquished His glory and power and became a servant in man's likeness. His purpose as man was to die for the sins of mankind. He was obedient to God's will, self-sacrificing, and loved men even to the death of the cross. He did everything with humility, obedience, compassion, and much prayer. Therefore God highly exalted Him (Philippians 2:9).

Jesus is your mentor and model to be followed. He was made in the likeness of men, so that we might be conformed into the likeness of God. As a disciple of Jesus, you have the opportunity to lay down your agenda, to give your life in service to others for the sake of the gospel. Self-sacrifice that God's will might be done and man might be saved, was Christ's life. It should be yours as well. You are called to work out this salvation of a Christ-like character with fear and trembling (Philippians 2:12). It is God who is working in you giving you the desire and the power to do what pleases Him (Philippians 2:13).

Having the mind of Christ isn't as impossible as it sounds. In fact Scripture tells you that you have the mind of Christ (1 Corinthians 2:16). If you don't learn to take every thought captive to the obedience of Christ, you won't live the life Jesus died to give you. You have been entrusted with the character of Christ. It is Christ who will give you the power to fulfill this high and holy calling.

AUGUST 25

*And some of them said, "Could not this
Man, who opened the eyes of the blind,
also have kept this man from dying?"*
—John 11:37

In the midst of your circumstances, when things appear to be at their worst, you begin to question where God is in the situation and why He did or did not do things the way you had planned them. When Lazarus had died, many Jews questioned his death and why Jesus did not prevent his death. They knew of His power, they knew that Jesus opened the eyes of a blind man, so they questioned in their hearts if Jesus could have kept Lazarus from dying.

You know that the answer to this question is "yes." Then why did Jesus allow Him to die? Jesus did not allow the need of even His closest friends, nor His own emotions to determine His actions. He followed the will of His Father. Jesus did not spare His friends the grief they suffered because He knew it would benefit them more in the end to witness His power over death.

Lazarus died and was raised from the dead in order to bring glory to God (John 11:40), and to those standing by, that they may believe that God had sent Jesus (John 11:42). There is always a reason why things don't turn out the way you expect them to. Look beyond what your eyes can see in the natural and ask the Lord to show you, in the spiritual, His purpose and His plan. There will be sufferings and hardships that you must endure but they will never compare to the glory which shall be revealed in you (Romans 8:18).

AUGUST 26

In the year that King Uzziah died, I saw the Lord
sitting on a throne, high and lifted up, and the train of
His robe filled the temple. So I said: "Woe is me, for
I am undone! Because I am a man of unclean lips, and
I dwell in the midst of a people of unclean lips; For my
eyes have seen the King, the Lord of hosts."
—Isaiah 6:1, 5

Isaiah had a life changing encounter when he saw the Lord seated on His Heavenly throne. Can you imagine the awesome vision of God, the train of His robe filling the temple? The vision so pierced Isaiah's heart and soul that he had to cry out, "I am a man of unclean lips. I am undone, for my eyes have seen the King, the Lord of hosts." In an encounter such as this, one truly grasps God's Holiness and begins to understand the fullness of His Glory. It can only lead one to a deep reverence for the Lord. Isaiah felt totally inadequate and unclean when his eyes saw the Lord of hosts. Then an Angel of the Lord touched Isaiah's lips with a hot coal from the altar and said that his sins were forgiven (Isaiah 6:6–7).

Many people today have had life changing encounters with the Lord and others are praying to have such an encounter. Seeing a vision is not the only way to have a life changing experience with the Lord. You can immerse yourself in His Word and allow the Word to build your faith. If you can truly grasp the deep meaning of the Words spoken by Jesus, His Holiness, and His Glory, and the depths of His love for you, you too can have life changing encounters. Lord, send an angel to touch my lips with a coal of fire, taking away my iniquity and purging me of my sins. Make me fit for service for You. Allow me to experience a life changing encounter that causes me to say, "Woe is me, for I am undone!" Pray that the Lord will take all of us to that point.

AUGUST 27

But no man can tame the tongue. It is an unruly evil, full of deadly poison. With it we bless our God and Father, and with it we curse men, who have been made in the similitude of God. Out of the same mouth proceed blessing and cursing. My brethren, these things ought not to be so.
—James 3:8–10

God knew from the very start that our tongues would be unruly, and he excludes no one. He says that no man can tame the tongue. How many times have you said something and in the midst of the breath you were speaking it, you knew that damage had been done. When you sin with your mouth, it defiles your whole body (James 3:6). If you examine a loaf of bread that has been left uncovered, you will notice mold beginning to form. If left unattended for a day or two, the mold will infect the entire loaf. So it is when you leave the sin of your mouth unattended for a day or two. The poison begins to infect your entire body.

James asks the questions, "Can a fig tree bear olives or a grape vine bear figs?" (James 3:12). Of course we know the answer is no, just as no spring yields both salt water and fresh. The words you speak sets the path for your life. You will live by the fruit of your lips, for good or for evil. Sowing words of blessings over your life and the lives of others is one of the greatest gifts you can give to yourself and others. Sowing words of forgiveness and turning a wrong into a right is another. When you have spoken damaging words to someone, make it right with that person. Attend to the deadly poison before it penetrates deep into the core of your being.

Guard your mouth. Speak carefully, realizing that words have the power to wound and to cause division and strife. Words have the power to either bless or curse. Use words to bless, encourage, and bring life to others. You will bring blessings, encouragement, and life to yourself when you do.

AUGUST 28

*"But when you do a charitable deed, do not let your
left hand know what your right hand is doing, that
your charitable deed may be in secret; and your Father
who sees in secret will Himself reward you openly."*
—Matthew 6:3–4

Can you imagine a world in which we all gave generously and unselfishly? What would that world look like? Surely would be many happy and thankful people. People who have never felt loved would begin to feel that there are people who really do care about them. Kind acts have a tendency to be passed onto others. Jesus was in favor of us doing charitable deeds in secret.

Many people do things for others to get attention or to gain something for themselves. But when you do kind acts anonymously, you will always have the right heart and reason for your giving. There will be no one to thank you or to boost your ego. The only rewards will be the gratification of knowing that a heart has been touched and possibly a life changed. Other people may not know what you have done, but your Heavenly Father will know. And in the end, God gives the only reward that really matters.

Be sensitive to the Holy Spirit and He will prompt you to do acts of kindness. Who knows, you may be that angel sent by God to change the life of a person. Always keep your heart open to the needs of others. Your Father who sees in secret will Himself reward you openly.

AUGUST 29

And you shall rejoice before the Lord your
God in all to which you put your hands.
— Deuteronomy 12:18b

God wants happy people who will rejoice in all they do. It is amazing to see the number of unhappy people in the world today. How many times have you done something grudgingly, wishing you were doing something else, hating the task at hand, or complaining the whole time you did it? I know I am guilty of this. It is easy to think negatively when doing tasks you do not enjoy and when your eyes are not focused on the Lord. But God calls us to rejoice in everything we put our hands to. Rejoicing really does change your attitude about many things.

Think of a situation at your work, or a task that you really don't want to do, and your resultant negative attitude. Would your attitude change if your boss were standing next to you as you performed the task? Would your attitude change if Jesus were standing there with you? Remember that Jesus sees all (Job 34:21) and hears all, even if the words have never been spoken. He hears the whispers of your heart (Matthew 9:4). And yet Jesus rejoices over you.

You live in a world where everything is not going to be hunky-dory. When you are faced with a task that you prefer not to do, ask the Lord to reveal things about the situation that can help change your attitude. If it is a task at your job that you are complaining about, rejoice that you have a job. Many people are without work and wish they had a job to go to. Rejoice in the mere fact that God is rejoicing over you (Isaiah 62:5).

AUGUST 30

Now may the God of hope fill you with all joy
and peace in believing, that you may abound in
hope by the power of the Holy Spirit.

—Romans 15:13

You enjoy the peace that comes from being right with God, but you still face daily problems that can lead to discouragement. Because of sin, there will always be disappointment, but hope does not disappoint us. As you hope in the Lord, it is the Holy Spirit who will impart to you the love, joy, and peace to sustain you as you continue to abound in this hope.

Hope is the confidence and expectation of something good happening. Because of Christ in you, the hope of glory (Colossians 1:27), you can expect the glory of God to shine in every aspect of your life including your health, finances, family, job, and ministry. Disappointment may come in these areas of your life, but when you allow God's love to penetrate in those areas as well, hope abounds and does not disappoint.

In faith, put your hope in God. Put your hope in God's Word. True hope does not disappoint because God has poured out His love within your heart through the Holy Spirit (Romans 5:5). This is His hope-filled promise to you, and He never disappoints. The more you walk in faith, the more hope arises within you. Put your faith in God and allow your faith to assure you that such hope in God does not disappoint.

AUGUST 31

Wisdom and knowledge will be the stability
of your times, and the strength of salvation;
the fear of the Lord is His treasure.

—Isaiah 33:6

Many Christians live in fear. They are afraid to step out in faith. Many question whether they actually heard from the Lord. Others fear getting out of their comfort zone. Many assignments have been given to you by the Lord and yet these opportunities have fallen by the waist side because of your inferiorities. We are all a part of God's plan and He has assignments for each of us. Do not let fear knock you down or keep your from moving forward in what the Lord has called you to do. Let wisdom and knowledge from the Lord be the stability of your time.

Has the Lord asked you to do something and you have hesitated stepping out in faith to do it? Is there fear in your life that is controlling your responses? Is the Lord tugging at your heart right now, beckoning you to do something, whether it be in words or actions? Whatever it may be, let the fear of the Lord be the treasure of your heart and allow that treasure to move you into obedience. Trust that God will let you know when you are veering to the left or right of where He wants you to be. No matter how small or how big the assignment, God is always there with you to carry you through. Do not delay an opportunity to be used by the Lord.

SEPTEMBER 1

The fear of God is to hate evil; pride and arrogance
and the evil way and the perverse mouth I hate.
—Proverbs 8:13

God is very clear of His stance about pride. He hates pride. Pride gets lumped together with arrogance, an evil way, and a perverse mouth. In another passage of scripture, pride is among one of the seven things that are an abomination to the Lord (Proverbs 6:16–19). God even puts pride in the same category with murder and blasphemy (Mark 7:21–23).

Why does God hate pride so much? Because pride renders us useless in the kingdom of God. When pride sets in your heart, you tend to do things your own way and fail to acknowledge God's hand in the matter. Pride prevents God from using you for His purpose because you are too busy doing things for your own purpose.

The Lord refuses to share His glory with anyone. When one starts to have thoughts like, "Look at what I have accomplished" or "Look at what I did," or "Look at who I am," pride has entered into the chambers of one's heart. Everything you accomplish comes about because God is the one who enables you and empowers you to succeed in all things. Anything short of giving God the glory for one's accomplishments is pride. You can still be proud of what you've done or how God has formed you without being prideful. Just be sure to recognize that everything you do and who you are is because of God's goodness on your life.

SEPTEMBER 2

But if you are led by the Spirit,
you are not under the law.
—Galatians 5:18

People who are led by the Spirit will do what is right freely, not by compulsion under the law. It is their love for God which causes them to live a pure and holy life. When you are led by the Spirit, you will not fulfill the lusts of the flesh (Romans 13:14). The Holy Spirit speaks to you constantly. Be obedient to His still, small voice. He will enlighten your soul and give you direction.

When you accepted Jesus Christ as your personal Savior and invited Him into your life, the Holy Spirit took residence inside of you. You are a temple of the Holy Spirit (1 Corinthians 6:19) and the Holy Spirit dwells within you (Romans 8:9). He is in your midst, dwelling deep within you. Search no further than your own heart for the Holy Spirit. When your flesh wants to do an unholy thing and your heart is telling you to do just the opposite, that voice you hear from the heart is the Holy Spirit speaking to you.

To be led by the Spirit of God, allow the Holy Spirit to have reign over your life. It is not an option, God expects this from you. God expects you to be led by the Spirit (Romans 8:14), pray in the Spirit (Ephesians 6:18), walk and live in the Spirit (Galatians 5:16), be fervent in the Spirit (Acts 18:25), worship in the Spirit (Philippians 3:3), be purposed in the Spirit (Acts 19:21), be instructed by the Spirit (John 14:26) and be renewed in the Spirit (Ephesians 4:23).

The Holy Spirit is your Friend and Helper. He resides within you to be your all. No matter what you need, He is there to meet that need. What a privilege you have. If you are not being led by the Holy Spirit, purpose in your heart today to dedicate your life fully unto Him.

SEPTEMBER 3

Blessed is the man who endures temptation; for when
he has been approved, he will receive the crown of life
which the Lord has promised to those who love Him.
Let no one say when he is tempted, "I am tempted by
God"; for God cannot be tempted by evil, nor does He
Himself tempt anyone. But each one is tempted when
he is drawn away by his own desires and enticed.
—James 1:12–14

Temptation is all around us. You see it on the Internet with different pop-up windows that try to lure you into places you should not go. You see it on billboards and advertisements. Even friends and family members may try to lure you into doing things that God has already spoken to your heart about.

Satan tempts people, but he does not make us sin. James tells us that enticement to evil is not from God either. "Let no one say when he is tempted, I am tempted by God; for God cannot be tempted by evil, nor does He Himself tempt anyone" (James 1:13). The whole satanic purpose of temptation is to entice people away from God. You choose to allow temptation to get the best of you and be drawn away from God by your own fleshly desires which you know are wrong. Satan indeed is the external source of temptation, but no one can blame him for the roots of sinful deeds which lie within each individual. When inner desires respond to outward enticement, sin is right around the corner. Sin begins with unholy desires and lusts which, if allowed to continue, produce sinful behavior.

Yield to the warnings of your conscience. Respond quickly to conviction of impure attitudes, thoughts, motives, or wrong behavior. Confess it and ask for forgiveness. Seek strength from God and endure the temptation. Receive the crown of life which is promised by God to those who love Him.

SEPTEMBER 4

And I fell at his feet to worship him. But he said to me, "See that you do not do that! I am your fellow servant, and of your brethren who have the testimony of Jesus. Worship God! For the testimony of Jesus is the spirit of prophecy."
—Revelation 19:10

"Worship God!" Such simple words, such a simple command, but many do not take the time to worship God. The only way to reach the nearness of God and fellowship with Him is through our worship. God inhabits the praises of His people. It is through your worship that chains of bondage are broken and prayers are answered. In our prayer time, our hearts are not set primarily on worshipping Him or on waiting for His presence, but they should be. Instead, you think mostly of yourself, your needs and weaknesses, your desires, your family, and the concerns of others. You forget that in every prayer, God must be first and the center of your focus.

First, give God the praise and worship due unto Him (Psalm 29:2) and give Him time to make Himself known to you. God wants to abide in your presence and wants to present Himself as a Hearer of your prayers. Prayer does not have its power in the number of words you speak or the volume in which you pray. The power lies in your faith that God inhabits the praises of His people. As you worship Him, God Himself is taking you and your prayers to the core of His loving heart. The power lies in your faith to believe that in His time, your prayers will be answered. Prayer is so important, but worshipping God is even more important. Have you worshipped God today?

SEPTEMBER 5

Now when the people complained, it
displeased the Lord; for the Lord heard
it, and his anger was aroused. So the fire
of the Lord burned among them, and
consumed some in the outskirts of the camp.
—Numbers 11:1

The Lord hears every word you speak and He is displeased when you speak in an ungodly manner. When you murmur and complain, you are actually murmuring and complaining against God, for it is He who has allowed the situation to occur in the first place. Accept whatever comes your way with grace and let your petitions be known to the Lord. You may not like the situation, but complaining will only make matters worse, for it fuels up iniquity in your heart.

If the behavior of Christians does not differ from the behavior of ungodly people in this crooked and perverse world, what is this telling the world? Instead of being a light that shines in the darkness, you blend into the darkness. Your reaction to situations says a lot about your character and has an influence on those around you. When you react ungodly, it not only displeases God but also adds fuel to a fire for the wicked to continue in their behavior.

Do not grumble and complain when you go through difficult times (Philippians 2:14). Just as the Lord loves a cheerful giver (2 Corinthians 9:7), the Lord loves those who are cheerful in the midst of their difficulties. Be content where you are, and the Lord who knows all, sees all and hears all, will meet your needs in His timing. Meanwhile, let your light so shine on the world around you and lighten the moral darkness of this world.

SEPTEMBER 6

Be silent, all flesh, before the Lord, for
He is aroused from His holy habitation!
—Zechariah 2:13

As long as you live on this earth there will always be a struggle between your flesh and spirit. You have all the intentions of living a holy life. However, when temptations come, the spirit is indeed willing, but your flesh is weak (Matthew 26:41) and your desires often win the battle. The battle between the flesh and spirit can occur in your prayer and devotional time as well. Much worship, even among believers, is not in the Spirit. You put a timetable on God and hastily enter into God's presence in the power of your flesh. Then because of your time constraints, you miss the opportunity of going deeper into fellowship with God because you do not wait on His Spirit to lift you up into the presence of the Lord.

Zechariah tells us that we must put all our flesh in silence before the Lord. The Lord is in His Holy temple and you need to keep silent before Him (Habakkuk 2:20). This means that when you desire to enter into the Holy presence of the Lord, put aside your agenda, your desires, your prayers, and anything within you that is led by your flesh and wait for the Spirit of God to take you deeper into His presence. It is when you surrender to God's Spirit, and allow the power of the Holy Spirit to direct you, that your prayers and worship flow from the spirit and not your flesh. Being silent before the Lord takes practice, but the more you do it, the easier it will become to silence the flesh and allow your spirit to be guided by the Holy Spirit.

SEPTEMBER 7

The Lord was with Joseph, and he was a successful
man; and he was in the house of his master the Egyptian.
And his master saw that the Lord was with him and
that the Lord made all he did to prosper in his hand.
—Genesis 39:2–3

Joseph was a faithful man and remained true to God even when he faced adversity. He disallowed his adversity to be a setback but rather used the opportunity to trust God in the midst of it. as a result, he was granted favor by the Lord. Joseph became very successful and his master saw that the Lord was with him. Others watch to and see how we handle adversity as well as success. In all things we are to give glory to God, no matter what the circumstance may be. When we look at the difficulties, inconveniences, and cares of life as potential assignments from God, our perspective about the situation will change. We will focus on what God can do through the difficult circumstance rather than on the details or seemingly impossibilities of the situation at hand.

Words of contentment, trust and faith in the midst of our trials have great power because they make people sit up and take notice. What are your words telling people about you? What are your words telling people about our God? Will they say, "We have certainly seen that the Lord is with you and He has granted you favor."? Will someone say to others, "I know someone, a mighty person of valor, prudent in speech and the Lord is with him. This person can help you" (1 Samuel 16:18–19)? Allow the Lord to use every trial that comes your way as a stepping stone to success and favor. Like Joseph, the Lord will make all you do prosper in your hand.

SEPTEMBER 8

Trust in Him at all times, you people; pour out your heart
before Him; God is a refuge for us. God has spoken once,
twice I have heard this: that power belongs to God.
—Psalm 62:8, 11

No matter what may come your way, God must be your refuge. Your trust must be in the Lord, for it is He who has the power to change every circumstance. While there is great comfort in sharing your problems and difficulties with a friend, you miss the greatest help if you fail to bring them to the Lord.

Are you faced with a situation at your work? Pour out your heart before God, for He is your refuge. Were you given a bad report from the doctor? Pour out your heart before God, for He is your refuge. Do you continue to revert to a sinful habit? Pour out your heart before God, for He is your refuge. Do you need a job or are you in a financial bind? Pour out your heart before God, for He is your refuge.

Many times you look to others for help when the Lord is already at work moving mountains, opening doors, and touching hearts on your behalf. No matter what the situation may be, pour out your heart before God, for He will be your refuge. Trust in the Lord and He will not fail you. Watch and see that the Lord is good and His mercy endures forever (Psalm 136). Allow the Lord to speak to you. Hear, believe, and see that the power belongs to God!

SEPTEMBER 9

"Speak to Aaron and his sons, saying, 'This is the
way you shall bless the children of Israel. Say to them:
"The Lord bless you and keep you; the Lord make His
face shine upon you, and be gracious to you; the Lord
lift up His countenance upon you, and give you peace."'
—Numbers 6:23–26

Jesus went around promoting good. He spoke with power and authority to change the lives and atmosphere around Him. You have that same power and authority within you. Many prophesy doom and gloom upon themselves and this nation because of words they speak into the atmosphere. But the Lord wants you to start promoting His goodness. There is a time and season for all things and this is the time to proclaim blessings upon your families, friends, Israel and your nation. Speak against the winds of adversity, doom and gloom. Speak life and blessings into the atmosphere. There is no greater feeling in a person's life than to know that the blessings of the Lord are upon them.

Lord Jesus, I proclaim Your blessings upon my family, friends, Israel, America and all nations. Bless them with Your glory and presence. Bless them with Your protection and increase prosperity in their lives. Bless them with Your grace and favor. Bless them with supernatural provision. Bless them with the outpouring of Your Holy Spirit. To all of God's children I pray, "The Lord bless you and keep you. The Lord make His face shine upon you and be gracious to you. The Lord lift up His countenance upon you and give you peace."

The goodness of God will overtake this nation when we proclaim blessings upon her. Hell will not be able to stop what God desires. Start promoting the goodness of God, the blessings of God, and watch America turn around for good. Get in alignment with God. God will breathe His Spirit into America again and raise it up and make it great again. I see the Lord high and lifted up and His glory filling the earth.

SEPTEMBER 10

Then the disciples came to Jesus privately and said, "Why could
we not cast it out?" So Jesus said to them, "Because of your
unbelief; for assuredly, I say to you, if you have faith as a mustard
seed, you will say to this mountain, 'Move from here to there,'
and it will move; and nothing will be impossible for you."
—Matthew 17:19–20

If I could physically be with each of you right now, I would give you a mustard seed. A mustard seed is so small, yet that is all the faith that is required to change the atmosphere or situation in your life. I can remember a situation in my former church where a gentleman would occasionally come to church and sit in the back. I would always speak to him when he came. I can't remember the conversations we had, but I remember telling him to have faith that God will change things. The next time I saw him, I put a mustard seed into his hand and told him to have the faith of this mustard seed, that's all it takes. Then I asked him if he wanted me to pray with him. He was not ready.

Every time he came to church, I would go up to him and say, "faith of a mustard seed." Finally the day came when he said "yes" to prayer, but asked that we wait until later in the service. He sat with his wife in the front of the church. When the altar call for prayer was made, he did not move. I went over and stood between the husband and wife, held his hand and began to pray for him. He squeezed my hand as I prayed and the power of God fell upon him that day and everyone was shocked and amazed because they knew his past. Little did they know what led up to that point, and how God was preparing his heart, and all it took was for him to have the faith of a mustard seed. He was a changed man that day.

If you do not have any mustard seeds, purchase a bottle. Tape a seed in places where you will see them, to remind you that it only takes the faith of a mustard seed to move mountains. Have them ready to give to others, and share with them what God can do for them, if they only believe. Keep reminding them—faith of a mustard seed, and over time, you will have testimonies to share as well.

SEPTEMBER 11

Remember the former things of old, for I am God, and there is no other; I am God, and there is none like Me, declaring the end from the beginning, and from ancient times things that are not yet done, saying, 'My counsel shall stand, and I will do all My pleasure,' calling a bird of prey from the east, the man who executes My counsel, from a far country. Indeed I have spoken it; I will also bring it to pass. I have purposed it; I will also do it.
—Isaiah 46:9–11

People put their hope in money, people, and idols of this world but the bottom line is that there is only one true God. He is Lord of all and there is none like Him. He is the God that controls all things. If indeed God has spoken it, it will come to pass. What God has purposed, He will also do it. He declares the end from the beginning and His counsel shall stand.

No one can understand the mind of Christ. There is no way you can begin to grasp the deep mysteries of God. With your finite mind and your self-centered views, you can't begin to know why God does what He does. People often look at tragedies and responded by blaming Him and turning their backs on Him. They assume their finite knowledge about the situation is wiser than His infinite wisdom.

God has given each of us the mind of Christ (1 Corinthians 2:16). Although we have the knowledge and mind of Christ, we do not automatically think the way He thinks or act the way God acts. His thoughts and ways are higher than ours (Isaiah 55:8–9). God has given us the freedom to choose and many tragedies occur because of man's sinful nature and poor choices in life. Often I have had to repent for questioning God and trying to lower His thinking to my own understanding. When life doesn't make sense, you still need to trust God. Ask Him to give you the strength to move forward beyond your own knowledge and pray that He will give you understanding.

SEPTEMBER 12

The earth is the Lord's and all its fullness,
the world and those who dwell therein.
—Psalm 24:1

The entire earth and all its fullness belongs to the Lord. Every person who dwells on this earth belongs to the Lord. All is under His control. The Lord God Almighty sees all, the good and the evil. Many times you can get distracted by the evil things happening in the world today: robberies, murders, gang rapes, no respect for the property or possessions of others. Although these things are disheartening, you should not be alarmed or disturbed by evildoers. They are in the hands of the Lord. All is under His control and He will see that justice is done. The Lord executes righteousness and justice to all who are treated unfairly (Psalm 103:6 NLT). Evil men do not understand justice, but those who follow the Lord understand completely (Proverbs 28:5 NLT). In due time, their wicked ways will catch up with them and justice will prevail.

Are you troubled by the things you see in the world? Pray about these situations and then give them to God. Remember that people are not evil, but it is the spirits that control them that cause them to do evil things. Pray that they would be delivered from these wicked spirits. Do not allow the wickedness of this world to overwhelm you. In the midst of all the evilness in this world, you are to keep your eyes focused on the Lord, for He truly is in control of the world and all those who dwell in it. Therefore know this day, and consider it in your heart, that the Lord Himself is God in both heaven on earth, and there is no other (Deuteronomy 4:39). And all the earth shall be filled with the glory of the Lord (Numbers 14:21).

SEPTEMBER 13

Let each of you look out not only for his own
interests, but also for the interests of others.
—Philippians 2:4

Where do you see yourself in two years? If you are struggling financially, emotionally or physically, do you see yourself walking in freedom? Most of us will see ourselves as having achieved goals and walking in victory. Now think of people you know who are struggling in life right now, whether it be physically, emotionally, spiritually, or financially. Where do you see them two years from now? Do you see them walking in their freedom or do you see them still struggling? During those two years, what do you see yourself having done to help them achieve victory?

God tells us that we are to seek after the well-being of others. Many times people do not achieve freedom because they think it is impossible and they will never get out of their situation. In the midst of their struggles, there is no one looking out for their best interest, encouraging them on to victory. Sometimes it can be a mere act of kindness, a word of encouragement at the right time, or giving someone a break with a job or finances that will lead them onto their road to victory.

Consider others more important than yourself and help them through their life's problems. Be concerned about things that are important to others and show them that you care. Be willing to sacrifice so that others may achieve victories in their lives. Let the love of God be revealed to others through your acts of concern, compassion and love. There is no greater feeling than knowing that you were part of someone's freedom and victory. To God be the glory for their freedom and victory.

SEPTEMBER 14

"And I will pray the Father, and He will give you
another Helper, that He may abide with you forever—
the Spirit of truth, whom the world cannot receive, because
it neither sees Him nor knows Him; but you know Him,
for He dwells with you and will be in you."
—John 14:16–17

When you go to a foreign country where you do not know the native language, it is very difficult to understand and communicate with the people of that nation. No matter how hard you try to communicate with them, nothing you say makes any sense to them. If you would spend extended time in that nation, you would start to learn their language and begin to understand each other.

Many things Christians say do not make sense to the world either, because there is a language barrier. You cannot expect those who are not filled with the Spirit of God to understand spiritual truth; it will sound foolish to them. Spiritual maturity comes only when the Spirit of God dwells within a person. It is important to not become frustrated or defensive when speaking with others about your faith. What looks plain and simple to you may sound foreign to another. Allow the Spirit of God to work in their lives as He has in yours. Pray that the Spirit of truth and understanding will fill their hearts and break the language barrier. Plant seeds of love into their lives and allow God to nurture and water those seeds with His Spirit. When you do, they will soon be speaking the same spiritual language as you, for the Spirit of God will be dwelling in them.

SEPTEMBER 15

And out of the ground the Lord God made every
tree grow that is pleasant to the sight and good for
food. The tree of life was also in the midst of the
garden, and the tree of the knowledge of good and evil.
—Genesis 2:9

God created man in His image to become like Him (Genesis 1:27). Adam and Eve walked with God daily in the very midst of His Glory. In the garden were many trees that were pleasant to the sight and good for food. Two other trees were also presented to Adam and Eve, the tree of life, and the tree of knowledge. The purpose of the tree of knowledge of good and evil was to test their obedience. Adam and Eve had to choose whether to obey God or break His commandment. God's way was the tree of life. But Satan deceived man into thinking that knowledge was what would make them like God. When Adam and Eve chose knowledge over obedience, they set the path that lead mankind to death.

The real question that Adam and Eve faced is the same one you face today. Which path are you going to choose? Will you choose obedience over breaking God's commandments. Under this same power of deception, Satan is leading many astray. Instead of living a life of obedience, men are seeking to gain knowledge, not by the Holy Spirit, but by the wisdom of man. Even when the Word of God is accepted, the wisdom of the world and fleshly desires always enter in and distort the truth of the God's Word.

In order for the truth to penetrate deep into your heart, lay aside your human understanding, worldly influences, and fleshly desires. Allow the Spirit of Truth to lead you to the tree of life with every choice you make. Seek God to make sure the decisions you are making are leading you to the tree of life and not to the tree of deception and death.

SEPTEMBER 16

*While he was still speaking, another also came
and said, "Your sons and daughters were eating
and drinking wine in their oldest brother's house,
and suddenly a great wind came from across the
wilderness and struck the four corners of the house,
and it fell on the young people, and they are dead;
and I alone have escaped to tell you!"*

—Job 1:18–19

Job was a righteous man, one who feared God (Job 1:1). The Lord's hedge of protection was upon Him and God blessed the work of his hand. Satan attacked Job's character and the Lord gave Satan the power over all he possessed (Job 1:12). In the midst of Job's prosperity, he lost his property and children. Job's response to the tragedy was to fall to the ground and worship the Lord. "Naked I came into this world and naked I shall return" (Job 1:20–21). He did not allow His possessions or his circumstances to influence the way he felt about God.

God's blessings and anointing does not exempt you from hardships and tragedy. It's easy to trust God when things are going great, but it takes faith to trust God when the flood gates open and it seems like your life or the lives of those around you are falling apart. When tragedy strikes, sometimes your situation actually gets worse before it gets better. But, regardless of the circumstances, know that God is moving on your behalf and knows the ending before you even see the beginning. All he asks is that you trust Him, even in the hard times. The Lord restored Job's losses and gave Job twice as much as he had before (Job 42:10). The Lord will restore that which the enemy has taken from you.

SEPTEMBER 17

*"Nevertheless I tell you the truth. It is to
your advantage that I go away; for if I do
not go away, the Helper will not come to you;
but if I depart, I will send Him to you. And
when He has come, He will convict the world
of sin, and of righteousness, and of judgment."*
—John 16:7–8

Jesus is always looking out for our best interest. He told the disciples that it would be to their advantage if He went away. They had to give something, in order to gain something. Jesus wanted the disciples to realize that the great work of the Holy Spirit, convicting the world of sin, could be done only if He had a dwelling place in them. They were to receive the power from on high, enabling them to be instruments through which the Holy Spirit could reach the world. They would receive power when the Holy Spirit came upon them. And they would be His witnesses, telling people about Him everywhere, in Jerusalem, throughout Judea, in Samaria, and to the end of the earth (Acts 1:8).

The Holy Spirit comes to you, so that through you, He may reach others. When He enters you, He does not change His character or lose His divine power. The power that was given to the disciples is not only the same power that raised Christ from the dead, but also the same power that resides in you today. You are an instrument through which the Holy Spirit can reach the world.

Jesus's primary purpose is to save lives. If His Spirit lives in you, your primary purpose should be to save lives as well. For what purpose was it that the Spirit of God fell upon you? Isaiah 61:1 tells us that the Spirit of God is upon us, for the Lord has anointed us to bring good news to the poor. He has sent us to comfort the brokenhearted, to proclaim liberty to the captives, and to open prisons for those who are bound. The purpose of the Holy Spirit dwelling in you is to continue to perform the works that Jesus did. Your goal must be to serve Jesus, being His hands, feet and mouthpiece, doing in Christ's power what Christ would do.

SEPTEMBER 18

For you have need of endurance, so that
when you have done the will of God, you
may receive what was promised.
—Hebrews 10:36

When I think of endurance, my first thoughts immediately turn to a vision of athletes in training. When they first start out, they can't run as fast or as far as they wish they could. It takes training, pushing oneself to build the stamina they need to run faster and longer. Fatigue and weariness may set in, but they have to push through the feelings knowing that better days lie ahead. What they eat, the amount of sleep they get, their mental attitude, and the amount of time they train all play a part in their ability to achieve their goal.

Your Christian walk and discipline can be compared to that of an athlete. When you first become a Christian, everything is new to you. You know where you want to be, but getting there takes time, discipline, and training. There will be times that you are weary and don't feel like working out, and may even feel like quitting, but endure the pressures, remain faithful, and tightly hold onto the promises of God.

What you feed your body is very important. Eat of the Word of God daily and let the nutrients from it, be absorbed by your heart and soul. A racer would not be successful if he ran only five minutes a day. Spend ample time in the Word of God, praying and soaking in God's presence, if you are to experience the riches of His Glory. It takes discipline to be an athlete of the Lord, but with commitment and determination, and setting your hope in the Lord Jesus Christ, victory awaits you. Do not grow weary in your pursuit of God. Do not grow weary while doing good. In due season, you shall reap if you do not lose heart and receive what was promised (Galatians 6:9).

SEPTEMBER 19

*"And he thought within himself, saying, 'What shall I do,
since I have no room to store my crops?' So he said, 'I will
do this: I will pull down my barns and build greater, and there
I will store all my crops and my goods. And I will say to my
soul, "Soul, you have many goods laid up for many years;
take your ease; eat, drink, and be merry."' But God said to
him, 'Fool! This night your soul will be required of you;
then whose will those things be which you have provided?'"*
—Luke 12:17–20

In the parable of the rich fool (Luke 12:13–21), Jesus warns us
of the dangers of materialism. Possessions neither give life nor
provide security, but instead, drives you to want even more. The
rich fool mistakenly looked upon his possessions as his own, not
achieved by the hand of God, not to be used for God's glory, but
to be laid up for many years so that he could take ease—eating,
drinking, and being merry. God called this man a fool, told him
his soul would be taken from him that very night, and asked him
who would get his possessions.

Continually search your heart and make sure it is right with
God. It is okay for you to gain wealth and possessions, but when it
becomes a focal point in your life and you are consumed with gaining more and more, you have entered into the dangers of materialism. While you can always accumulate more things and be more
successful, there will always be room for more. Where there's room
for more, there's room for wanting more; and wanting more leads
to buying and accumulating more. The cycle never ends.

God is the One who allows you to be blessed with materials
and wealth, and He expects you to share them with others. When
you bless others, God in turn will bless you. It is in the heart of
giving that keeps you out of the danger zone of possessing and
wanting more. Be thankful for what God has blessed you with and
share your blessings with others.

SEPTEMBER 20

*"Now, Lord, look on their threats, and grant to
Your servants that with all boldness they may speak
Your word, by stretching out Your hand to heal, and
that signs and wonders may be done through the name
of Your holy Servant Jesus." And when they had
prayed, the place where they were assembled together was
shaken; and they were all filled with the Holy Spirit,
and they spoke the word of God with boldness.*
—Acts 4:29–31

The apostles knew that it was not their preaching that would provide the victories but it was their cry to God. They asked God to stretch forth His hand so that there might be healings and miracles done through the name of Jesus. They knew that it was only through the power of Jesus that they would bring forth victories. God does amazing things in response to faith filled prayers. God heard their prayers and acted according to their faith. He filled them with His Spirit and they spoke the Word with boldness, and signs and wonders accompanied them.

How bold are you in sharing the Word of God and leading others to salvation? God has commissioned each of us to go into all the world and preach the gospel to everyone (Mark 16:15). And these signs shall follow them that believe…they will cast out demons in My name, they will speak in new languages, they will lay hands on the sick and they will recover (Mark 16:17–18). Pray the same prayer that the disciples prayed. Lord, grant me, Your servant, boldness that I may speak Your word and stretch forth Your hand to bring healing, that signs and miracles may be done through the name of Your holy Servant Jesus. Father, I receive this promise and claim it in my life. I shall lay hands on the sick and by the power of Your Spirit and Your spoken Word, they shall recover. Grant unto Your servant your spoken Word. I activate the gift of healing in my life through Your spoken promise. Use me Lord to bring salvation and healing to Your people in Jesus's name, I pray.

SEPTEMBER 21

For sin shall not have dominion over you,
for you are not under law but under grace.
What then? Shall we sin because we are not
under law but under grace? Certainly not!

—Romans 6:14–15

W hen you think of grace, you think of the favor of God upon you. There is nothing you can do to earn God's grace. It is a free gift founded in love. Salvation and grace are His gifts given in love to you. You just have to receive them. When the Spirit empowers your life, you can fully possess and enjoy the riches of grace that are yours in Christ. His grace flows into your life each moment bringing hope, peace and security. God thinks, sees and responds to you through the eyes of grace.

When you think about your life before God, sins can capture your attention and cause you to feel separated from God. But there is nothing that can separate you from the love of God (Romans 8:39). His grace washes over your sins. If you would only grasp the fullness of His divine love and grace. It's the secret of how your freedom from sin and the law may become a living and abiding experience. Every believer who wants to live in this freedom will understand the path in which he must learn to walk.

As the grace of God falls upon you, you learn to walk in freedom. You become dead to sin and alive in Christ. You receive freedom from sin and the laws of man and become married to Christ. You will begin to see that every good thing that comes your way is an act of His grace. Every answered prayer is an act of His grace. Every forgiven sin is an act of His grace. His grace does not depend upon circumstances. His grace does not depend upon whether you do or do not do certain things. His grace is a gift and always will be. Receive His gift of grace in all areas of your life.

SEPTEMBER 22

Fear not, for I am with you; Be not dismayed,
for I am your God. I will strengthen you. Yes,
I will help you, I will uphold you with My righteous
right hand. For I, the Lord your God, will hold your
right hand, saying to you, 'Fear not, I will help you.'
—Isaiah 41:10, 13

Satan has so many people in bondage because of their fears. Fear is false evidence appearing real. It is a panic that grips people causing them to become anxious and scared. Fear causes people to not move forward in their destiny in life. Each of us will face fear at some point, but what we do with that fear will determine victory or defeat.

Claim your position as child of God and trust that God is with you at all times. He will strengthen you, help you and uplift you. When you are given a bad medical report, fear usually sets in. But no matter what the report may show, God is bigger than any physical illness or disease. In Proverbs 29:25, we are warned that fearing people is a dangerous trap, but trusting the Lord means safety. The fear of man will entrap you and hold you back. That is why it is so important to not look at the storms of your life through your own wisdom and understanding but to keep your eyes focused on Jesus.

So how do you overcome fear when it comes knocking at our door? First, trust God's Word. God tells you to not be afraid, for He is with you. He will strengthen you and help you. When adversity strikes, do not fear what man can do to you, for God will uphold you with His victorious right hand. Cast your fears upon the Lord and He will strengthen you. Secondly, come to experience God's love. There is no fear in love, but perfect love casts out fear (1 John 4:18). Thirdly, be filled with God's Spirit, for God has not given you a spirit of fear, but of power, love, and a sound mind (2 Timothy 1:7). Overcome fear by facing your fear head on. Speak truth to the false evidence that appears real and be free from the bondage of fear.

SEPTEMBER 23

I will betroth you to Me forever; Yes I will
betroth you to Me in righteousness and justice, in
lovingkindness and mercy. I will betroth you to
Me in faithfulness and you shall know the Lord."
—Hosea 2:19–20

Many people are walking around in life with unfulfilled dreams. They are dissatisfied, feel sad and lonely, and have many unfulfilled expectations. The origin of their malcontent is a hunger for what they cannot see. Ddeep within them is a hunger to fully know God. The only way to a fulfilled life is to desire less of worldly things and to passionately seek after God.

No matter how much you know about God, there is always more to discover about Him. The Lord wants to betroth you. Betrothal is the period of engagement preceding marriage. As you build your relationship with Christ, He reveals more about Himself to you and your love relationship with Him grows deeper. He is preparing you for the marriage of the Lamb. During this preparation time, He will betroth you to Himself in righteousness, justice, lovingkindness and mercy. He will betroth you in faithfulness to Him and you shall know Him as your Beloved. He promises to be faithful to you forever until that day when the marriage of the Lamb has come, and His wife has made herself ready (Revelation 19:7). He is making you ready for that special day. Blessed are those who are called to the marriage supper of the Lamb! (Revelation 19:9)

The Lord will show you the path of life and in His presence you will experience the fullness of joy. As you pursue your desire for God, He will fill you with pleasures forevermore (Psalm 16:11). If you find yourself dissatisfied, search deep within your heart to see if what you are really longing for, is a deeper relationship with God.

SEPTEMBER 24

My son, if you receive My words, and treasure My
commands within you, so that you incline your ear to
wisdom, and apply your heart to understanding; Yes,
if you cry out for discernment, and lift up your voice
for understanding, if you seek her as silver and search
for her as for hidden treasure; then you will understand
the fear of the Lord, and find the knowledge of God.
—Proverbs 2:1–5

Living a godly life in an ungodly world can be very trying. The book of Proverbs provides guidance for successfully living a godly life every day. Many people incline their ear to wisdom, but they are seek wisdom from man and not from God. They strive to satisfy their own passions and desires without regard for their future or the consequences of their actions. Solomon asked God for wisdom and God answered his prayer. In Proverbs 2, Solomon shares this sound wisdom on seeking God for his direction and spiritual insight. The first four verses are filled with actions that you are to do. The fifth verse tells you the rewards of your obedience.

First, Solomon tells you to receive God's word and to treasure His commands. When you treasure something, it has value to you and it is something you cherish. You are to cherish His commands. You are to listen to God's Word for wisdom and apply it to your heart so that you may gain in understanding. You are to cry out for insight and ask for understanding. If there was a large sum of money buried in a field, you would seek after it with might and determination to find that hidden treasure because you know the value of it. Solomon tells you to seek after God's wisdom with the same passion you would if you were seeking hidden treasure. He knew the value of finding this Godly treasure. God's wisdom brings life, blessings, honor, the fear of the Lord, and the favor of God upon you. Seek diligently and earnestly after God's wisdom and you will find the knowledge of God.

SEPTEMBER 25

Not that I speak in regard to need, for I have learned in whatever state I am, to be content: I know how to be abased, and I know how to abound. Everywhere and in all things I have learned both to be full and to be hungry, both to abound and to suffer need.
—Philippians 4:11–12

Can a man really be content? When it's cold outside, we want it to be hot. When it's hot outside, we want it to be cooler. Curly haired people want their hair straight. Straight haired people want their hair curly. Short people want to be taller and tall people want to be shorter. Can man really be content? Ray Stedman writes, "Contentment is not having all that you want. True contentment is wanting only what you have." In the scripture for today, that is what Paul had found. He had learned to be content no matter what state he found himself in. Paul's relationship with God superseded whatever he had or did not have. His contentment was based on his relationship with Christ and not on the circumstances around him.

Contentment doesn't happen overnight. It is something you have to learn. Compared to the way some people live, you are blessed, but you do not see how blessed you are because you have so much. It takes going to a third world country where people are living in poverty, to put one's life into prospective. As you draw closer to God and learn the true values in life, you begin to appreciate life in a different way. It is more about sharing the love of the Father with others and being appreciative for what you have. You begin to realize that things are of less importance and your relationship with God and others is what is important in life. You begin to trust God more and lean less on yourself.

Contentment comes when you know who you are in Christ and what Christ can do for you and through you. No matter what you may face today, if you lean on God, He will give you strength to be content. Base your contentment on your relationship with Christ, not on your circumstances. Learn to be content in whatever state you are in.

SEPTEMBER 26

So when they continued asking Him, He raised Himself
up and said to them, "He who is without sin among you,
let him throw a stone at her first." And again He stooped
down and wrote on the ground. Then those who heard it,
being convicted by their conscience, went out one by one,
beginning with the oldest even to the last. And Jesus
was left alone, and the woman standing in the midst.
—John 8:7–9

In the beginning of John 8, the Pharisees brought an adulterous woman to Jesus and wanted to know what they should do with her. They were testing Him with the law, for Moses would have had her stoned. No one knows what Jesus wrote in the sands, but we do know that He was listening for His Father's advice on the matter and then spoke the words He heard (John 12:50). He responded with the Father's wisdom and said, "He who is without sin, let him throw a stone at her first." Those who heard it were convicted of their own sin, and one by one they walked away.

We are so quick to judge. Instead of showing mercy and compassion toward others, we want to write them off as sinners. But Jesus reminds us that we are all sinners. In James 1:19, we are told to be quick to hear, slow to speak, and slow to get angry. You need to listen to people with compassion and hear both sides of a story before making a judgment or speaking your thoughts. As you listen to others, you need to seek the Holy Spirit to see what wisdom the Spirit of the Lord would say about the matter.

Live a life that is constantly seeking after God's wisdom. The greater the sin, and the more compassion you show toward the person in sin, the deeper the gratification for forgiveness you will receive from that person. You have the power through the Holy Spirit to change the course of action of others by simply learning to forgive, extending God's mercy, and speaking words of wisdom from the Father. How many lives will you impact this week?

SEPTEMBER 27

Then Moses answered and said, "But suppose they will not believe me or listen to my voice; suppose they say, 'The Lord has not appeared to you.'" Then Moses said to the Lord, "O my Lord, I am not eloquent, neither before nor since You have spoken to Your servant; but I am slow of speech and slow of tongue."
—Exodus 4:1, 10

Why is it that when you are asked to do something, you find yourself making excuses or justifying to others and yourself that you can't do what was asked of you? Surely the other person thought you were qualified, or they wouldn't have asked you to do it. Yet the fear and insecurity keeps you from having confidence that God will see you through. God had called Moses to lead His people out of Egypt. The Lord told Moses that He would be with Him on this journey (Exodus 3:10, 12). Immediately, Moses began imagining what others would think and say instead of trusting God and being confident that he was the man for this task.

To prove to Moses that God was going with him, God performed signs (Exodus 4:2–7). Even then, Moses made an excuse that he was not very good with words, that he gets tongue-tied, and his words get tangled. Moses was afraid that he was inadequate and would not be persuasive when confronting others. When Moses spoke the words, "Neither before nor since," he had already convinced himself that his speech problem was beyond what Yahweh could do and from his perspective, this would never change.

Too often, you are like Moses. You view things through your eyes and perspective instead of looking at the tasks through God's eyes. Persevere through your fears and trust that God will give you the skills to perform the task at hand. Forget about your own strength and capabilities and look at each situation with God's strength and power moving through you. God has chosen each of us with specific tasks for the advancement of His kingdom. Move forward in the power of God and do what He has called you to do.

SEPTEMBER 28

And we have known and believed the love
that God has for us. God is love, and he who
abides in love abides in God, and God in him.
—1 John 4:16

God is love (1 John 4:16) and God is Spirit (John 4:24). You cannot have one without the other. You have only as much of the Spirit as you have the love of God. We have only as much of the love of God as you have of His Spirit. The two are inseparable. The Spirit in you is the love of God abiding in you.

In 1 John 5:7, we read "For there are three that bear witness in heaven: the Father, the Word, and the Holy Spirit, and these three are one." Throughout the Word we read about the love of God and the relationship that the Father had with His Son. The two were inseparable. In this love between the Father and Son, the Spirit is the bond of their love. No one knows the things of God except the Spirit of God (1 Corinthians 2:11). Jesus said, "I and My Father are one" (John 10:30). It is only through God's Spirit that they are one.

The Father is the loving One, the fountain of all love. The Son is the Beloved One, the reservoir of the Father's love, always receiving and always giving. The Spirit is the living love that makes them one. The outpouring of the Spirit is the in-pouring of His love. God is in you because He has put His Spirit within you. It is the Spirit of God that enables you to love Him and others. Abide in the love of Jesus and you will be a reservoir of His love—always receiving and always giving of His love to everyone you meet.

SEPTEMBER 29

Therefore humble yourself under the mighty
hand of God, that He may exalt you in due time.
—1 Peter 5:6

Pride will cause you to move ahead of God and out of God's will for your life. When things don't go the way you think they should, you try to make them happen. People strive to make a name for themselves whether it be in the workforce or in ministry. Pride hardens a person's spirit so that he can no longer hear from God. Like any sin, pride defiles a man (Mark 7:22–23). God hates prideful and arrogant people (Proverbs 8:13). Eventually a man's pride will catch up with him and bring him low (Proverbs 29:23). Those who walk in pride, God is able to put down (Daniel 4:37).

You are to be content with the place of service and leadership that the Lord assigns to you. Self-promotion usually leads to heartache and sets one up for failure. If you want to advance in God's kingdom, do not strive to make things happen, but rather humble yourself before God. It is He who will exalt the humble in due time. The same is true in the work place. Be content with your current position and do the best job you can, not striving, but allowing the Lord to promote you in His timing.

Live in humility and God will exalt you. Repent of any pride, for pride will cause God to resist you. Humble yourself, knowing that God will give you grace and equip you with what you need to succeed in His promotion for you. Wait upon the Lord and know with confidence that in due time, He will exalt you.

SEPTEMBER 30

Then behold, they brought to Him a paralytic lying on a bed. When Jesus saw their faith, He said to the paralytic, "Son, be of good cheer; your sins are forgiven you." And at once some of the scribes said within themselves, "This Man blasphemes!" But Jesus, knowing their thoughts, said, "Why do you think evil in your hearts? For which is easier, to say, 'Your sins are forgiven you,' or to say, 'Arise and walk'? But that you may know that the Son of Man has power on earth to forgive sins"—then He said to the paralytic, "Arise, take up your bed, and go to your house."
—Matthew 9:2–6

Jesus is in the healing business. He cares about your entire being—mind, body, and soul. In the eyes of God, sin and sickness are as closely united as the body is united to the soul. They form a strong bond. Jesus is the only one who has the power to forgive sin. When Jesus's listeners heard Him say "your sins are forgiven," they were shocked and responded, "Who can forgive sins but God alone?" (Luke 5:21) It was more difficult for Jews to believe in the pardoning of their sins than it was to believe in their healing.

Today, it is just the opposite. The church has heard so much about forgiveness of sins that the soul easily receives the message of grace. But divine healing for today is rarely mentioned. Many do not believe that the signs, wonders, and miracles of yesterday are here for the church today. Unbelief separates the free gifts of the Lord's healing and forgiveness. Christ has made a provision for the well-being of your total person—mind, body, soul, and spirit. In order to receive healing, it is usually necessary to begin by confessing sin and desiring to live a holy life. Having dealt with his sin, Jesus healed the paralytic. Immediately the paralytic arose and departed to his house (Matthew 9:7).

Jesus is the same Savior both of the soul and of the body and awaits your response to grant pardon and healing. Let us all be ones to proclaim, "Bless the Lord, O my soul, who has forgiven me of all my iniquities and healed all my diseases." Praise be to the Healer of both body and soul.

OCTOBER 1

*Shadrach, Meshach, and Abed-Nego answered and said
to the king, "O Nebuchadnezzar, we have no need to answer
you in this matter. If that is the case, our God whom we serve
is able to deliver us from the burning fiery furnace, and He
will deliver us from your hand, O king. But if not, let it be
known to you, O king, that we do not serve your gods, nor
will we worship the gold image which you have set up."*
—Daniel 3:16–18

Shadrach, Meshach, and Abed-Nego had a decision to make.
They could give in to the pressures of the king and worship his
golden idol or face the fire. They chose the latter and honored
God. They were ready to face the fiery furnace because they
believed that the God they served would deliver them. Although
they did not really know what the outcome would be, they yielded
their bodies, understanding that they should not serve nor worship
any god except their own God! Their faith was built on serving
God and obeying His commandments.

Notice that God did not remove the fiery furnace from
Shadrach, Meshach, and Abed-Nego. Instead, He walked in the
midst of the fire with them (Daniel 3:24–25). Too many times
when you feel a little heat, you want instant comfort and want
God to remove the fire. But it is in the midst of a fire that hearts
are changed.

Are you in a heated fire right now? Are you only feeling the
heat and seeing the flames grow, or are you seeing the Lord in the
midst of the burning? Do not pray to be brought out of the fire
until after you have found the Lord in the midst of it. The God
who delivered Shadrach, Meshach, and Abed-Nego from the fiery
furnace will walk with you in the midst of your fire and deliver
you.

OCTOBER 2

But the manifestation of the Spirit is
given to each one for the profit of all.
—1 Corinthians 12:7

It is God who distributes spiritual gifts as He sees fit. Each one of us receives at least one spiritual gift that is to be used to build up the faith of the church. There are nine specific gifts necessary for a full manifestation of the Spirit (1 Corinthians 12:7–11): the word of wisdom, the word of knowledge, the gift of faith, gifts of healing, the working of miracles, the gift of prophecy, discerning of spirits, different kinds of tongues, and interpretation of tongues.

Learn the value of these spiritual gifts and set your heart to attain them. The word of wisdom—God giving you utterances through the Holy Spirit at a given moment disclosing His mind and will to a specific situation. The word of knowledge—revelation of information pertaining to a person or event given for a specific purpose. The gift of faith—supernatural faith beyond normal faith. Gifts of healing—healings which God performs supernaturally by the Spirit. The working of miracles—manifestation of power enabling you to do something beyond normal means. The gift of prophecy—sudden insight of the Spirit prompting exhortation, comfort, or warning. Discerning of spirits—the ability to detect the true source of circumstances or motives of people. Different kinds of tongues—the gift of speaking supernaturally in a language not know to the individual. Interpretation of tongues—the gift of translating the message of the Spirit.

We all will operate in at least one of these gifts if we allow the Holy Spirit to manifest through us. The Holy Spirit distributes to each one individually as He wills (1 Corinthians 12:11). Allow the Holy Spirit free access in your life to teach you, to give you gifts, and to use you for His purpose. Welcome the manifestation of the Holy Spirit in your life. Be willing and available to receive any of the gifts of the Spirit that He would minister through you. Earnestly desire the best gifts (1 Corinthians 12:31).

OCTOBER 3

They soon forgot His works; they did not wait for
His counsel, but lusted exceedingly in the wilderness,
and tested God in the desert. And He gave them
their request, but sent leanness into their soul.
—Psalm 106:13–15

How easy it is for you to forget. Unfortunately as we age, we seem to become even more forgetful. The Israelites soon forgot about the mighty power of God that had freed them from slavery. They constantly murmured and complained along their journey to freedom. God finally tired of hearing their complaints and gave them the desires of their heart, but He sent leanness into their souls. To be lean means to lack richness or productiveness, to be deficient. Their souls no longer had the richness of God's glory. It reminds me of the scripture in Mark 8:36, "For what will it profit a man if he gains the whole world and loses his own soul?" At what cost are you willing to obtain something you want? At what cost are you willing to be defiant and not wait on the counsel of the Lord? For the Israelites, it cost them their souls.

It's hard to wait on the Lord when you want an answer now. At times you may even murmur and complain, wanting things your way. But you must not move ahead of God nor should you test God. He may answer your prayers and satisfy your heart, but you may lose your soul in the process. As you wait upon the Lord, meditate on His works, remembering all the other times that He has answered your prayers. Trust that He knows what is best and that His timing is perfect. If a prayer is not answered right away, reflect on your prayer to see what it would cost for you to obtain it. Make sure it is worth the price. Thank the Lord for the many times He did not answer your prayers when they would have brought destruction to your soul.

OCTOBER 4

For I have given you an example,
that you should do as I have done to you.
—John 13:15

Right after Jesus shared the Lord's Supper with His disciples, He demonstrated to them what was lacking in their lives. Jesus rose from supper and poured water into a basin to wash the disciples feet (John 13:4–5). The task of washing the feet of guests was typically done by a slave. But there was no slave to do the work. None of the disciples thought of humbling themselves for such a task. Jesus arose, humbling Himself, and began to wash their feet.

Just before His death, in one significant act, He demonstrated the whole work of His ministry. Jesus symbolically showed them what He had done for souls in cleansing them from sin while also demonstrating to them that love willingly gives up all. It was love that made Jesus a servant. He humbled Himself to do a lowly task that a slave would typically do. After washing their feet, He sat down and said, "Do as I have done to you."

For those who know that Jesus has washed away their sins, He commands that we do as He has done. Are you serving in humility? When asked to do something at your job, do you humbly accept even though you do not feel like doing it? When a pastor calls for volunteers, do you step up to the plate and serve because you see the need? Christ humbled Himself and became obedient to the point of death, even the death of the cross. He always did what the Father asked Him to do. His heart was to love, to serve, and to save that which was lost.

Are you living like Christ? He who says he abides in Christ should live his life as Jesus did (1 John 2:6). Do you rise to the occasion without being asked? The higher you rise in being like Christ, the lower you will stoop to serve those around you. Live each day rising to the occasion to be like Christ. Open your heart to the Lord and be willing to say, "Lord, even as You have done, so I will do also."

OCTOBER 5

Now when Daniel knew that the writing was signed,
he went home. And in his upper room, with his windows
opened toward Jerusalem, he knelt down on his knees three
times a day, and prayed and gave thanks before his God,
as was his custom since early days.

—Daniel 6:10

When Daniel heard the fate of his future, the first person He turned to was God. He did not allow his circumstances to influence the way he lived. He was accustomed to praying to God three times a day, and He continued to do so, even though He could have faced grave consequences. Over your lifetime, you will face many difficult situations. Whatever life sends your way, you can be sure that God cares. God wants and expects you to call upon Him (Jeremiah 33:3). He is bigger than any problem you face and will guide you through the difficulty. When a trial hits, your first response should be to go to prayer before Him.

Prayer and praise are two weapons that a believer can use when faced with a challenge. In prayer, we profess our need for God and ask for His solution to the problem. In praise, we acknowledge that God is our Lord and give Him honor for who He is. As we acknowledge Him, faith builds inside of us and reassures us that God is in control. God honors the prayers of His people. He sees every tear we cry and will give us insight and revelation to guide us along the way. Open your heart to God when you are hurting, discouraged, anxious, oppressed or just needing some love. There is no place you will feel more accepted or secure than in the arms of Jesus. Call upon Him and He will answer.

OCTOBER 6

*Jesus said to him, "If you can believe, all things
are possible to him who believes." Immediately
the father of the child cried out and said with
tears, "Lord, I believe; help my unbelief!"*
—Mark 9:23–24

Jesus didn't say—some things are possible. He said all things are possible to him who believes. When your faith starts to waiver, you need
to take hold of this scripture and keep repeating it to yourself until
faith arises in you to believe that your situation is not unique, that "all
things are possible." Why is it that you have great faith to believe in
the signs, miracles, and healing for other people, but you lack it for
yourself? When you begin to question your healing, when you begin
to doubt that you will see victory, confess to the Lord the difficulty
you have in believing Him. Tell Him you want to believe and ask
Him to remove your unbelief. Say the prayer the father said in the
above scripture, "Lord I do believe, help me overcome my unbelief."

Jesus has the power to heal, save, and do miracles. What He
does for one, He will do for all. He is the same yesterday, today,
and forevermore (Hebrews 13:8). Jesus is ready to heal, save and
do miracles but He is waiting for us to call upon Him. He is waiting on us to act so that He can react. The responsibility lies upon
us. We must pray and believe. Prayer without faith is powerless. It
is prayer offered in faith that will heal the sick (James 5:15).

Come to believe in the divine power of Jesus. Believe what
the Lord says He can and will do. Believe in who He is and lean
completely on His divine grace to conquer all unbelief within you.
The Lord will give you victory. Are you seeking the Lord for an
answer to prayer right now? All things are possible to those who
believe. Tell Him, "Yes, Lord, I believe" and watch the power of
God move on your behalf. Keep repeating those words until faith
arises in your heart and soul for your situation. Yes, Lord, I believe.
Yes, Lord, I believe. Yes, Lord, I believe. All things are possible
through You Lord Jesus.

OCTOBER 7

Do you not know that your bodies are members of Christ?
Shall I then take the members of Christ and make them
members of a harlot? Certainly not! Or do you not know
that he who is joined to a harlot is one body with her?
For "the two," He says, "shall become one flesh." But
he who is joined to the Lord is one spirit with Him.
—1 Corinthians 6:15–17

Our bodies are members of Christ. They are temples of the Holy Spirit and belong to Christ (1 Corinthians 6:19). God formed man from the dust of the earth and breathed the breath of life into his nostrils, and man became a living soul (Genesis 2:7). The soul is what binds the body and the spirit together. It is the soul that must choose between the voice of God (the Holy Spirit speaking to your spirit) or the voice of the world (external world speaking to your flesh, your senses).

Immoral conduct defiles your body. It is not only a sin against your body but also a sin against the Holy Spirit who dwells within you. One would never think of deliberately defiling the Holy Spirit, but that is exactly what you are doing when you chose to live ungodly. Do not give in to immoral sin of any kind. Choose to be joined with Christ. Rely on the power of the Holy Spirit to help you live godly.

If you are joined to the Lord, you are one spirit with Him. It is the Holy Spirit who joins your spirit to the Spirit of God and the life of Jesus. It is the Spirit of God that imparts to you His holiness, His strength, His joy, His peace. The Holy Spirit imparts to you all that you are willing to receive. When you have fully surrendered your body and soul to Christ, desiring nothing but to be one in spirit with Him, it is then that He can manifest His power in you and through you. Choose to be one in spirit with Him. God bought you with a high price, so honor God in your body and in your spirit (1 Corinthians 6:20).

OCTOBER 8

But thanks be to God, who gives us
the victory through our Lord Jesus Christ.
—1 Corinthians 15:57

Has God ever failed you? Has there ever been a time where God was not your refuge and strength? At times it may seem like God is far away, but God is always there when you need Him. Whatever you face today, the Lord's purpose will be fulfilled in spite of your weaknesses, if you rely on His strength. Jesus said that in the world you will have tribulation but be of good cheer, He has overcome the world (John 16:33). It's not easy being happy and cheerful when it feels like your world is in chaos, but that is exactly what you are to do. Sometimes it's going to take your praise to win the battle you are facing and to thank the Lord for the victory that has already been won.

It is Christ who gives you the victory, and it is your faith in Christ that helps you to achieve that victory. You can't have victory without faith in Jesus Christ to give you the victory. Regardless of your flaws, God's will shall be done if you lean on the Lord and not on your own abilities. Your lack of faith in Christ is the thing that only holds you back from victory. God takes delight in bringing victory in those places where victory seems nowhere in sight. Rely on God. You are more than a conqueror through Christ who loves you (Romans 8:37). Ask God for the victory and watch the Lord show Himself strong on your behalf. Thanks be to God who gives you the victory through our Lord Jesus Christ (1 John 5:4).

OCTOBER 9

"What man of you having a hundred sheep, if he loses one of them, does not leave the ninety-nine in the wilderness and go after the one which is lost until he finds it? And when he has found it, he lays it on his shoulders, rejoicing. And when he comes home, he calls together his friends and neighbors, saying to them, 'Rejoice with me, for I have found my sheep which was lost.'"
—Luke 15:4–6

The tax collectors and sinners were all gathered around Jesus to hear Him. But the Pharisees were muttering among themselves how Jesus welcomed sinners and ate with them (Luke 15:1–2). As a result, Jesus told the parable of the lost sheep (Luke 15:3–7). The parable illustrates Christ's attitude toward the self-righteous as well as toward the saved sinner. The ninety-nine sheep represent the Pharisees who considered themselves righteous and with no need of being saved from sin. The lost sheep represents a sinner who realizes his lost condition and seeks forgiveness from the Lord. The shepherd represents Jesus Christ.

In the parable, the shepherd leaves the ninety-nine to find the one lost. The shepherd's highest priority is the lost sheep, knowing it's defenselessness in a dangerous world. Just as a shepherd is concerned about one lost sheep and goes out and searches for it, so God's mission in Christ is to seek and to save the lost (Luke 19:10). He does not want any of us to perish (2 Peter 3:9).

The focus in the parable is on the effort it took to find one lost soul and the joy experienced when that lost sheep was found. The lesson is clear, heaven rejoices when a sinner repents and is restored to fellowship with God, but there is no joy over self-righteous people who have never been convicted of their sinful nature (Luke 15:7). All men are sinners and all must repent in order to be saved. Jesus's ministry was one of seeking the lost. Jesus calls you to be like Him, to reach out to the lost. How much effort are you exerting to find one lost soul?

OCTOBER 10

Repay no one evil for evil. Have regard for
good things in the sight of all men. Do not be
overcome by evil, but overcome evil with good.
—Romans 12:17, 21

Why is it that all we read about in the newspapers or hear on television are headlines of what is wrong with the world. Rarely do we hear the good that is going on. The more evil that people hear about, the more they begin to feel powerless. But we are not powerless. Repaying evil with more evil only compounds the matter. Instead, we should overcome evil with good. If more people would step up to the plate and determine to make a difference in this world, we would begin to see a change in our society.

Evil gets all the headlines. Why? Because that is what people want to hear. They are glued to the news wanting to hear what else is going wrong with America. The only way we can turn this trend around, is to stop talking about the bad, the ugly, and the evil, and start talking about the good things that people are doing. We can change the mindset of people if we all pull together and speak and do that which is good. We need to be of one mind, having compassion for one another; love as brothers, being tenderhearted and courteous to one another. We should not return evil for evil or insult for insult, but on the contrary, sow blessing, knowing that we were called to this that we may inherit a blessing (1 Peter 3:8–9).

Be quick to speak good about someone. Evil may be lurking all around you, but God's goodness is more powerful and stronger and He wants you to do good on His behalf to overcome evil. Jesus said that in the world you will have tribulation, but to be of good cheer, He has overcome the world (John 16:33). As light overcomes darkness, so goodness can overcome evil.

OCTOBER 11

*For what I am doing, I do not understand. For what
I will to do, that I do not practice; but what I hate,
that I do. For I know that in me (that is, in my flesh)
nothing good dwells; for to will is present with me but
how to perform what is good I do not find.*

—Romans 7:15, 18

I think all of us can relate to the internal struggle that Apostle Paul describes. You know how you should live and desire to live a holy righteous life, but sin still has that powerful force over you. You simply do not have the power within you to conquer sin. For the flesh lusts against the Spirit, and the Spirit against the flesh; and these are contrary to one another, so that you do not do the things that you wish (Galatians 5:17). You constantly face a battle between your flesh and the Spirit.

Sin is an option. Those who live according to the flesh set their minds on the things of the flesh, but those who live according to the Spirit, set their minds on the things of the Spirit. You need to learn to say no to the power of sin, trust in God to give you the strength to walk away from it, and set your mind on things of the Spirit. There are forces all around you that try to lure you away from God. Recognize those forces and break their strength over you. Although you experience setbacks and failures, you have a Savior who stands ready to forgive. Once you realize you have sinned, seek forgiveness from the Lord. He stands ready to pour out His grace and mercy upon you.

You have great potential to live a holy life through Christ Jesus. When you sin, you should not only recognize that you have sinned, but also determine why you gave into its power. If you deal with the root cause of why you sin, you will lessen the powerful force that sin has over you. Allow Christ to free you from the powers of sin and learn to walk in the power of the Holy Spirit.

OCTOBER 12

He who does not love does not
know God, for God is love.

—1 John 4:8

God is love. His love is unconditional. You cannot do anything to gain His love nor can you do anything that would cause Him to take His love away from you. While we were yet sinners, Christ died for us (Romans 5:8). No matter where you are in your walk of life, God loves you and no one can take that love away from you. Many people do not know or believe that they are loved by God. They come from abusive or dysfunctional families that never showed love. Some come from loving families, but they have never allowed themselves to feel love because of past wounds. Others know that God loves them, but they will not allow themselves to receive His love because they feel they are unworthy due to their sins.

God knew us before He even formed you in your mother's womb (Jeremiah 1:4–5). He had already set in place His mercy and grace for your shortcomings. His love saw you as you are—a child of God. And as your Father, He longs for you to experience His love.

What about you? Do you have a hard time believing that God loves you? Do you want to know and believe the love that God has for you? Are you ready to experience God's love in a deeper way? Take the time to meditate on these words "God is love" and "I am loved by God." Allow God to pour out his love upon you. You don't have to do anything but receive His love.

Come to the full realization that God really loves you. Go to the website www.FathersLoveLetter.com and read the Father's Love Letter. It's the cry of the Father's heart from Genesis to Revelation that He has written for you. Believe and experience the love that God has for you.

OCTOBER 13

"No weapon formed against you shall prosper, and every tongue which rises against you in judgment you shall condemn. This is the heritage of the servants of the Lord, and their righteousness is from Me," says the Lord.
—Isaiah 54:17

Are you not a servant of the Lord? Then by birthright, no weapon formed against you will prosper. It is the Lord who fights your battles and brings vindication upon every tongue that rises up against you. You are already victorious before the battle even begins. The only one who can defeat you is you yourself if you allow your carnal mind to think defeat. Decree your victory through Christ Jesus. He is the one who always causes you to triumph. It is the Lord strong and mighty who goes before you as a consuming fire. He will destroy and subdue your enemies (Deuteronomy 9:3).

It is the Lord who places a hedge of protection around you and your home and helps you to prosper in everything you do (Job 1:10). He orders His angels to protect you wherever you go (Psalm 91:11). It is the Lord who has given you the authority to tread upon every spirit and over the power of the enemy (Luke 10:19). He has given you the weapons of defense, you just have to use them in battle. Know therefore today, that it is the Lord who goes before you in battle. In all things, you are more than a conqueror through Christ (Romans 8:37). Victory belongs to the Lord and to you. You are an overcomer by the blood of the Lamb (Revelation 12:11). Thanks be to God who always leads you in triumph (2 Corinthians 2:14).

OCTOBER 14

I tell the truth in Christ, I am
not lying, my conscience also bearing
me witness in the Holy Spirit.

—Romans 9:1

There is a harmony that must exist between your conscience and the Holy Spirit. It is your conscience that condemns sin and lets you know when things are right in your spirit. God's work of redemption begins with your conscience as the Holy Spirit moves upon your heart. If you think of your heart as a chamber in which your life dwells, it is lined with the very image of God since you were created in God's image (Genesis 1:27). His laws are engraved in your heart and the fragrance of His love fills the air. Your conscience is a light to that chamber that allows you to look and see into the inner depths of your heart.

As you allow the Holy Spirit to speak to your conscience, the light that shines into the chamber reveals the true image of God and reveals every sin you commit. If you choose to ignore what the Holy Spirit is telling you, your conscience becomes defiled because your mind refused the prompting of the Holy Spirit. As the Holy Spirit exposes each sin and you ignore your conscience speaking to you, the light within the chamber of your heart gets dimmer and dimmer, until the light no longer shines in the chamber. Your conscience is no longer in harmony with the Holy Spirit. Conviction has been totally darkened because your conscience is now blinded from the light. The laws of God are always hidden deep within your heart and it is only through the Holy Spirit that your heart can be renewed and sanctified.

When your body is sick, it can self-heal if you give it the proper food and nutrients it needs. Likewise, your mind and conscience can renew themselves too if you allow the Holy Spirit to restore what sin has defiled. By restoring the conscience back to health, you are able to live a life in harmony with the Holy Spirit.

OCTOBER 15

My people have committed two evils: They
have forsaken Me, the fountain of living
waters, and hewn themselves cisterns—
broken cisterns that can hold no water.

—Jeremiah 2:13

In this scripture we are told that the people committed two evils. The first evil was that they had forsaken God. The second was that they had replaced God with broken cisterns. A cistern is a man-made reservoir dug into the earth to hold water. The problem with man-made reservoirs is that they end up cracking and cannot hold the rainwater that is collected. God was using an illustration to the Israelites that their man-made idols and religious beliefs were like cisterns, cracked and useless. Instead of choosing God, the fountain of living waters, who constantly refreshes them, they chose cracked and dried-up reservoirs, worthless idols which gave no life, but instead empty promises.

Jesus intentionally stopped at a well in a city of Samaria knowing that a Samaritan woman needing salvation would be there to draw water. In their conversation, Jesus told the Samaritan woman that He has living water, and whoever drinks of the water that He gives, will never thirst again. The water that He gives will become in them a fountain of water springing up into everlasting life (John 4:5–14). This same fountain of water offered to the Samaritan woman is available to you to freely draw from forever, whenever you like. Many people dig wells and try to find salvation in other ways, but there is only one way to salvation and that is by drinking from the cup of Living Water. Why build wells that cannot hold living water? Rather, go to the fountain and freely draw from the well that never dries up, where you can drink and be full.

OCTOBER 16

And he said to his servant, "Go up now, look toward the sea." So he went up and looked, and said "There is nothing." And seven times he said again "Go again." Then it came to pass the seventh time, hat he said, "There is a cloud, as small as a man's hand, rising out of the sea!" So he said, "Go up to Ahab, Prepare your chariot, and go down before the rain stops you.' Now it happened in the meantime that the sky became black with clouds and wind, and there was a heavy rain. So Ahab rode away and went to Jezreel.
—1 Kings 18:43–45

Elijah received from God the promise that it was about to rain (1 Kings 18:1). He did not wait around for it to happen, but took that promise from God and went and prayed with perseverance and faith. God willed for it to rain, but it did not happen until Elijah activated his faith and birthed it forth in prayer. Elijah sent his servant to look toward the sea. The servant went and looked and returned to Elijah and told him he didn't see anything. Elijah repeated his request seven times until the appearance of the first cloud was rising out of the sea.

This is how you should pray for your promises from God, with faith and perseverance. This is how you should pray for your circumstances. This is how prayer for the sick should be made. Whatever things you ask for in prayer, if you believe that you've received it, it will be yours (Mark 11:24). God is a rewarder to those who believe and diligently seek after Him. Prayer by faith receives what God has promised before it manifests itself. Elijah prayed with perseverance, never losing sight of God's promise, and in time, watched his promise manifest.

When healing is delayed, do not lose hope of the promise from God. Only perseverance in prayer can remove the obstacles that may be delaying your victory. Do not let faith be shaken by those things which are not yet seen. God's promise remains the same. So I say to you, look toward your sea and see what you see. If you see nothing, go again and again until it comes to pass that you see a cloud of hope as small as man's hand. Then know that your promise is about to manifest.

OCTOBER 17

*Then Jehoshaphat stood in the assembly of Judah and Jerusalem,
in the house of the Lord, before the new court, and said: "O
Lord God of our fathers, are You not God in heaven, and do
You not rule over all the kingdoms of the nations, and in Your
hand is there not power and might, so that no one is able to
withstand You? Are You not our God, who drove out the
inhabitants of this land before Your people Israel, and gave
it to the descendants of Abraham Your friend forever?"*
—2 Chronicles 20:5–7

King Jehoshaphat was afraid. All around him people were preparing for battle against him. Instead of giving into his fear, Jehoshaphat sought the Lord and proclaimed a fast (2 Chronicles 20:1–3). As he gathered the people of Judah together, he publically proclaimed his trust in God, acknowledged who God was, the power that God possessed, and what God had done for Abraham. He declared that he was putting all his trust and hope in the Lord who had power over all.

When you are faced with battles of your own, you need to stop what you're doing, fast and seek the Lord in prayer. Cry out to God in humility. Acknowledge your weaknesses and declare the power and authority He has to change any situation. Thank Him for what He has done for you in the past and ask Him to move on your behalf. Acknowledge to God that you have no power, you do not know what to do, but your eyes are fixed on Him. Like Jehoshaphat, do not allow doubt and fear to rule in your heart but set you hopes in the power of the Almighty God. He has never failed you in the past and will not do so now.

OCTOBER 18

We are hard-presses on every side, yet not crushed;
we are perplexed, but not in despair; persecuted, but
not forsaken; struck down but not destroyed—always
carrying about in the body the dying of the Lord Jesus,
that the life of Jesus also may be manifested in our body.
—2 Corinthians 4:8–10

W hen you are faced with hardships, you may sometimes forget who you have on the inside to strengthen and sustain you. The power of our Lord Jesus Christ lives within you. We all face difficulties in life, some more than others. When you do, look deep within yourself and call upon the Holy Spirit to help you, sustain you, and to give you the victory.

You will be hard-pressed to the limit but you will not be crushed. Do not give in to the difficulty or strain you are faced with. Do not give in to defeat by saying, "Lord, I can't take it anymore. I give up." Instead, call upon the Lord and acknowledge that He is God and that He will sustain you—"Lord, your grace is sufficient for me to get through this. I trust in you." Then lean on His strength.

When your mind is overwhelmed with uncertainty, bewilderment or confusion, do not fall into despair, but instead, hope in the promises of God. Ask the Holy Spirit to bring clarity to your mind. When you are faced with persecution, remember that Jesus was persecuted too (John 5:16), but He was not forsaken and neither will you be forsaken. The Lord sees all and is in the midst of your persecution. When life seems to knock you down, continue to get up. When you do, yesterday's fall will lead to today's victory. There will be times that you will face hardships so that others may come to know the power of God. Allow the life of Jesus to be manifested in you and through you so that others may come to know Christ.

OCTOBER 19

Therefore we do not lose heart. Even though our outward man is perishing, yet the inward man is being renewed day by day. For our light affliction, which is but for a moment, is working for us a far more exceeding and eternal weight of glory, while we do not look at the things which are seen, but at the things which are not seen. For the things which are not seen are temporary, but the things which are not seen are eternal.
—2 Corinthians 4:16–18

In every situation, God controls the forces that come upon your life. You are not to lose heart nor are you to question the circumstances. Rather, you are to look to God for understanding. You look upon the natural physical world and the circumstances around it. God looks at your spiritual well-being. Consider that the sufferings of this present time are not worthy to be compared with the glory which shall be revealed in you (Romans 8:18). Do not give up or be discouraged. Do not look at your circumstances and what you see in the physical, but set your focus and faith on things which are unseen and eternal.

While you are praying for a problem to be solved, a need to be met, or a thorn to be removed, God is watching for true faith and to see how you will react to the situation. There is always a lesson to be learned through each trial you face. Walk by faith and not by what can and cannot be seen with your natural eyes (2 Corinthians 5:7). Know that the trials and difficulties you face today will seem light compared to the immeasurable glory that awaits you in eternity.

OCTOBER 20

I beseech you therefore, brethren, by the mercies
of God, that you present your bodies a living
sacrifice, holy, acceptable to God, which is your
reasonable service. And do not be conformed
to this world, but be transformed by the renewing
of your mind, that you may prove what is that
good and acceptable and perfect will of God.
—Romans 12:1–2

W hen we think of sacrifice, we usually think of an inconvenience or giving up something that is of value. But in Hebrew, it involves the offering of a life. In the Old Testament, animals were placed on the altar as a sacrifice for the atonement of sins. People willingly sacrificed a lamb without blemish to make reconciliation with God. Jesus, the Lamb without blemish, became the ultimate sacrifice for the atonement of your sins (1 Peter 1:19).

Paul encourages you to present yourself as a living sacrifice each day before God. Presenting your body as a living sacrifice means that you bring your body before God, lay it on the altar in His presence and ask Him to use this sacrifice for His glory. You are to lay down your anxieties and trust Him for everything. You are to lay down your will and seek the will of God. Do not live according to the ways of the world, but allow God and His Word to transform your mind to the mind of Christ.

Many times the Lord seeks after you, but you continue in pursuit of your own ways. He has put obstacles in your paths, and yet you ignore those obstacles thinking that the enemy placed them there. You continue to move forward with your own agenda. Have the mindset of Christ. Do not be conformed to this world, but be transformed by the renewing of your mind. If you lay yourself down on the altar as a living sacrifice, the Lord will show you what is acceptable and the perfect will of God.

OCTOBER 21

For you know the grace of our Lord Jesus Christ, that
though He was rich, yet for your sakes He became poor,
that you through His poverty might become rich.
—2 Corinthians 8:9

Jesus was very rich, not in a material sense, but His richness was in recognition of His eternal status as Lord of heaven and earth. For our sake, He became poor—He gave up His richness in Heaven, totally giving of Himself, and became man. Jesus willingly became a human being on our behalf, relinquishing His Glory though retaining His deity. And being found in the appearance as a man, He humbled Himself and became obedient to the point of death, even the death of the cross (Philippians 2:6–8). It is through His poverty; His self-giving, that we are able to become rich in His glory.

It does not matter how little you have of the treasures of this world, for you are blessed with the abundance of His grace. God could have shown His anger upon you to make His power known. You could be enduring, with much longsuffering, the vessels of wrath prepared for destruction (Romans 9:22). Instead, He has made known to you the richness of His glory in the vessels of mercy, which He has prepared beforehand for you whom He called (Romans 9:23). If you could only grasp what was done for you, you would truly realize how rich you really are. There is no want for him who is a follower of Jesus. There is never any lack. Although you may be poor in the world's eye, you are rich in the Spirit of Christ Jesus.

OCTOBER 22

"Therefore come out from among them and
be separate, says the Lord. Do not touch
what is unclean, and I will receive you."
—2 Corinthians 6:17

The Lord calls you to separate yourself from the world, to be a part of the world but to not engage in the activities that would cause you to compromise your walk with Him. There are ways to witness without compromising your walk with the Lord. However, there is no way to compromise your Christian values and at the same time be an effective witness. You are a vessel of the Lord and must keep yourself holy, sanctified for the Lord's use.

Separation from the world involves you distancing yourself from sinful influences and staying close to God. You are to cleanse yourself from everything that can defile your body and spirit (2 Corinthians 7:1). There are two steps to cleansing: turning away from sin and turning toward God. The Lord calls you to come out, to depart from darkness. He calls you to come out lest you share in their sins and receive the consequences of those sins (Revelation 18:4).

Those who seek the truth and the light will be drawn out into the light. You are a light, a city on a hill (Matthew 5:14) and God will draw people to you who are ready to come out of darkness. You cannot go back into darkness hoping to save them. It will only give the evil one an opportunity to attack your soul. Light always overcomes darkness. Turn on a light switch in a dark room and the light prevails. So it is when Christians walk among the unsaved. There is a light that permeates from us. If we allow our light to shine, we will prevail over darkness.

OCTOBER 23

*"Pardon the iniquity of this people, I pray according to
the greatness of You mercy, just as You have forgiven
this people, from Egypt even until now." Then the Lord
said, "I have pardoned, according to your word."*

—Numbers 14:19–20

Moses was a man who always went before the Lord to defend the people. He knew God was a God of mercy full of grace who had forgiven the iniquity of his followers in the past. Moses begged for mercy for their present condition of heart because he knew that intercession for the people would touch God's heart. The Lord heard his cry and pardoned the people according to the prayer Moses had spoken.

Many people are numb to their spiritual condition and do not realize they are living in sin. The Lord is counting on you to intercede for His people that He might pardon their sins as well. Many people are dying and going to hell each day because no one has interceded for them. The Lord is merciful and gracious, slow to anger, and abounding in mercy (Psalm 103:8). Like Moses, He will pardon sins according to your prayers.

God calls you to stand in the gap and intercede for those who are lost, those who are too weak to pray for themselves, those who are being persecuted, or those who are in bondage. Whatever the circumstance or whoever the Lord places upon your heart, you need to take the time to birth victory on behalf of His people. Prayer does make a difference. It will change the course of direction in people's lives and the state of our country and nation. Who has the Lord placed upon your heart to pray for? Are you beckoning to the call on their behalf?

OCTOBER 24

These six things the Lord hates, yes seven are an
abomination to Him: a proud look, a lying
tongue, hands that shed innocent blood, a heart
that devises wicked plans, feet that are swift in
running to evil, a false witness who speaks lies,
and one who sows discord among brethren.
—Proverbs 6:16–19

It is so important that we guard our tongue. Three of the seven abominations in these scriptures deal with the tongue, and two of them can cause us to sin with our mouth as well. The Lord classifies these sins with murder (Galatians 5:20–21). We would never consider murdering a person, but we are quick to tell a lie, spread rumors and gossip, or speak words that kill a person's hope, dreams and self-esteem. What causes us to fall into this trap? More than likely, it is our unhealthy attitudes or unhealed past wounds. Anger, resentment, frustration, impatience, disappointments, stress, guilt, insecurity, and jealousy all contribute to the damaging words we speak. As we lash out at others, we wound and divide friendships and relationships, including our relationship with God. When we cut into the heart of another, we are also cutting into the heart of God.

When you realize that you have committed an abomination to the Lord, immediately seek forgiveness from the Lord and make amends to the one you have hurt. Rid yourself from all gossip and slander. Replace words that may hurt a person with words that will heal their heart, extend love, and bring forth forgiveness. Boasting, lying, and the rest of the ways you use words to hurt and divide need to be removed as well. Search deep within yourself and determine why you engage in these abominations. Then deal with the root of the issue that is in your heart. When you examine your own attitudes, pain and hurts, you will be less apt to speak words that will cause pain and hurt to others.

OCTOBER 25

"Now there was a widow in that city; and she came
to him, saying; 'Get justice for me from my adversary.'
And he would not for a while; but afterward he said
within himself, 'Though I do not fear God nor regard
man, yet because this woman troubles me I will avenge
her, lest by her continual coming she weary me.'"
—Luke 18:3–5

In Luke 18, Jesus tells a parable of a persistent widow to encourage His disciples that men always ought to pray and not lose heart. He tells of a judge who is reluctant to bestow justice, but does so for fear of her tiring him with her persistence. Then Jesus contrasts God to this judge and God's willingness and readiness to speedily answer petitions of His own people. In Luke 18:7, God responds, "And shall God not avenge His own elect who cry out day and night to Him, though He bears long with them?" Notice that God hears every cry you petition day and night. If a godless judge responds to constant pressure, how much more will a loving God respond to you.

Pray with perseverance! Persistence is what causes a heart to move. To persist in prayer does not mean you spend long hours praying endless repetitions for a request. It means that you continually keep your requests before God as you live for Him day by day believing He will answer. What a blessing it is to be able to ask the Lord for an answer to prayer and to know with all certainty that it is His will to answer that prayer. Sometimes your answer to prayer is immediate; other times you must wait. God's timing is perfect. He can delay answers to prayer as He sees necessary and then instantly bring the answer at just the right time. There may be a delay, the reason for which only God knows, but trust that God's timing is perfect. Pray with perseverance and faith until your prayer is answered.

OCTOBER 26

"But the very hairs of your head are all numbered.
—Matthew 10:30

Have you ever tried to count the number of hairs on your head? The first time I read this scripture, I remember trying to count mine and it wasn't soon afterward that I knew it was an impossible task. I can also remember asking the Lord, "How do you do it?" How could He remember the count of everyone's hairs on their head? His response was, "Because I am God." Need He say anything else?

Can you imagine trying to count the sand crystals on the beach? And yet God's thoughts toward you are as countless as the sand on the seashore (Psalm 139:17–18). Then I ponder how often I think of God. It is nothing compared to how often He thinks of me. I am so thankful that His love and devotion to me is not based on my love and devotion to Him. O Lord, increase the love and devotion in my heart toward you.

God cares about every detail of your life. He knows when you sit and when you rise (Psalm 139:2). No matter what is going on in your life, He knows about it. He has the answer for the problems you are facing right now. He loves you with an everlasting love (Jeremiah 31:3) and He will never stop loving you. He carries you close to His heart (Isaiah 40:11) and His answer to your situation is only a heartbeat away.

The Lord knows that we are busy people. But in your busyness, He wants you to pause and think of Him. Think of His goodness, mercy, everlasting love, and His thoughts toward you. All He wants from you is for you to love Him back. Take the time to show your love to Him. Remember Him throughout your day with praise and thanksgiving. You will never be able to think of Him as often as He thinks of you. But when you do remember to think of Him, keep this one thought in mind…He's already thinking of you.

OCTOBER 27

"Your kingdom come. Your will be
done on earth as it is in heaven."
—Matthew 6:10

How can you know whether or not something is God's will? How can you pray in faith when you are not sure that you are asking according to the will of God? Sickness is one area that many of us struggle with. We pray fervently for healing for ourselves and for others and healing does not come. Then we begin to question and ponder whether it is God's will that we remain ill and what is the purpose for our suffering. So how do you determine what is the will of God?

To know God's divine will, be guided by the Word of God and by the Holy Spirit. What does the Word say about healing? What does the Word promise you? In James 5:15, the Word promises you that the prayer of faith will save the sick. In Isaiah 53:5, the Word promises you that by His stripes you are healed and in Isaiah 53:6, the Word promises you that the Lord has laid upon Himself the iniquity of us all.

Jesus Christ has already obtained for you the healing of your diseases. He has borne your sicknesses and iniquity. According to His promises, you have the right to be healed because it is a part of salvation that you have in Christ. We need not tell yourself "if it be the Lord's will, then I will get healed." Putting "if" in your prayers only delays your prayers being answered. It questions whether God is really able to do it. You need to quit saying "if" and start saying "when." Claim the promise that is already guaranteed to you—yes, it is God's will that I be healed and by His stripes I am healed. Declare your "When," When the Lord heals me…When my son is free from drugs…When the Lord restores my marriage…When the Lord…

Do not let your heart be influenced by the doctor's report, by the pain you feel, by results not yet seen, or by the discouraging words of others. Allow your faith to rise up to the fact that God wills for you to be whole and to live a prosperous life. Sickness and iniquity leave in the Jesus's name. Restoration come in Jesus's name. Receive your healing in Jesus's name.

OCTOBER 28

*Because what may be known of God is manifest
in them, for God has shown it to them. For since
the creation of the world His invisible attributes
are clearly seen, being understood by the things that
are made, even His eternal power and Godhead,
so that they are without excuse.*
—Romans 1:19–20

Before I committed to spending a lifetime with my husband, I wanted to know him first, to see if He was the man I wanted to share my life with. I had to learn his ways, his character, what he believed and how he would treat me. Spending time with him allowed me to know who He was and that I wanted to spend my life with Him. God knows all about you and has already committed Himself to spending a lifetime with you. He is waiting for you to commit to Him. Have you courted the Lord to see if you want to spend eternity with Him? God delights in revealing to His people who He is. He has chosen to make Himself known. God has revealed who He is through Scripture by declaring His names, His character, His ways, and His works. You were made to know God, to love God, and to spend eternity with Him.

There are many hidden secrets waiting for your discovery. The secret things belong to the Lord but the things revealed belong to us and to our sons forever (Deuteronomy 29:29). You have a great opportunity to know God if you spend time with Him. Many are content to settle for just talking about God. I personally would rather know Him than just talk about Him. When God reveals Himself to you in a new way, He is opening Himself up to you to embrace. It is a new promise from Him so that you may grow in knowledge of God and learn that He is beyond what you could ever have imagined. How hungry are you to know God and find the secret things of God?

OCTOBER 29

*"I have been crucified with Christ; it is no longer I
who live, but Christ lives in me; and the life which
I now live in the flesh I live by faith in the Son of
God, who loved me and gave Himself for me."*

—Galatians 2:20

How have you been crucified with Christ? If you look at the works of Jesus, then legally you have died with Christ because your sins died with Him. God cancelled the record that contained the charges against you. He took it and destroyed it by nailing it to Christ's cross (Colossians 2:13–14). Because you have been crucified with Christ, you have also been raised with Him (Romans 6:5). You have legally been reconciled with God (2 Corinthians 5:19) and free to grow into Christ's likeness.

Before you believed in Christ, your nature was evil. You disobeyed, rebelled, and ignored God. After you became a Christian and gave your life to Jesus, you became a new creation (2 Corinthians 5:17); Christ came into your heart and He lives in you. Once a slave to your sinful nature, but now you are free to live for Christ (Romans 6:6).

God did not take you out of the world. You are still free to choose and you will sin at times, that is your human nature. But the more you surrender your life and allow Christ to live in you, the less often you will sin. You have Christ's resurrection power in you to empower you as you continue to fight sin (Ephesians 1:19–20).

In your daily life, regularly crucify sinful desires that keep you from following Christ. You cannot do this on your own, will it in your heart for it to be done. As you do so, God will work with you and within you to bring it to pass. Will it in your heart that— it is no longer I who live, but Christ who lives in me.

OCTOBER 30

And Asa cried out to the Lord his God, and
said, "Lord, it is nothing for you to help, whether
with many or with those who have no power; help
us, O Lord our God, for we rest on You, and in
Your name we go against this multitude. O Lord,
You are our God; do not let man prevail against
You!" So the Lord struck the Ethiopians before
Asa and Judah, and the Ethiopians fled.
—2 Chronicles 14:11–12

When you go to battle in the name of the Lord, you win every time. What looks impossible to you is nothing to the Lord. As Asa prayed for God's help, he recognizing that he was powerless against this mighty army unless God intervened. His army did not fight with their own power and strength. In the name of the Lord they went against their enemy. They rested on God to win their battle. God heard Asa's prayer, stuck the Ethiopians, and they fled.

If you are facing battles you feel you can't possible win, don't give up. The secret to winning the battle is to admit that you are helpless without God. Cry out to God and then trust Him to save you. His strength is made perfect in your weakness (2 Corinthians 12:9). God likes to step in when you recognize our own limitations and depend on Him. He is there for you in each of your battles. No matter how great or how small your battle may be, rest upon the Lord. Cry out to God for His help and let Him fight your battle. You will win every time.

OCTOBER 31

Whatever the Lord pleases He does, in heaven
and in earth, in the seas and in all deep places.
—Psalm 135:6

God has the power and wisdom to accomplish everything and anything He desires. He rules the entire universe. He has established His throne in heaven and His kingdom rules over all (Psalm 103:19). Whatever the Lord pleases He does. What does the Lord want to do? The Lord desires that all be saved and live eternally with Him. He will do everything in His power to help you find the way, but the ultimate decision to accept His invitation is yours. He wants to shower you with His love and to have intimacy with each and every one of us. He wants you to live a prosperous life (Job 36:11). But most of all, the Lord desires your heart.

What pleases the Lord? It pleases the Lord to do good, to show mercy, and to bestow grace upon His people. The Lord was pleased to make us His people (1 Samuel 12:22). It pleases the Lord to see His children obedient and honoring Him. It pleases the Lord when you walk in humility, serve others, and show compassion to others. He takes delight in showing compassion to you. Solomon asked the Lord for an understanding heart to judge the people and discern between good and bad. His request pleased the Lord
(1 Kings 3:9–10). It pleases the Lord when you seek Him for wisdom, understanding, and discernment, and He takes pleasure in granting you your request.

The Lord takes delight in blessing His people, defending His people, healing His people, and delivering His people. He has the power and wisdom to accomplish it all. Our God is in heaven and He does whatever He pleases.

NOVEMBER 1

Then the disciples came to Jesus privately and said, "Why could we not cast it out?" So Jesus said to them, "Because of your unbelief; for assuredly, I say to you, if you have faith as a mustard seed, you will say to this mountain, 'Move from here to there,' and it will move; and nothing will be impossible for you. However, this kind does not go out except by prayer and fasting."
—Matthew 17:19–21

A man came to Jesus and asked Him to have mercy on his son for he was an epileptic and suffered severely, falling into fires and waters. He told Jesus he had brought his son to His disciples but they were not able to heal him. Jesus rebuked the demon in the boy, it left him, and the boy was well thereafter (Matthew 17:14–18). The disciples asked Jesus why they weren't able to cast out the demon. Jesus told them it was because of their unbelief; that it took not only faith, but also prayer and fasting to remove this stronghold.

I believe that fasting is the lost key to hidden treasures. Fasting is something you rarely hear about and many do not understand its importance. If fasting were not important and biblical, Jesus would not have fasted. Before He even began His ministry, Jesus was led by the Spirit into the wilderness and fasted forty days (Matthew 4:1–3). It is important for you to develop a lifestyle of prayer and fasting.

The purpose of fasting is to humble yourself before the Lord. Through prayer and fasting, you are seeking His face to invoke God's mercy, healing and deliverance. Fasting is used for spiritual warfare to loose chains of wickedness, untie heavy burdens, to set the oppressed free and to break yokes (Isaiah 58:6).

Fasting is the lost key to unleashing the Holy Spirit's power. This lost key is found throughout the Bible, yet somehow has been set aside or misplaced. It is time that you find this lost key, apply it to your life, and unlock the hidden treasures that the Lord has stored up for you.

NOVEMBER 2

*"For what great nation is there that has God so near
to it, as the Lord our God is to us, for whatever reason
we may call upon Him? And what great nation is
there that has such statutes and righteous judgments
as are in all this law which I set before you this day?"*
—Deuteronomy 4:7–8

If ever America needed to turn back to God, it is now. Just as we are able to seek God individually, corporately this nation needs to turn back to the ways of God. It is only through repentance that God will hear the cries of His people. Moses told the Israelites that they must observe the decrees and regulations so that they may live and go in and possess the land (Deuteronomy 4:1). Corporately, we must turn back to God, observe the laws and possess the land.

The Ten Commandments, the heart of God's law, are just as applicable today as they were years ago because they proclaim a lifestyle endorsed by God. He wrote them on the stones when He spoke them to Moses (Exodus 34:28). They were written by God to tell man how He wants him to live. God's laws are designed to guide all people toward lifestyles that are healthy, upright, and devoted to God. Their purpose is to point out sin and to show the proper way to deal with sin. They are the foundation with which we must live.

Pray that America will return to the foundation on which it was built, observing God's ways and pledging alliance to God. If America does not turn back and serve the one and only God, the Lord Jesus Christ, we will lose God's hand of protection upon us, and this land will be possessed by others. Wake up America to the calling of the Lord. Wake up and possess the land today, for tomorrow may be too late.

NOVEMBER 3

Also with moisture He saturates the thick clouds;
He scatters His bright clouds. And they swirl about,
being turned by His guidance, that they may do what-
ever He commands them on the face of the whole earth.
—Job 37:11–12

The greatest forces in nature, the winds, the rains, and the thunders, give nothing but the tiniest hint of God's immeasurable power. He wraps the rain in His thick clouds and the clouds do not burst forth with the weight until the Lord calls them forth. He loads the clouds with moisture and they flash forth with His lightening. The clouds turn around and around under the Lord's direction. They do whatever He commands throughout all the earth. The greatest forces in nature are just a whisper of God's power, and yet He makes all that power available to you through prayer.

Nothing can compare to God and His immeasurable power. If God can hold back the rains until their time, He can hold back the forces that are coming against you. Cry out to Him that the thunder of His voice may be heard in your storm. As the winds and clouds turn around and around under His direction and do what He commands, so it will be with the forces that are against you. They must bow down to His voice and move under His direction.

The Lord spoke to Job from a whirlwind (Job 38:1). Allow the Lord to speak out of the whirlwind in your life. God said he was reserving the treasuries of the snow and hail for times of trouble (Job 38:22–23). God has all the forces of nature at His command and He can unleash or restrain them at will. You can't even begin to know all of God's treasures that He reserves for you and is ready to unleash at will.

NOVEMBER 4

Therefore I exhort first of all that supplications, prayers,
intercessions, and giving of thanks be made for all men,
for kings and all who are in authority, that we may lead
a quiet and peaceable life in all godliness and reverence. For
this is good and acceptable in the sight of God our Savior.
—1 Timothy 2:1–3

God has chosen us to help change the world through our prayers. Pray earnestly for our leaders in government and those in authority over us. Our heartfelt prayers delight the Lord and will have powerful results (James 5:16). And so Lord, we pray for our government officials right now.

Guide them into Your truth. Give them wisdom to make the right decisions. Lead them in straight paths and help them live their lives with integrity. May they trust in You and not lean on their own understanding. May they acknowledge You in all their ways. Set their hearts, minds, and will to follow You Lord and to walk in Your ways.

Place a hedge of protection upon them and their families. Expose every plot of the enemy that would bring harm to them. Grant favor to those who serve You. Convict them when they want to pass laws contrary to your Word. May no bill or legislation pass that is against Your ways. Guard their hearts from corruption so they may not be persuaded by peer pressure or false pretenses.

Give our elected officials wisdom and guidance on building this nation. Remove all corruption from our government. Make our officials accountable for their decisions. Be near to them as they cry out to You. May they all come to know Your saving grace. We pray for the souls of those who don't know You; grant them salvation this very day. We pray this in the name of Jesus Christ, our Savior and our Lord.

NOVEMBER 5

And those who know Your name will
put their trust in You; for You, Lord,
have not forsaken those who seek You.
—Psalm 9:10

Do you trust God? Most of the time we all can say that we trust Him. However, when we are in the heat of a spiritual battle, and it seems like everything is caving in on us, do we still trust God? It's easy to lose hope and allow doubt to set in when there seems to be no end in sight. No matter how long the battle may last, we must trust and lean on God for the victory. Those who know His name will put their trust in God for He will not forsake those who seek him. In the heart of every person is a desire to know God, a hunger that only God Himself can satisfy. When we ask God to tell us His name, we are asking to know Him as He really is. When we come to know His name, we will put our trust in Him. When we come to know God as the Healer, we will rely on Him and believe in Him to heal our body.

Throughout scripture, there are many names of God. Discovering God's name and attributes will alter the course of our lives and build our trust in God. When we discover His names, we begin to trust in the names of God, declare His names, depend on His names, delight in His names, and begin to see God work in our lives in astounding ways. We begin to express what we feel in our hearts about God.

As you read your Bible each day, always look for truths about God. Focus your thoughts on Him. Tune out the demands of your job, financial worries, family and health issues, and the cares of life and tune into God. Discover who God is, what He does, and what He says. Discover the names of God and watch your faith arise as you call out to God by His names. Your heart will replace fear and worry with a new confidence in God.

NOVEMBER 6

"Again I say to you that if two of you agree
on earth concerning anything that they ask,
it will be done for them by My Father in heaven.
For where two or three are gathered together in
my name, I am there in the midst of them."
—Matthew 18:19–20

The Spirit of God lives in each individual Christian, but He promises to be with us in a special way when we gather together "in His name" for worship, service, prayer, or just to encourage one another. This is the confidence that we have in Him, that he hears us whenever we ask for anything that pleases Him. And since we know He hears us when we make our requests, we also know that He will give us what we ask for (1 John 5:14–15). Two or more believers, filled with the Holy Spirit, will pray according to God's will, not their own, and thus their requests will be granted.

If our hearts do not condemn us, we can come to God with bold confidence. We will receive from him whatever we ask because we obey him and do the things that please him (1 John 3:21–22). Jesus tells us to keep on asking and it will be given to us (Matthew 7:7). Keep on believing and we will receive whatever we ask for in prayer (Matthew 21:22). We are not to give up in our efforts to seek God. Jesus assures us that we will be rewarded (Matthew 7:8–9).

Jesus, our role model, prayed, "Everything is possible for you...Yet I want your will not mine" (Mark 14:36). We must pray with God's interests and desires. When we pray, we can express our desires, but we should want His will above ours. Jesus promises us that He is with us always, even to the end of the age (Matthew 28:20). Jesus is with us today through His Spirit. When we seek God in prayer, the Holy Spirit will align our spirits with His so that we may pray according to the Father's will. Allow the Holy Spirit to speak to you as you quiet yourself in prayer.

NOVEMBER 7

Who gave Himself for us, that He might redeem
us from every lawless deed and purify for Himself
His own special people, zealous for good works.
Speak these things, exhort, and rebuke with all
authority. Let no one despise you.

—Titus 2:14–15

Imagine a person in a car accident, trapped and not able to get out of the vehicle, but with the help of another, escapes from the car moments before the car explodes. The gratitude the trapped person has for the person who risked their life to free them, giving them another chance at life. Now imagine Christ nailed on the cross for sins He did not commit. He didn't risk His life to free us; He gave His life willingly, taking the punishment for our sins so that we could have freedom to live for Him and with Him. Many are unaware of the price that was paid for their freedom. Some that do know the price Christ paid take it for granted and show no gratitude for what was done for them. Others are grateful but are not committed to doing what is right.

Christ freeing us from sin opens the way for Him to purify us. We are not only free from the death sentence for our sins, but we are also purified from sin's influence as we grow in Christ. The more we learn and understand about Christ, the more we will be whole-heartedly committed to serving the One who saved us. It is Christ's desire that none should perish (2 Peter 3:9) and it is our responsibility to spread the gospel to those around us. Demonstrate the love of Christ to others and teach them about the freedom that is theirs because of what Christ did for all.

NOVEMBER 8

So be truly glad! There is wonderful joy ahead, even though
it is necessary for you to endure many trials for a while.
—1 Peter 1:6, NLT

We all face many trials. We are no different than the people in the Bible who faced many challenges, yet endured the suffering and persecution. They didn't know how their circumstances would end and neither do we, but they held onto the understanding that God knew how everything would turn out. You must hold onto that understanding as you face your battles. As a child of a Sovereign God, you are never a victim of your circumstances. There is always a purpose and lesson to be learned. You must accept trials as part of the refining process that burns away impurities and prepares you to meet Christ. Trials teach patience and help you grow to be the kind of person God wants you to be.

God knows that the Christian life is not easy. There is always a battle, whether you are dealing with your flesh, the world, or the devil. Satan is very perseverance. If he can't cause you to fall in one area, he will try in another and if that doesn't work, he will get to your heart by attacking loved ones in your family.

When the going gets rough, you must not run, or quit, but push through. Even though you may feel that you are in a seemingly hopeless situation, know that God has an entirely different view of the outcome. He knows what goal He has set for us and how much we can endure. The One who endured the cross lives in us so we can endure ours. If we stumble, He is there to pick us up. If one door closes, He is there to open another. Recognize that God is with you and He will use every situation that happens to you for your blessing and for His glory.

NOVEMBER 9

Then Jesus said to His disciples, "If anyone
desires to come after Me, let him deny himself,
and take up his cross, and follow Me."
—Matthew 16:24

To deny self is the opposite of pleasing self. The Webster's dictionary defines the word deny as: to declare untrue, to refuse to recognize or acknowledge, to disavow, and to reject as false. It is no wonder Peter went away weeping bitterly after denying Christ three times (Matthew 26:69–75). When Peter denied Christ, he said, "I do not know the Man." Peter did not want anything to do with Jesus. He did not wish to be counted His friend. The fear of man drove him to deny Christ.

How many times have you denied Christ? You may say, "I am His friend, I would never deny Him." Peter was His friend and He denied Him three times. You deny Christ when you do not speak about Him to others when you have the opportunity to. You deny Christ when there is a need and you do not allow God to use you in that circumstance. You deny Christ when you do not order your life around godly principles. We are to deny ourselves and not Christ.

To deny yourself is to reject the old self, your old ways of thinking, your old habits and interests, anything of the sinful nature you no longer want to be a part of. You disengage and refuse to permit the old self to be your friend. There will always be two sides to a Christian life. On the one hand, you are complete in Christ when you have accepted Jesus as your Lord and Savior. On the other hand, you are growing in Christ, becoming more and more like Him as you deny yourself. You feel both the presence of Christ and the pressure to sin. If you remember these two sides of a Christian life, you will not grow discouraged as you face temptations and problems. Instead you will learn to deny yourself and depend on the power of Christ that is in you to disengage from your old nature.

NOVEMBER 10

O Lord, You have searched me and known me. You
know my sitting down and my rising up; You understand
my thought afar off. You comprehend my path and my
lying down, and are acquainted with all my ways.
—Psalm 139:1–3

Too many times people do not go to the Father because of the condemnation the devil places upon them. We see ourselves as unworthy and too ashamed to go before His Holiness. Whether we go before Him, or not, does not change the fact that God already knows everything about us. He knows our thoughts and is acquainted with all our ways. As a parent, we know our children pretty well. We know that they are not perfect, but that does not stop us from loving them. Parents just naturally want to be a part of their children's lives to love upon them and to nurture and guide them along life's journey. Our Heavenly Father is no different.

You are a child of God, and your Heavenly Father eagerly waits to speak to you, to love upon you and to nurture you. His Spirit is ready and willing to work within you. He wants to give you guidance every day of your life. We all need love and God loves us unconditionally. He knows how you are made; after all, He created you. He knows your strengths and your weaknesses and wants to help you so that your weaknesses become your strengths. He wants to heal your innermost hurts, fears, and frustrations.

Later in this psalm, David asked God to search him and know his heart, even to the level of testing his anxious thoughts (Psalm 139:23). Be willing to pray the same prayer so that God will reveal sin in your life. As God shows you your sins and you repent of them, you will be continuing on the path to everlasting life.

NOVEMBER 11

So Jesus said to them again, "Peace to you!
As the Father has sent Me, I also send you."
—John 20:21

Jesus knew what His mission was. He knew the Father had chosen Him and sent Him into the world with one purpose: to make known the Father's love and His will in the salvation of sinners. Jesus never questioned the Father or wondered how He would accomplish that which He was called to do. He knew the Father would give Him all that He needed to do it.

God never gives us something without wanting us to give it away. Jesus fulfilled His mission and has shown us the Father's love and granted us salvation. He now passes the torch to us to be the front runners of carrying out His mission. As the Father has sent Jesus, Jesus sends His followers, and that includes you and me. We are called to be salt and light (Matthew 5:13–16). Jesus saved us so that we may in turn lead others to Christ. We must portray the image of Christ so that the world may know what Christ is like. Do you reflect the image of Christ? The Lord needs you to be His representative in the circle in which you live. You are called to be a light for Jesus. Is your light hidden under a basket, or have you placed yourself in a place where it gives light to everyone in your circle (Matthew 5:15)?

Many people are living in fear; they have erected walls around themselves. The pain, hurt, rejection and betrayal run so deep that they are no longer willing to take a risk with anyone else. They allow people to only get so close and then the walls go up. You may be one of those people. The Lord wants to set His people free. It is going to take the Father's love to tear down those walls and allow people to walk in freedom. If you are one of those people who is living in a box, the Lord is beckoning you to take a risk right now. Are you willing to take the risk to be free so that in turn the Lord will use you to set others free?

NOVEMBER 12

*God's purpose was to show his wisdom in all its rich
variety to all the rulers and authorities in heavenly realms.*
—Ephesians 3:10, NLT

Just as the earth is filled with good and evil, so are the heavenly realms filled with good and evil. The rulers and authorities in the heavenly realms are either angels sent by God, or hostile spiritual forces opposed to God. Those who are not "flesh and blood" are demons over whom Satan has control. We face a powerful army whose goal is to defeat Christ's church. When you believe in Christ, these hostile spiritual forces become your enemies and they try every scheme to turn you away from Christ and back to sin. The devil does not seek to destroy the defiled as much as he seeks to destroy those who choose to live a holy life. Satan is constantly battling against all who are on the Lord's side.

When the enemy attacks, fight back with full force. The enemy has come to destroy you (John 10:10) and you will have to use a stronger force if you hope to defeat him. God has provided this force by giving you His Holy Spirit and His armor (Ephesians 6:13–18). All hell trembles when God's people take command in the name of Jesus over evil powers. Those who do are hated by the adversary. Although all hell may seem like it is rising against the church body, God will give us power to stand. Put on all of God's armor so that you will be able to stand firm against all strategies of the devil. For you are not fighting against flesh and blood, but against principalities and powers of the unseen world, against spiritual forces of darkness intruding into heavenly places (Ephesians 6:11–12). When you feel discouraged, remember Jesus's words to Peter: "Upon this rock I will build my church, and all the powers of hell will not conquer it" (Matthew 16:18). God is on your side to help you be victorious over the enemy.

NOVEMBER 13

And so it was, after the Lord had spoken these words to Job, that the
Lord said to Eliphaz the Temanite, "My wrath is aroused against you
and your two friends, for you have not spoken of Me what is right,
as My servant Job has. Now therefore, take for yourselves seven bulls
and seven rams, go to My servant Job, and offer up for yourselves
a burnt offering; and My servant Job shall pray for you. For I will
accept him, lest I deal with you according to your folly; because
you have not spoken of Me what is right, as My servant Job has."
—Job 42:7–8

Thank God that He is merciful and does not pour out His
wrath upon us when we deserve it. Eliphaz, Bildad, and Zophan
heard about Job and felt a burden to comfort him. But when they
got there and saw the condition Job was in, they gasped and were
silent for seven days. Once they finally opened their mouths, they
judged his pitiful condition and insisted that it was Job's sinfulness
that had caused his adversity. Then God stepped in and made it
clear that Job's friends were wrong. Job's friends had made an error
of assuming his suffering was caused by some great sin. They were
judging Job without knowing what God was doing.

Be careful to avoid making judgments about a person because
God may be working in ways you know nothing about. The three
men could have pleaded to God for mercy but God would not
have heard their cry for His wrath was upon them. God knew that
Job was a devout and upright man (Job 1:1) and He would accept
Job's prayers. Their lives could have ended in tragedy had Job
taken revenge instead of praying for his friends. In spite of much
criticism, Job was still able to pray for his friends. It's difficult to
forgive someone who has accused us of wrong doing, but Job did
so, and God expects us to do so as well. Follow Job's actions and
pray for those who have wronged you. Never judge something by
its appearance, for you never know what God's intentions are in a
situation.

NOVEMBER 14

"Am I a God near at hand," says the Lord, "And
not a God afar off? Can anyone hide himself in
secret places, so I shall not see him?" says the Lord;
"Do I not fill heaven and earth?" says the Lord.
—Jeremiah 23:23–24

No matter what we face today, God is near at hand to give us the wisdom to make the right choices, to give us revelation about His Word, or the matter at hand, to give us peace in the midst of our storm, and to bring healing to those who are suffering. No matter what our need may be, God is close by and ready to lend a helping hand.

Many try to flee from God because of their sinfulness, or try to hide from God to avoid an assignment from Him. We may escape for the moment, but God always finds a way to bring us to our senses to make us realize we cannot flee from His presence. Jonah tried to hide from God but God did not give up so easily on him. It took a great fish to bring Jonah back to his senses (Jonah 1–4). God gave Jonah a second chance to fulfill his God-given assignment. Like Jonah, we allow fear to stop us from doing what God has called us to do. In His mercy, God gives us a second chance to carry out His assignment.

We serve a God who fills heaven and earth. Everywhere we are, He is there. Where can I go from your Spirit? Or where can I flee from Your presence? (Psalm 139:7) The answer of course is "nowhere." Instead of fleeing, or trying to hide from God, realize that the God who knows all and sees all is the One who has you dear to His heart. He has filled the earth with His Glory for us. Repent of your wrongdoing and walk in the Glory of the Lord. His hand is there to guide you. Have faith in God that He has chosen you for the assignment and that He will see you through.

NOVEMBER 15

He will take these weak mortal bodies of
ours and change them into glorious bodies like
His own, using the same mighty power that
He will use to conquer everything, everywhere.
—Philippians 3:21, NLT

Aging is one aspect about ourselves that we cannot change. It is one of the ways God keeps us headed homeward. For those of us who still have parents living, we appreciate the moments we can spend with them for we never know when the Lord will call them home. Letting go of loved ones is not easy, but if we can imagine them receiving their heavenly reward, it eases the loss we feel when they are no longer with us.

If you have ever experienced the Holy Spirit in your life, it is only a foretaste of our future glory. We will be resurrected with glorified bodies like the body Christ now has in heaven (1 Corinthians 15:50–58). Our resurrected bodies will be transformed. Our spiritual bodies will not be weak, will never get sick, and will never die like our physical bodies.

We all face limitations, but our attitude about our weaknesses will make us or break us. Some may have physical, mental, or emotional disabilities. Some may be blind, but they see a new way to live. Some may be deaf, but they hear the Lord speaking to them. Some may be lame, but they can walk in God's love. They live with those limitations knowing that they are only temporary. This gives us hope in our suffering. For we know that when we die and leave these bodies, we will have a home in heaven, an eternal body made for us by God himself and not by human hands (2 Corinthians 5:1). This truth should give us great courage and patience to endure anything we might experience.

NOVEMBER 16

*"And he said to him, 'Son, you are always
with me, and all that I have is yours.'"*
—Luke 15:31

When we read the parable of the prodigal son (Luke 15:11–32), what usually speaks to us is the father's love for the prodigal son. But what is hidden in this parable is the heart the father had for the elder son as well. The elder son was always with the father; he had never-ending and unlimited fellowship with him. Although he was home and with his father all the time, he never understood, received, or enjoyed this privilege with his father. Many Christians are like the elder son. They are with the Father but they do not understand, receive, or enjoy the privilege of salvation and the Father's love. There are many benefits that come with salvation, but many do not read the Word, or fellowship with God to find out what those benefits are.

When the elder son complained of the reception the father had for the prodigal son, the father lovingly answered, "Son, you are always with me, and all that I have is yours." This is what our Heavenly Father says to all His children. God is telling us that all He has is ours. He has given it to us in Christ. All the love of the Father and the riches of Christ are ours. There is nothing that He has that is not ours. Even His glory is for all to see and experience. Are you experiencing the fullness of your salvation and the unlimited love and never-ending fellowship we have with the Father? If not, you can. Just ask. Father, manifest Your love upon me. I want to see Your glory. Show me Your glory. Allow me to see and experience Your glory and all the riches of Christ that are mine.

NOVEMBER 17

Then Jesus, being filled with the Holy
Spirit, returned from the Jordan and was
led by the Spirit into the wilderness
—Luke 4:1

Jesus fulfilled His entire ministry by relying on the power and direction of the Holy Spirit. When you rely on the Holy Spirit as Jesus did, you can be sure you are walking in the will of God. Many times you hear from the Lord and the Holy Spirit is directing you to do something. Then someone comes along and shatters your dreams because they believe that you have not heard clearly from the Lord. You begin to question yourself and allow doubt to set in. Before long, you decide to believe man instead of God and do not follow through with His original instructions.

Once you have heard clearly from the Lord, never waver but determine to do what God has asked of you. Satan will put fear, confusion, and people in your life to try to stiffen you and to get you out of the will of God. He wants to cloud your vision, blind your eyes, and deafen your hearing to what the Lord is revealing to you. You are to continue to be led by the Holy Spirit and not by man. There will be times that you may miss the mark, that the Lord hadn't spoken to you what you thought you had heard from Him. But I would rather go to the Lord and ask for forgiveness for not hearing clearly and ask Him to sharpen my spiritual ears than to fail for not even listening, or trying at all. The Lord will sharpen your spiritual ears if you allow Him to and you will learn to recognize the traps of the enemy. Do not let fear, confusion, or another person keep you from being led by the Holy Spirit.

NOVEMBER 18

*O Timothy! Guard what was committed to
your trust, avoiding the profane and idle
babblings and contradictions of what is falsely
called knowledge — by professing it some have
strayed concerning the faith. Grace to you. Amen.*

—1 Timothy 6:20–21

Timothy warns us that we are to guard that which the Lord has entrusted to us. Many have strayed from their faith because they were not strong in the doctrine of Jesus Christ. They have allowed godless foolish discussions with people to cause them to wander from the truth. Many are slick and smooth with their words that sound promising and true but eventually lead people down the wrong path. The only way to know you are headed down the right path is to compare how you are living to the Word of God. Hold fast to the sound doctrine of the Bible and be loyal to your faith. Guard what was planted in your heart by the Holy Spirit. Avoid profane and idle babblings and contradictions of what is falsely called knowledge. True knowledge comes only from the Holy Spirit.

Come judgment day when you meet your Creator, you will not be judged whether you lived your life by what was taught by someone else; you will be judged by how you lived your life according to God's Holy Word, the Bible. No matter what anyone tries to tell you, the Holy Bible is the Word of God. In the beginning was the Word, and the Word was with God, and the Word was God (John 1:1). Who is the foundation of your faith? If your faith is not built on the foundation of Jesus Christ, then someone has led you down a wrong path. If anyone or even an angel from heaven preaches any other gospel to you than what is in the Bible, then he is accursed (Galatians 1:8–9). Read the Bible daily and there you will find Truth. Allow God's truth to lead you down the right path.

NOVEMBER 19

"For if you forgive men their trespasses, your
heavenly Father will also forgive you. But if
you do not forgive men their trespasses, neither
will your Father forgive your trespasses."
—Matthew 6:14–15

The key to forgiving others is remembering how much God has forgiven you. In God's grace, forgiveness is one of the first blessings we receive from God and should be one of the first blessings we extend to others. Yet we tend to forget about the grace and mercy that was extended to us when another has offended us, or done injustice to us. Love conquers all. It is love that enables you to forgive as Christ has forgiven you. If we do not forgive others, the Lord in turn does not forgive us. The two are inseparable: God's forgiveness of us and our forgiveness of others.

He who only seeks forgiveness but has not accepted forgiving love from others, proves that God's forgiveness has never really penetrated his heart. He who has really accepted forgiveness from Christ will allow forgiveness to rule in his heart and be quick to forgive others. It is easy to ask God for forgiveness but difficult to grant it to others. Whenever we ask God to forgive us for sin, we should ask, "Is there anyone that I need to extend forgiveness to?" Is it difficult for you to forgive someone who has wronged you a little when God has forgiven you so much? Realize God's infinite love and forgiveness can help you love and forgive others. Extend unto others what God has graciously extended unto you.

NOVEMBER 20

"Do not judge according to appearance,
but judge with righteous judgment."

—John 7:24

I can remember years ago walking down to a market store at lunch time to buy some fruit for lunch. My eyes caught a big shiny red apple. It looked so delicious and I couldn't wait to bite into it. I purchased the apple and took it back to the office. When I started to eat the apple, I became very disheartened. Immediately I could see that the inside of the apple was nothing like the outside; it was rotten to the core. To my disappointment, I was deceived by the outward appearance. This reminded me of how easily we can be deceived when we judge by what we see instead of what is in the heart of the matter. How easy it is to make wrong first judgments. Based on incomplete or inaccurate information, we can jump to wrong conclusions, and make poor value judgments about people and situations.

Scripture warns us that we should not judge by appearance but with righteousness. We are to judge the way God will judge—with fairness and truth. We dislike those who base their judgments on appearance, false evidence, or hearsay. However, we are sometimes quick to judge others using these same standards. Only Christ can be the perfect fair judge. Only as we allow Him to govern our hearts can we learn to be as fair in our treatment of others as we expect others to be toward us. Reflect on the last week and determine if you have judged someone unfairly. If you have, seek God for forgiveness. Lord give us eyes of compassion and hearts of mercy so that we may judge with righteousness.

NOVEMBER 21

"Now, therefore," says the Lord, "Turn to Me with
all your heart, with fasting, with weeping, and with
mourning." So rend your heart, and not your
garments; return to the Lord your God, for He is
gracious and merciful, slow to anger, and of great
kindness; and He relents from doing harm.

—Joel 2:12–13

God does not delight in sending hardship, but to bring rebellious people or a disobedient believer to repentance, He will use trials and even tragedies if He must. He wants to bless His people not judge them, and at times, it takes serious measures. In Joel 2, God was warning the people to turn to Him while there was still time. Destruction would soon fall upon them if they did not repent and turn back to God. Because we do not know when our lives will end, we should trust and obey God now while we can. Deep remorse was often shown by tearing one's clothing. But God didn't want an outward display without a true inward repentance. The Lord looks at a person's thoughts and intentions (1 Samuel 16:7). We must be sure our expression of repentance is genuine and not just an outward action. While everyone can see our outward appearance, only God knows what our heart really looks like.

The Lord tells us that we are to weep, mourn, and to fast. To weep is to express your sorrow by shedding tears. To mourn is to feel grief or deep sorrow for your sinfulness and disobedience. You must truly be sorry in your heart for turning away from God. The Lord also calls us to fast. Fasting is simply an outward indication of an inward sincerity, evidence of urgency you feel when praying for a need. You are willing to give up something that feeds your natural man to show God you are serious about rendering your heart to Him. Don't let anything, or anyone hinder you from turning back to God. If you need forgiveness, render your heart and seek God now while you have the chance.

NOVEMBER 22

Therefore, as the elect of God, holy and
beloved, put on tender mercies, kindness,
humility, meekness, longsuffering.
—Colossians 3:12

There are many scriptures that warn us about pride. James 4:6 tells us that God resists the proud, but gives grace to the humble. Prideful people are never humble and pride can ruin a person's life. Pride makes you self-centered and self-sufficient. Pride leads you to conclude that you deserve all you can see, touch, or imagine. It creates greedy appetites; the more you have, the more you desire, and the more you pursue it. When you are prideful, you are never satisfied and convince yourself that you deserve more. The cure from pride is humility. A humble spirit is not proud, or haughty. A person with a humble spirit is meek, modest, and lowly. God resists the proud, but gives grace to the humble. To the humble, all God does is right and good. Humility is always ready to praise God for the simplest of things and does not take His mercy for granted. A humble person submits unconditionally to all that God says.

In Colossians 3, Paul offers you a strategy to help you live for God each day: imitate Christ's compassionate, forgiving attitude (3:12–13); let love guide your life (3:14); let the peace of God rule in your heart (3:15); always be thankful (3:15); keep God's Word in you at all times (3:16); and live as a representative of Jesus Christ (3:17). All the virtues that Paul encourages you to develop are bound together by love. As you clothe yourself with these virtues, the last garment you are to put on is love (3:14) which holds all of the others in place. Have you clothed yourself with love today?

NOVEMBER 23

Not that we are sufficient of ourselves to
think of anything as being from ourselves,
but our efficiency is from God.
—2 Corinthians 3:5

Without God you can do nothing (John 15:5). Everything you do is because God has given you the gifts and abilities to perform those tasks. The gifts that He has given to you are not about you, but about Him and are to be used for His purpose. No one is too talented or capable that he or she can succeed in life without depending on God every step of the way. All your talents and skills can be taken away in a heartbeat. When you hesitate on doing something the Lord has asked you to do because you feel you don't have the knowledge, or skills to do it, then you need to examine your heart. Such hesitation indicates that you are relying on your own strength and abilities instead of believing that God will provide everything you need to accomplish the task.

Your trust must not be in your own self confidence but in confidence that your efficiency comes from God. The Lord will perfect that which He puts your hands to do. Is there something in your life that God has asked you to do that you have been putting off? Do you feel a tugging in your spirit that God wants you to do something right now but you have resisted His Spirit? Spend some time alone with God and ask Him to reveal to you things that He has asked you to do that you have neglected. Seek God for forgiveness and then set out to do that which God has asked you to do. Rely on God and not on yourself to complete the task. Then thank the Lord for His efficiency and provision every step of the way.

NOVEMBER 24

And I, brethren, when I came to you, did
not come with excellence of speech or of wisdom
declaring to you the testimony of God. For I
determined not to know anything among you
except Jesus Christ and Him crucified.
—1 Corinthians 2:1–2

Many people want a powerful relationship with God, but they will not discipline themselves to seek God in order to obtain it. Therefore, they feel defeated before they even begin. They cannot see themselves ever having an intimate relationship with God. The key to finding and knowing God is to put Him first. In all your ways you must know, recognize and acknowledge Him and He will direct and make straight and plain your paths (Proverbs 3:6). Everything is worthless compared to the infinite value of knowing Jesus Christ. Like Paul, you must count all things as garbage, so that you can gain Christ and become one with Him. It is not through your righteous deeds, but you become righteous through faith in Christ. For God's way of making you right with Himself depends on faith (Philippians 3:8–9). Passionately seek after Him to know Him and the power of His resurrection.

There is a vast difference between knowing a person's actions and knowing what is deep in his heart. Knowing God is going beyond the recognition of His character and qualities but experiencing them as well. God is looking for people whose hearts are devoted to Him for who He is, and not for what He does. The people who want to bring delight and pleasure to the heart of the Father and who seek Him diligently will come to understand His ways. When you know Him, you can effectively make Him known to others. Purpose in your heart to know Him. Seek Him and search for His wisdom as you would for treasure (Proverbs 2:4). Know Him and then make Him known.

NOVEMBER 25

I will praise the name of God with a song,
and will magnify Him with thanksgiving.
This also shall please the Lord better than
an ox or bull, which has horns and hooves.
—Psalm 69:30–31

Thanksgiving Day is a time we should reflect on the goodness and blessings of the Lord and to come before Him, honoring Him with praise and thanksgiving. God loves to hear the praises of His people. It delights Him more than any sacrifice we make. And so we take the time right now to give thanks unto the Lord.

We thank You God, for giving us victory over sin and death through Jesus Christ our Lord (1 Corinthians 15:57)! You are worthy, O Lord, to receive glory and honor and power, for You created all things and it is for Your pleasure that they exist and were created (Revelation 4:11). We give thanks to You, for Your faithful love endures forever (Psalm 107:1). Thank You Lord for every prayer that You have answered. Thank You for the wisdom You give us to make wise choices. Thank You for the trials we go through that make us stronger and help our faith to grow. Thank you for always being there with us, guiding us and protecting us from danger. Thank You Father for Your mercy, love, and forgiveness and teaching us to be merciful, loving, and forgiving toward others.

Thank You Lord for the gift of life. Thank You for our salvation through Christ Jesus and may we never take our salvation for granted. Thank You Jesus for showing us the way and being an example for us to live by. Thank You for giving us the Father's heart that we may share the love of the Father to others. Thank You Lord for family and friends. May we never take another for granted but also show compassion to each and every one of them as You have shown it to us. I thank You Lord for each person who reads this Whisper of Hope. Happy Thanksgiving to you all and may the Lord truly bless you this Thanksgiving day.

NOVEMBER 26

Therefore I rejoice that I have
confidence in you in everything.
—2 Corinthians 7:16

Who does your confidence lie in? Is the Lord your security, or do you rely on your own strength and ability to accomplish things? Do you react to the situations around you, or do you wait upon God with quietness and confidence? Do you step out in confidence that the Lord is your provider when He asks you to do something, or do you hesitate because of your inadequacies? If God has confidence in you to ask you to do something, then you need to respond in confidence to Him knowing that He shall supply everything you need to do whatever He asks you to do.

If you do not act in response to God's directive, you will never receive His blessings in the matter. God gives you strength according to the task, but He gives it to you as you do the work and not beforehand. To hesitate is to become more weak and timid, for it is a sense of inadequacy that causes you to draw back with fear and not move forward. This draws attention to yourself, and because there is never sufficient power within you to do the Father's work, any focus on your own strength or ability will soon persuade you that the task is impossible. Never delay receipt of the blessings that God has waiting for you. He can only fill that which you give Him. Are you doing the work that God has called you to do, or has your doubts stopped you short? Walk in confidence knowing that God has confidence in you.

NOVEMBER 27

My soul melts from heaviness; strengthen me
according to Your Word. Remove from me the
way of lying, and grant me Your law graciously.
—Psalm 119:28–29

When you are hurting or heavy laden, everyone wants to make you feel better. Some speak words of encouragement, while others bring more confusion and pain. And then there is the voice inside your mind which speaks to you as well, the all familiar negative self-talk the enemy tries to speak to you during your pain. "You won't get through this. God does not hear your prayers. I am always overlooked and someone else gets the promotion. I will never receive healing. I will never recover financially." The negative talk goes on and on once you allow it to start. The psalmist must have recognized this voice and knew it was a voice that could not be trusted. In the midst of his pain, he wanted to hear the truth. He asked the Lord to remove from him the way of lying. He knew the voice inside was speaking lies to himself.

So how do you keep from lying to yourself in the midst of your pain? How do you take control of your thoughts before they get out of control? Instead of believing the voice you hear inside, or the negative talk from others, hold onto the promises of God. Speak the way Jesus spoke to the enemy…But it is written (Matthew 4:4, 7, 10). God will never forsake you and He heals the broken-hearted, binding up their wounds (Psalm 147:3). Allow the Word of God to soothe your soul and quiet your heart. Remember that the Lord is with you in the midst of your pain. His truth will remove your fears, change your beliefs and attitudes, and speak life into your heart. Allow the Word of God to speak and strengthen you today.

NOVEMBER 28

As for you, my son Solomon, know the God of your father,
and serve Him with a loyal heart and with a willing mind;
for the Lord searches all hearts and understands all the intent
of the thoughts. If you seek Him, He will be found by you;
but if you forsake Him, He will cast you off forever.
—1 Chronicles 28:9

David told his son Solomon the key to success in life was to serve God with a loyal heart and a willing mind. If he sought the Lord, He would be found. God promises us that we will find Him when we seek Him with all our hearts (Jeremiah 29:13). If we draw near to God, He draws near to us (James 4:8). Our ability to know and serve God begins with humility. Many seek God's wisdom but are not willing to humble themselves and follow wisdom's path. They are not willing to let go of earthly desires for spiritual gain. Many fall into the trap that Solomon fell into. Solomon asked God for wisdom and God gave him abundant wisdom. Growing in God's wisdom, Solomon soon relied more on his own wisdom instead of leaning on God to give him the wisdom. Eventually Solomon stopped relying on the Lord and relied entirely on his own ability. This led to his downfall (1 Kings 11:1–13).

When you fail to humble yourself and take time to hear from God, you become your own God. You become easily deceived because you are following after your passions and you make decisions that appeal to your own desires and not the Lord's. By doing so, you miss out on God's very best for you. So how do you avoid these pitfalls? Daily surrender your heart and passions to the Lord. Ask God to open your heart to the truth and give you a willing heart to obey Him. Then obey what God has asked of you. Like David giving advice to his son, so I too give advice to you, my daughters. Yvonne and Jennifer, serve the Lord with a loyal heart and with a willing mind. Seek and search for Him with all your heart and He will be found (Jeremiah 29:13). Lord, bless my children with Godly wisdom and may they always serve You and You alone.

NOVEMBER 29

*"Every branch in Me that does not bear fruit He
takes away; and every branch that bears fruit
He prunes, that it may bear more fruit. If anyone
does not abide in Me, he is cast out as a branch
and is withered, and they gather them and throw
them into the fire and they are burned."*

—John 15:2, 6

Pruning has always been mysterious to me. In my carnal mind, I think that if you trim something back, you are taking away from the bush. Why bother trimming something back when it looks fine the way it is? There is a hesitation of letting go in fear that it may not grow back and look as good. But it never fails; the bush always produces new growth. Jesus makes a distinction between two kinds of pruning: cutting back and cutting off branches. Fruitful branches are cut back to promote growth. Many times we do not want to be trimmed; we are fine just the way we are. But without pruning there is no new growth. God must sometimes discipline us or take us out of our comfort zone in order to strengthen our character and faith.

Branches that don't bear fruit are cut off at the trunk because they are worthless and could infect the rest of the tree. People who do not bear fruit for God will be cut from His life-giving power. Many people try to be good, honest people who do what is right. But Jesus says that the only way to live a true and good life is to stay close to Him like a branch attached to a vine. Apart from Christ your efforts are unfruitful. Are you receiving the nourishment and life offered by Christ? Are you allowing yourself to be pruned to promote new growth? Are you producing much fruit? Allow Christ the Vine, and God the Gardener to make you fruitful. Daily He sends sunshine and rain to make you grow and constantly nurtures and prepares you to blossom. Align yourself daily to receive from God and you will begin to produce much fruit.

NOVEMBER 30

*"Blessed is the man who trusts in the Lord, and
whose hope is the Lord. For he shall be like a tree
planted by the waters, which spreads out its roots by
the river, and will not fear when heat comes; but its
leaf will be green, and will not be anxious in the
year of drought nor will cease from yielding fruit."*
—Jeremiah 17:7–8

When you pray, you are to find a quiet place where you can shut the door to distractions around you and spend some quality time with the Lord (Matthew 6:6). Worship music can help you enter into His presence where you can fellowship and listen for the Lord's promptings. It is these times of closeness to God which causes your roots to reach deep into God. Deep roots make strong healthy trees. Most trees have as much under the ground root systems as they have above the ground in branches and leaves. You can compare the roots to your private life with God and the branches and leaves to your public life with others. Deep roots create stability and confidence in times when strong winds come. There is tranquility within because you have tapped into the source of strength.

When everything in your Christian life is above the ground, you have very little depth of stability. You will be easily tossed back and forth and will lack confidence in God. For many, the vast majority of their time with God is in a public setting, going to church, Bible studies, or prayer meetings. You need as much time with the Lord below the surface in your secret place as you have above the ground with fellow Christians. When a life of private fellowship is developed with the Lord, it will be evident. Your life will be rooted in the promises of God and no matter what may come your way, you will withstand firm.

DECEMBER 1

*But the priests, the Levites, the sons of Zadok, who kept charge of
My sanctuary when the children of Israel went astray from Me,
they shall come near Me to minister to Me; and they shall stand
before Me to offer to Me the fat and the blood," says the Lord
God. "They shall enter My sanctuary, and they shall come near
My table to minister to Me, and they shall keep My charge."*
—Ezekiel 44:15–16

Come near to Me. Come near to Me. Hear the Lord echoing in
your heart, "Come near Me and minister to Me." This is an invitation for you and me from Almighty God to come into the inner
chambers and spend time with Him. God wants some of our time
reserved just for Him, to minister unto Him. We become busy ministering to others and not meeting the Lord's needs. Moses went
up to the mountain to spend time alone with God. When he came
down from the mountain, his face shone from the glory of God
(Exodus 34:29).

It is in the inner court that our life and attitudes will be affected
in such a way that people will know that we have spent time alone
with God. Our face may not shine as Moses's did, but the proof of
our time with Him will be evident. You cannot be in the presence of
God and not be changed. His very presence will saturate you with His
influence, His passion and His love. He will put in you the things that
He wants to flow through you. As you become comfortable being
alone with God, it forms a beautiful relationship that continues to
increase.

DECEMBER 2

Let the word of Christ dwell in you richly in all wisdom,
teaching and admonishing one another in psalms and hymns
and spiritual songs, singing with grace in your hearts to the Lord.
And whatever you do in word or deed, do all in the name of the
Lord Jesus, giving thanks to God the Father through Him.
—Colossians 3:16–17

Scripture teaches us to let the richness of Christ's words live in our hearts and use His words to teach, counsel, and encourage others. Whatever we do in word or deed must bring honor to Christ in every aspect and activity of our daily living. As a Christian, we represent Christ to those around us. All of our daily interactions should reflect the light of Christ in us. This includes the desire to have a healing ministry.

Many desire to have a healing ministry. They want to be able to lay hands on people and have the power of God move through them and bring healing and miracles to others. Let us each start a healing ministry that first touches the souls of people and then physical healings will follow. We should not be content to heal bodies while wounding souls. We must learn to minister blessings and comfort to other's spirits through our words and actions. Let the Word of God inhabit your conversation with others. Allow the Word of God to become a part of your spiritual DNA so that His Word influences all aspects of your life. Let your words bring glory to God. Desire to be used by God in the healing ministry of body, soul and spirit.

DECEMBER 3

For this is he who was spoken of by the
prophet Isaiah, saying: "The voice of one
crying in the wilderness: 'Prepare the way
of the Lord; make His paths straight.'"

—Matthew 3:3

John the Baptist quoted a prophecy from Isaiah (Isaiah 40:3). Like Isaiah, John was a prophet who urged the people to confess their sins and live for God. To those who would listen, they both taught the message of repentance and seeking the forgiveness through God's love. John the Baptist prepared the way for Jesus. John did not want to baptize Jesus and felt unworthy to do so, because He knew that Jesus was the Messiah. But Jesus answered and said to him, "Permit it to be so now, for thus it is fitting for us to fulfill all righteousness." And so, John baptized Jesus (Matthew 3:13–15). We are to prepare ourselves for the coming of the Lord. People who do not know Jesus in a personal way need to prepare to meet the Lord. We are to make our paths straight, follow the Lord, and not take any side trips along the way.

We need to prepare the way not only for ourselves, but also for others. There are many who are being led astray by misconceptions, false teachings, and ignorance. We can make a straight road for them by correcting the misconceptions that might be hindering them from coming to Christ. Many are turned away from serving God because of Christians whose actions do not match their words. God looks beyond our words and religious activities to see if our conduct backs up what we say. He judges our words by the actions that accompany them. Other people judge us the same way. We must prove by the way we live that we have turned from our sins and are living the path that leads to the Lord. Examine the path you are traveling and make sure your path is straight.

DECEMBER 4

*Who is the man that fears the Lord? Him
shall He teach in the way He chooses. The
secret of the Lord is with those who fear Him,
and He will show them His covenant.*

—Psalm 25:12, 14

Friendship with the Lord is reserved for those who fear Him. God offers intimate and lasting friendship to those who reverence Him. The more we revere the Lord, the deeper the friendship with God will grow. To fear the Lord is to recognize His attributes: He is holy, almighty, righteous, pure, all-knowing, all powerful, and all wise. When we truly come to know who God is, we gain a clearer picture of ourselves: sinful, weak, and frail and in need of a Savior. When we recognize who God is and who we are, we will fall to His feet in humility for we know our true condition.

There is nothing profound in knowing the secrets of God. All we have to do is fear Him for who He is and choose to fellowship with Him. The Lord will teach us the way to choose and will share with us hidden treasures and secrets that He reserves for His chosen ones. We are all God's chosen people. He loves each of us the same and will not hold back anything from us. How much do you desire to know the secrets of the Lord? Desire Him! Desire to follow Him. Desire to seek Him with your whole heart, mind, and soul. Desire to love Him with an everlasting love that changes who you are and what you do. Let Him capture your heart and He will capture yours. The secret of the Lord is with those who fear Him, and He will show them His covenant.

DECEMBER 5

Thank God for His Son—
a gift too wonderful for words.
— 2 Corinthians 9:15

The greatest gift that has ever been given is Jesus Christ. God so loved the world that He gave His only begotten Son so that whoever believes in Him should not perish but live in eternity with Him (John 3:16). We are here because of Christ's willingness to be given as a Gift—a gift too wonderful for words. This is the season where we are busy looking for that perfect gift for friends and family. Having trouble finding that perfect gift? Here are a few suggestions:

- The gift of genuine friendship—be true and honest no matter what the cost.
- The gift of time—Be there for someone who is sick, lonely, elderly, or depressed.
- The gift of sincerity—say what you mean and mean what you say.
- The gift of love—let others know that they are loved and that God loves them.
- The gift of peace—let peace rule in your heart and share the Gospel of peace to those around you.
- The gift of joy—let others see the joy of Christ in you and be willing to help them find this joy in themselves.
- The gift of thanks—let people know that they are special and thank them for being a part of your life.
- The gift of forgiveness—let go of offenses, forgive others, and be the first to say I'm sorry.

As we begin this month in preparation for Christmas, remember the reason for the season. Offer the gift of Jesus Christ to someone this year.

DECEMBER 6

You keep track of all my sorrows.
You have collected all my tears in your bottle.
You have recorded each one in your book.
—Psalm 56:8, NLT

Tears are a good thing. They release the pressure of the pain we feel on the inside. Some see tears as a loss of control, or a lack of faith. They will say to themselves, "If I had more faith in God, I wouldn't be feeling this sad or hurt." But there will be times that sadness will come and we just have to allow ourselves to be sad. We have to allow the tears to flow and allow God to work in the situation. God sees every sorrow we feel and collects all our tears in a bottle. He sees the sorrow we feel when we have lost someone dear to us, or when we've been forced to let go of a dream, or live through a nightmare. Even in our deepest sorrow, God cares. When we are discouraged and feel like no one understands, we must remember that God knows every problem and sees every tear.

When the Lord speaks, He does what He says. He will wipe away every tear (Isaiah 25:8), no matter how painful the situation may be. Not only will all our tears be wiped away, He will remove all the sorrow that caused them (Revelation 21:4). Are you hurting inside? Has someone caused you much pain, or are you going through a nightmare that has shattered your dream? Do you feel like you need a good cry? Take the time right now and allow yourself to cry. Allow the tears to release the pressure you feel inside and then allow God to work in your circumstances to remove the sorrow that caused the pain and tears. Allow God to minister to you in your deepest sorrow, for God really does care.

DECEMBER 7

Do not remember the sins of my youth, nor
my transgressions; according to Your mercy
remember me, for Your goodness' sake, O Lord.
—Psalm 25:7

How do you want people to remember you? How do you want God to remember you? When you think about others, how do you remember them? David knew all too well his past sinfulness and transgressions and asked the Lord to not remember them, but to remember him according to His mercies. In order for God to show mercy upon us, we must be willing to show that same mercy to others. Make a list of different people that have crossed the path of your life, include friends, family, and acquaintances. Now think of each person and what is the first thing that you remember about them? If it is something negative, then you have not extended mercy to that person.

The best way to get rid of offenses we hold against another person is to pray for that person. Ask the Lord to work in that area of their life. Ask the Lord to help you to forgive and to extend mercy to that person, and then ask the Lord to extend His mercy upon them too. The only way to truly let go of offenses is to bless the person. Speak promises from scripture upon their life and as you do, you will begin to have a change of heart toward that person. Ask the Lord to help you to remember the good in that person's life. We all want to be remembered for the good things we have done in life. I want to be remembered as an encourager, someone showing the Father's love to others and leading them to a deeper, closer walk with the Lord. I want to be remembered as someone who not only knows Truth, but walks in God's truth. Think of how you want to be remembered and then walk accordingly.

DECEMBER 8

So David said to Nathan, "I have sinned against
the Lord." And Nathan said to David, "The
Lord also has put away your sin; you shall not die.
However, because by this deed you have given great
occasion to the enemies of the Lord to blaspheme,
the child also who is born to you shall surely die."
—2 Samuel 12:13–14

What happens when we sin and delay asking God for forgiveness? Are there consequences? Are the consequences the same if we would have repented immediately? When David committed adultery with Bathsheba, he didn't repent immediately. It was some time later that he repented and only after the Lord sent a prophet to confront him with his sin (2 Samuel 12:1–14). No matter how terrible we have sinned, we can pour out our heart to God and seek His forgiveness. When God forgives us and restores our relationship with Him, he doesn't eliminate the consequences of our wrong doing. There may be irreversible consequences in our sin.

David confessed and repented of his sin but God's judgment was that his child would die. Why did his child have to die? We have to remember that this was not a judgment on the child being conceived out of wedlock, but a judgment on David's sin. Could it be that the child's death was a greater punishment for David than his own death would have been? Discipline is designed to change our hearts and obey God. David returned to God and the Lord forgave him, opening the way to begin a new life again with Him. When we return to God, accept His forgiveness, and change our ways, the Lord gives us a fresh start. Remember that the consequences of our sins not only affect us, but those around us as well. Is there something in your life that you have not sought the Lord for forgiveness? Repent now, receive His forgiveness and then move ahead with a new and fresh approach to life.

DECEMBER 9

Pray, too, that we will be rescued from wicked
and evil people, for not everyone is a believer.
But the Lord is faithful; he will strengthen
you and guard you from the evil one.
—2 Thessalonians 3:2–3, NLT

The Lord warns us that the time is coming when there will be a great rebellion against God and many will abandon sound doctrine and will instead embrace whatever teaching seems popular at that moment (2 Thessalonians 2:3). In our daily walk with God, there is a fierce struggle among invisible spiritual powers. As the end times approach, we will see more and more violence, hatred and destruction. It will be a power struggle between good and evil until the very end, but we know that our Lord has already won the battle and it is just a matter of time before the evil one receives his just reward.

You must not be caught off guard, nor should you be afraid of the things to come. Instead, anchor yourself in the Word of God and pray for God's protection against the evil one and for those who reject God's Word. If you stay close to God, He will not allow the adversary to swallow you up. He will deliver you, honor you, and be glorified through you. Although the battle may seem fierce at times and all hope is gone, do not despair, for the Lord is on your side and will win the battle for you. You need to protect yourself from the evil one. How do you prepare and protect yourself? First, take the threat of spiritual attacks seriously. Many do not believe that there are invisible spiritual powers waging war against the souls of people. America never believed that we would be attacked by terrorism, but it happened on 9/11. Then fight hard! Pray that God will give you strength and help you when you are personally attacked. Stay alert. Study God's Word to recognize Satan's style and tactics. Use the Word of God as a weapon against the evil one. Trust in God. He is faithful and will guard you against the evil one.

DECEMBER 10

*For "He who would love life and see good days,
let him refrain his tongue from evil, and his lips
from speaking deceit. Let him turn away from
evil and do good; let him seek peace and pursue it."*

—1 Peter 3:10–11

There is always a lot of talk about peace this time of year. You sing it in Christmas carols and hear many tell you that Christ came to bring peace on earth and good will to men. But how many of us really live in peace. Even in the season when we should feel it the most, many are stressed out from shopping and getting ready for Christmas. So how does one find peace? The scripture above gives us four things a person can do to find peace. First we have to keep our tongue free from evil. Death and life are in the power of the tongue (Proverbs 18:21) and we can bring blessings, or misery upon ourselves with the words we speak. We must choose our words wisely. The second step to finding peace is to turn away from wickedness. We commit more sins with our tongue than any other part of our body. Turning away from wickedness means that we remove ourselves from people who gossip, lest we get caught in their trap as well. We must examine ourselves to see if there is any wickedness in our hearts and then take action to remove it.

The third step to finding peace is to do good. The decision to do right must follow the decision to stop doing wrong. Some people turn from their sin but never make the decision to start doing right. This will eventually cause a person to fall back into their sin. The last step to finding peace in this passage is to search for it, to pursue it, to go after it. Peace will not come to you, you have to find it. You must take actions in order to achieve peace in your life. If, in the midst of shopping and preparing for Christmas, you find yourself stressed out, take some time in your busyness to find peace. Take the time to be alone with God and ask Him to restore inner peace.

DECEMBER 11

My soul longs, yes, even faints for
the courts of the Lord; my heart and
my flesh cry out for the living God.

—Psalm 84:2

God has a wealth of knowledge and spiritual power that He desires to give us. You are the only one who can determine how much of that depth will be obtained. How far are you willing to go to quench the thirst that is within you? The more deeply we yearn for God to pour Himself through us, the more deeply He will cultivate us. Some people are not determined or desperate enough to seek Him. They want His presence without putting any effort into seeking His face. Rarely do your find a lost diamond without putting the effort into finding it. We must be willing to put some effort into finding the deep things of God if we are to experience His glory. Deep calls unto deep (Psalm 42:7). The deeper we go, the deeper He goes.

Are you yearning to find purpose in your life? Are you longing or thirsty for something lasting in your life? Is your soul longing to enter the courts of the Lord? God alone is the only one who can satisfy your deepest longing. We are all destined for a purpose. Spending time alone with God will help you determine and fulfill that purpose. Do not deny yourself the privilege of communion and fellowship with the Father. Oh Lord, my heart and flesh cry out for You, the living God. You are my hope, my joy, and the living water that quenches my thirst. It is You and You alone that I desire. Take me deeper into Your holy presence. May I experience You in a way that will change me forever.

DECEMBER 12

Though the fig tree may not blossom, nor fruit be on the veins; though the labor of the olive may fail, and the fields yield no food; though the flock may be cut off from the fold, and there be no herd in the stalls—Yet I will rejoice in the Lord, I will joy in the God of my salvation.
—Habakkuk 3:17–18

You must trust in God in the dark times. Crop failure and death of animals would devastate any person. Yet Habakkuk rejoiced in the Lord even in the times of starvation and loss. His feelings were not controlled by the events around Him but by faith in God's ability to give Him strength. He took his eyes off his difficulties and looked to God. In difficult times, faith becomes a matter of devoted allegiance to the Lord Jesus Christ. You must have confidence in Him regardless of the circumstances. Disappointments are inevitable; discouragement and hopelessness is a choice.

God has a unique plan for your life, one that does not change with unexpected events. When things don't go as you planned, rejoice in the Lord anyway. Sometimes God allows disappointments to occur so that we learn to rely on Him more fully, to walk by faith and not by sight. In the daily disappointments that threaten to consume your emotional well-being and take your attention away from the Lord, you have a choice to make. You can allow the circumstances to control you or you can allow Jesus to do so. You do not have to be a victim of your feelings or circumstances. You can choose to look to God. Let go of disappointments. God holds your future in His hands and the best is yet to come. Cling to God and His Word. Allow the scars of disappointments to fade away as you look forward to what the Lord has in store for you. Allow Christ to be your strength, stability and hope.

DECEMBER 13

Behold, the eye of the Lord is on those who
fear Him, on those who hope in His mercy.
—Psalm 33:18

God is constantly watching over His people. The eye of the Lord is on those who fear Him, on those who hope in His mercy. Fear and hope are generally thought to be contrasts with each other. But in the presence of God in worship, they are found side by side in harmony. There is a fear that involves torment, but that fear is cast out by perfect love for there is no fear in love (1 John 4:18). There is a fear that is found in the heavens, a holy fear. The deeper we bow before His holiness in holy fear, in deep reverence and awe, the more His holiness rests upon us.

When you cry out to God in prayer, where are your eyes focused? Are they focused on the Lord, or are they focused on your circumstance? God's eyes are upon His people and our eyes should be focused on Him. When you look into the innocence of a child as he cries out his heart to you, it is hard to say no to him. When we cry out to God, and our eyes are focused on Him, it is very hard for God to say no to His children. When our eyes are focused on Him, the Holy Spirit will lead us to pray according to the Father's will and His ears are open to our cry. When our eyes are focused on the Lord, it takes our eyes and thoughts away from ourselves and causes us to center our thoughts toward God.

Pay attention to how you pray and see where your eyes are focused. If your eyes are not looking up to the Lord, meeting Him looking down upon you, refocus your eyes before you begin to pray. As your train your eyes to focus on the Lord and look into His gazing eyes, the deeper the reverence, awe and holy fear you will feel. The eye of the Lord is on those who fear Him. The eyes of the Lord are on the righteous and His ears are open to their cry (Psalm 34:15).

DECEMBER 14

And because you are sons, God has sent
forth the Spirit of His Son into your
hearts, crying out, "Abba, Father!"
—Galatians 4:6

Just because someone lives in a household doesn't mean that the person communicates and fellowships with the other members of the family. There are some families who do not get along. People live together for the physical needs so that they have a roof over their heads and someone to help pay for the bills. Outside of that, there is no fellowship or communication. God has sent His Holy Spirit to dwell in our hearts. Some have accepted the Holy Spirit into their hearts, but the relationship has faded away. They call upon the Holy Spirit when there is a physical need, but outside of that, the Holy Spirit dwells alone in the corner of their hearts while they go about their own business.

The Holy Spirit wants to be an active participant in our lives. He dwells in the center of our hearts ready to respond to our needs, but the relationship needs to go well beyond that. He wants to sit down and sup with us, to share things over a cup of coffee or tea. He wants to know everything, the good, the bad, and the ugly. We have been taught to release our burdens to the Lord, and we do a good job at that. We give the Lord liberty to take away all that is displeasing to Him. But God is asking us to give Him the priceless things which He has given us. All the blessings, all the good things the Lord has given us He wants us to give to the Holy Spirit, not to take them away from us, but to keep them for us, that He may bless them further. He wants to guard our treasures. How is your relationship with the Holy Spirit? Does He sit dormant in your heart, or is He actively a part of your life? It is never too late to rekindle a relationship that has become dormant.

DECEMBER 15

Yes, they spoke against God: They said, "Can God prepare a table in the wilderness. Behold, He struck the rock, so that the waters gushed out, and the streams overflowed. Can He give bread also? Can He provide meat for His people?"
—Psalm 78:19–20

How do you approach God when you pray? Do you go before Him with confidence knowing that He is able to do immeasurably more than all we ask or imagine, according to His power that is at work within us (Ephesians 3:20)? The Israelites knew what God could do, but their expectation could not rise beyond their experience of what they had already seen God do, or their own thoughts of what might be possible. They tested God in their hearts, the Lord heard it, and He was furious and His anger came against Israel (Psalm 78:21). They did not believe in God and did not trust in His salvation (Psalm 78:22)

What do you believe deep down inside of you? Do you limit the Holy One? You must think and believe the impossible, no matter how impossible it looks. Allow God's heart to touch your heart, heart-to-heart, so that His infinite ways become a reality to you. Confess how little you understand about what God is willing to do for you. Confess how you have limited God by your own thoughts and understanding of what He is able to do. Then wait upon God to do the impossible. Lord, my thoughts are so limited and my heart does not know the true reality in this matter. But my hope is in You Lord. I wait upon You to accomplish exceedingly abundantly above all that I ask or think because Your mighty power is at work within me.

DECEMBER 16

Let integrity and uprightness
preserve me, for I wait for You.

—Psalm 25:21

In order for food to last, you must preserve it. You can't put vegetables from a garden into a jar and think that they will be healthy to eat in a few months. There is a process that needs to take place to properly preserve food. In order to not become contaminated, we too must take precautions to preserve our walk with God. Two powerful forces that need to be applied to our lives to preserve us along life's way are integrity and honesty.

Integrity is a term used to describe a person's level of honesty, morality, and willingness to do right. Integrity is being what we say we are. It keeps us from claiming to be honest while living as if we do not know God. Integrity means doing the right thing at all times even if no one is watching. A person of integrity keeps his promises, is truthful, and takes responsibility for his mistakes or failures.

Honesty is truthfulness, sincerity, or frankness; freedom from deceit or fraud. A person can be honest and still not have integrity but a person cannot have integrity without having honesty. Honesty is giving your word while integrity is keeping it. Honesty makes us learn God's ways and strive to fulfill them. Honesty says this is God's way and integrity says I will walk consistently in it.

When we are willing to seek God, learn from His Word, and obey His commands, then we will know the true meaning of what it means to walk with integrity and honesty. When we walk in the two powerful forces of integrity and uprightness, the Lord will preserve our lives and we will live in His presence forever (Psalm 41:12). Let integrity and uprightness preserve you.

DECEMBER 17

Therefore, holy brethren, partakers of the
heavenly calling, consider the Apostle and
High Priest of our confession, Christ Jesus.
—Hebrews 3:1

For Jews, the highest human authority was the high priest. The high priest was the mediator between God and his people. His job was to regularly offer animal sacrifices and to intercede with God for the forgiveness of sins on behalf of the people. For Christians, the highest human authority was the apostles. Jesus, the Apostle and High Priest, is the ultimate authority in the church. Jesus Christ is now our High Priest (Hebrews 4:14). He came to earth as a human being and once and for all paid the penalty for our sins by His own sacrificial death and by His atonement, restored the broken relationship with God. Like the high priest, Jesus mediates between God and us. He intercedes for us before God (Romans 8:34). As God's representative, He assures us of God's forgiveness.

We are released from sin's dominion over us when we commit ourselves fully to Christ, trusting completely in what He has done for us. It is God working in us, giving us the desire and the power to do what pleases him (Philippians 2:13). Because of Christ, we can go boldly to the throne of our gracious God. There we will receive his mercy, and we will find grace to help us when we need it most (Hebrews 4:16). As one of the partakers of a heavenly calling, our destination is heaven (Hebrews 3:1). We are set apart for God. Our appearance, wealth, profession, and ministry do not define us. Only our identity in Christ defines us and makes us complete. We cannot add to it and the world can take nothing from it. Praise be to God! May the God of peace who brought up our Lord Jesus Christ from the dead, through the blood of the everlasting covenant, equip you with all you need for doing his will. May he produce in you, through the power of Jesus Christ, every good thing that is pleasing to him (Hebrews 13:20–21). To God be the glory forever and ever.

DECEMBER 18

In everything give thanks; for this is the
will of God in Christ Jesus for you.
—1 Thessalonians 5:18

In everything we are to give thanks to God. This does not mean that we are to thank Him for everything that happens to us. Evil is not from God, so we should not thank Him for it. But when evil strikes, we can still be thankful for God's presence and for the good that He will accomplish through the distress. Sickness is not from God, so we should not thank Him for it. But when sickness strikes, we can still be thankful for God's presence in the midst of our illness and for the miracle or healing that He will accomplish through the sickness.

When our heart is directed toward God, there is no calamity or sickness that does not work for our blessing. When we do not strive against adversity, its power to hurt us is destroyed. Instead of devoting all our energy fighting the affliction, we must show courage in the face of our adversity. God will give us strength while He walks through it with us. The greater the opposition, the greater the opportunity for God to show Himself strong on our behalf. Suffering through adversity may be painful, but it will make our victory all the sweeter. The flesh may suffer, but the spirit will be blessed. God will not fail anyone. His voice speaks through every situation to the ear that is yielded to His Spirit. His love flows freely through every sorrow to the heart that is devoted to Him. Leave every burden, stress, concern, worry, and unsolved problem with the Lord. Praise Him and rejoice while He works all things out for His glory. I will bless the Lord at all times, His praise shall continually be in my mouth. My soul shall make its boast in the Lord for I put my trust in Him (Psalm 34:1–2).

DECEMBER 19

"Be strong and of good courage, for to this people you shall divide as an inheritance the land which I swore to their fathers to give them. Only be strong and very courageous, that you may observe to do according to all the law which Moses My servant commanded you; do not turn from it to the right hand or to the left, that you may prosper wherever you go."

—Joshua 1:6–7

Many people think that prosperity comes from having power, money, influential personal contacts, and working hard to get ahead. But the strategy for gaining prosperity that God taught Joshua was to be strong and courageous because the task at hand would not be easy. He was to obey God's law and to read and study God's Word. How the world views success and prosperity does not line up with how God views success; in fact, you may not succeed by the world's standards. But in God's eyes, you are a success and His opinion is what counts and lasts forever. When you apply God's Word to your life, it will produce great success.

The phrase "be strong and of good courage" occurs four times in Joshua 1 (vs. 6–7, 9, 18). It was God's encouragement to Joshua as He led the people into the Promised Land. Do you want to be prosperous? God's Word tells us that if our hearts would always fear Him and obey His commands, then we and our children would be prosperous forever (Deuteronomy 5:29). The road ahead may not always be easy, but if you trust in God, be strong and very courageous, God will lead you to victory. Are you facing a difficult task right now? My encouragement to you is to be strong and be courageous. Do not be afraid or terrified for the Lord your God goes with you. He will never leave you nor forsake you. There is a light at the end of the tunnel, and the Lord is preparing the way for prosperity.

DECEMBER 20

*Now the birth of Jesus Christ was as follows: After His
mother Mary was betrothed to Joseph, before they came
together, she was found with child of the Holy Spirit. Then
Joseph, her husband, being a just man, and not wanting
to make her a public example, was minded to put her away
secretly. But while he thought about these things, behold, an
angel of the Lord appeared to him in a dream, saying, "Joseph,
son of David, do not be afraid to take to you Mary your wife,
for that which is conceived in her is of the Holy Spirit. And
she will bring forth a Son, and you shall call His name Jesus,
for He will save His people from their sins."*
—Matthew 1:18–21

What would be going through your mind if you were Mary
or Joseph? How would you explain to your husband-to-be that
although you were pregnant, you did not have an affair? When
Mary told Joseph about her pregnancy, Joseph knew the child was
not his. He had a choice to make. Joseph decided he would break
the engagement, but to do it in a manner that would not cause
public shame to Mary. He intended to act with justice and love.
The birth of Jesus Christ is a supernatural event beyond human
logic and reasoning. Because of this, God sent angels to help
Joseph understand the significance of what was happening and to
confirm Mary's story. Joseph obeyed God, married Mary, and honored her virginity until the baby was born. His willingness to obey
empowered him to be Jesus's chosen earthly father.

When our decisions affect the lives of others, we must always
seek God's wisdom. Joseph had two options: to divorce Mary quickly
or have her stoned. But God gave Joseph a third option—to marry
her. God often shows us that there are more options available than
we think. That is why it is so important to not act out of haste, out of
human wisdom, or out of pressure from others. Sometimes we avoid
doing what is right because of what others might think. Like Joseph,
we must choose to obey God rather than seek the approval of others.

DECEMBER 21

*"Not everyone who says to Me, 'Lord, Lord' shall
enter the kingdom of heaven, but he who does the
will of my Father in heaven. Many will say to me
in that day, 'Lord, Lord have we not prophesied
in Your name, cast out demons in Your name,
and done many wonders in Your name?' And
then I will declare to them, 'I never knew you;
depart from Me, you who practice lawlessness!'"*
—Matthew 7:21–23

I never want to be one whom Jesus tells, "I never knew you,
depart from Me." That is why it is so important that we examine
ourselves to see if our faith is genuine. We are to test ourselves, to
know ourselves, that Jesus Christ is in us lest we be disqualified (2
Corinthians 13:5). Jesus said, "Because you are lukewarm, and neither cold nor hot, I will vomit you out of My mouth" (Revelation
3:16). On Judgment day, only our relationship with Christ, our
acceptance of Him as Savior, and our obedience to Him will matter. Being good and doing religious activities will not reward us
with eternal life. Many are afraid to examine themselves in fear
of what might be exposed by the Holy Spirit. How do we know
whether we are living a lukewarm, half-hearted life if we don't
examine ourselves? What does a lukewarm Christian look like?

Isaiah 29:13 states one condition: they honor Me with their
mouth and lips but their hearts are far from Me. Their worship
of Me is made up of rules taught by men. Lukewarm people tend
to choose what is popular, what is acceptable over what is right.
Scripture is filled with many examples of lukewarm people, those
who are not willing to give everything to follow the Lord all the
way. Examine your heart. Ask the Holy Spirit to reveal any area
in your life where you are living a lukewarm, half-hearted life and
then give that area to the Lord.

DECEMBER 22

"Wash yourselves, make yourselves clean;
put away the evil of your doings from before
My eyes. Cease to do evil. "Come now, let
us reason together," says the Lord, though
your sins are like scarlet, they shall be as
white as snow; though they are red like
crimson, they shall be as wool.

—Isaiah 1:16, 18

When we have worked hard all day outside in the yard, the first thing we want to do is take a shower and wash off the dirt. There is nothing more refreshing than a nice hot shower. In the spiritual realm, there is nothing more refreshing than having the Lord wash away our sins and make us white as snow. Of all the colors that can fade or stain, red has got to be the worse. The stain of our sin seems equally permanent, but God can remove the stain of our sins from our lives if we are willing and allow Him to cleanse us. God is asking us to go before Him, to talk to Him about our sin. He is willing and able to remove every trace and stain of sin… though our sins are red like crimson, they shall be as wool. Sin separates us from God. In His mercy, He calls us to return to Him and be cleansed, forgiven and fully restored to fellowship with Him.

Throughout scripture we see how people continually fell into sin, and yet in His mercy, God continually reached out to them in order to bring His people back to Himself. God is a God of judgment (Romans 2:5), but He is a God of mercy (Deuteronomy 7:9) who wants His people restored unto Himself. Scripture reminds us to wash ourselves and be clean. We are to stop sinning and cease from doing evil (Isaiah 1:16). Sin is always lurking at our back door, and out of our weakness we fall into its grip. Restoration is always awaiting us at the front door. Though our sin may be scarlet, if we open the door and allow restoration to cleanse us, He will make us white as snow.

DECEMBER 23

While Peter thought about the vision, the Spirit
said to him, "Behold, three men are seeking you.
Arise therefore, go down and go with them,
doubting nothing; for I have sent them."
—Acts 10:19–20

W hy is it so easy to believe in the wisdom of man, but when the Holy Spirit speaks to us, we question whether we have heard from God and start doubting ourselves? God desires to make His will known to us and He wants us to trust the Holy Spirit as our daily Guide, doubting nothing. I can remember having to make an important decision in my life about two years ago. I believed that I had heard from the Lord and I asked Him for confirmation. The Lord gave me confirmation, so I made my decision based on what was confirmed in my spirit. Even though I had stepped out in faith, I continued to question whether I had heard correctly. Some of my friends insisted that I had not heard from the Lord and that I was making a huge mistake.

One Sunday while I was in service, the thought of whether I had made the right decision came to my mind again. I told the Lord that I just wanted to do His will. Then the Lord gave me the scripture from Luke 9:62, "No one, having put his hand to the plow, and looking back, is fit for the kingdom of God." The Lord was telling me that I was moving in the right direction and to never look back again regarding this matter. I started to cry, repented for doubting, and never questioned again whether I had heard correctly from God.

Rely on the Holy Spirit to give you specific personal guidance and say "yes" when He prompts you to take a certain action, or speak a certain word. The Holy Spirit will speak to you in the stillness of your heart. Actively listen for the Holy Spirit to speak to you. God rewards those who diligently seek Him (Hebrews 11:6). Diligently seek the Holy Spirit for His guidance, asking for it, expecting it, receiving it, and then obeying it.

DECEMBER 24

"Where is He who has been born King of the
Jews? For we have seen His star in the East and
have come to worship Him." When they heard the
king, they departed; and behold, the star which they
had seen in the East went before them, till it came
and stood over where the young Child was.
—Matthew 2:2, 9

The wise men eagerly journeyed to Bethlehem to welcome the newborn King. They followed the star which led them to the exact location of the child Christ. The star that is placed on the top of Christmas trees is symbolic of the star that the wise men followed. God promised a Savior for the world and the star was the sign of that promise fulfilled on the night that Jesus Christ was born. God always fulfills His promise. Those who are wise still seek Him.

When the wise men entered the house, they saw the young Child with Mary His mother, and fell down and worshiped Him. And when they had opened their treasures, they presented gifts to Him: gold, frankincense, and myrrh (Matthew 2:11). After seeing the star brightly shining, the wise men knew by faith the importance of this birth and they brought only their finest. They did not give gifts to each other. They did not have a Christmas tree at home with presents for their family and friends. The only gift giving that went on during the birth of Christ was to Christ.

Upon entering the home, the wise men felt the power of the Christ child and humbled themselves to Him, worshipping, and laying at his feet the best they had to offer. Even though the wise men brought their finest gifts, they really gave themselves. They traveled long and far to see the Savior of the world and humbled themselves before the Christ child. That is all God wants from us, the gift of ourselves. Are you willing to give of yourself to Christ?

DECEMBER 25

For the wages of sin is death, but the gift of
God is eternal life in Christ Jesus our Lord.
—Romans 6:23

Christmas is a time of giving. Ever since the wise men from the East arrived at the stable carrying gold, frankincense, and myrrh, people have been exchanging gifts at Christmas time. A gift is something that is freely given to you with one specific purpose in mind—that you receive it. The Bible tells us that Jesus is God's gift to you. Eternal life is not found in a certain place we go to when we die, but rather, eternal life is found in a certain person, and that person is Jesus Christ. When you believe in the Lord Jesus Christ and receive Him as your Savior, His very life enters into yours. Truly Jesus Christ is God's indescribable gift. On Christmas, we celebrate the fact that God gave us the gift of His Son, Jesus Christ, so that through faith in Him, we can be forgiven of our sins and have eternal life.

Jesus is the gift that perfectly fits every heart. It is with His love that the celebration of Christmas begins. We rejoice in Him as we remember His birth and thank God for sending His only Son to earth. He is the reason for the season. Christmas in America is mostly about the gifts we give and receive. Millions of dollars are spent on getting the perfect gifts for loved ones and friends. Many will open gifts today without even knowing the true meaning of Christmas. It is our responsibility to let others know about this gift that is waiting for them. Not everyone who is given this gift receives it. We have to take the package, open the box, and each of us has to make the decision to receive Jesus Christ into our lives. Maybe that gift is still under the tree, wrapped and ready to be opened by you. What better day than Christmas to renew your commitment to Christ, or to begin a new life of fellowship with Him. What better way to celebrate Christmas than to offer the gift of Christ to someone.

DECEMBER 26

"Do not lay up for yourselves treasures on earth, where moth
and dust destroy and where thieves break in and steal; but
lay up for yourselves treasures in heaven, where neither moth
nor rust destroy and where thieves do not break in and steal.
For where your treasure is, there your heart will be also."
—Matthew 6:19–21

It's the day after Christmas. Many will be rushing to stores to return gifts that were given to them. Others will be seeking those after-Christmas bargains. Some will be storing another addition to their collection, a sports card, comic book, or some other must-have item. While collecting can be a fun hobby, we must keep in mind that once we leave this earth, our treasures become someone else's collection. Jesus warns us that we should not lay up for ourselves earthly treasures, which can be easily destroyed or stolen, but we are to lay up eternal treasures which cannot be stolen or destroyed.

What eternal treasure did you give or receive this Christmas? Did you make a difference in someone's life? Did you lead someone to Christ, or did someone lead you to a closer walk with Christ? Did you break the tradition of giving lots of gifts and just spend time with family and friends. Jesus gave of Himself to each and every one of us. What did you give to Jesus this Christmas? If you haven't thought about it, it's not too late. Is there something that the Lord has been asking you to do that you have been putting off? Give it to Jesus this Christmas. Is there a habit that you want to break? Give it to Jesus this Christmas. Is there someone that the Lord has placed upon your heart to talk to them about salvation? Do it for Christ this Christmas. Storing treasures in heaven is not limited to tithing, but is accomplished by all acts of obedience to God. Seek to please God by fulfilling God's purpose in all you do.

DECEMBER 27

"Behold, I stand at the door and knock. If anyone
hears My voice and opens the door, I will come
in to him and dine with him, and he with Me."
—Revelation 3:20

Jesus did not counsel us to try harder but rather He counseled us to let Him in. We are so busy enjoying worldly pleasures that we don't even notice that God is trying to enter. The pleasures of this world—money, sports, fame, and material possessions have a temporary satisfaction that is chocking out God's offer of lasting satisfaction and is making us indifferent to the things of God. Many people fear failure, but our greatest fear should be succeeding at things in life that don't really matter—those things that do not have eternal value. God wants our best, deserves our best, and demands our best. It's easy to fill ourselves with other things and then give God whatever time is left over. How would you feel if you were served leftovers every night for dinner? It would become old after a while. Why would you think it would feel any different to God?

How we spend our time, what we spend our money on, and where we invest our energy reflects where our heart is with God and is equivalent to choosing God, or rejecting Him. How do you think God feels when we choose to follow worldly pleasures rather than to seek Him? Are you giving your best to God? If not, purpose in your heart to desire to draw near to God. If you draw near to God, He will draw near to you (James 4:8). Do you wonder if God is knocking at your door? God is patient and persistent with us, not breaking and entering, but knocking. He allows us to decide whether or not to open the door of our life to Him. If we leave the door of our heart open at all times, we won't have to worry about hearing His knock, He will simply come in.

DECEMBER 28

Now faith is the substance of things hoped for, the evidence of things not seen.

—Hebrews 11:1

Faith is not wishful thinking. It is confidence that God will always do what He promises regardless of the circumstances. Faith is having the confidence that even though you don't see it, it will come to pass (Romans 8:24–25). Begin declaring those things which are not as if they were. Declare the outcome of your circumstances and then believe that God will see it through. The more we declare by faith, the stronger our faith becomes. The more we walk in faith, the more we become free in Christ. The more we become free in Christ, the more confident we become in who we are in Christ—holding onto the promise of our eternal life, never losing sight of our heavenly home. God's greatest promise is that we can be saved through Jesus.

Without faith it is impossible to please God (Hebrews 11:6). Lack of faith insults God. How do you feel when someone does not think you are qualified for the job? How do you feel when someone tells you they don't believe you? Now, how do you think God feels when you doubt and say I don't think You are qualified for the job? When doubts begin to form, ask God to give you greater faith. Do not believe the lies of the enemy. When you think that God is too slow in answering your prayers, consider that He might be testing you. No matter how grim your circumstance may be, never lose faith in who God is and what God can do. Hebrews 11 is filled with great examples of faith, heroes of faith who lived and died without seeing the fruit of their faith on earth and yet continued to believe. We too must hold onto our faith, encouraging each other, and looking forward to Christ's return.

DECEMBER 29

So take a new grip with your tired hands and strengthen your weak knees. Mark out a straight path for your feet so that those who are weak and lame will not fall but become strong.
—Hebrews 12:12–13, NLT

We earn the respect of others by setting an example. Be an example to all believers in what you say, in the way you live, in your love, your faith, and your purity (1 Timothy 4:12). No matter how young or old we are, or how long we have followed Christ, we all are to be an example to others by submitting our lives to Christ and learning how to rely upon His power and the leading of the Holy Spirit. God can and will use us if we allow Him to. People look to see how we respond to pressures and calamities. Although we may not feel strong enough to push on to victory, we will be able to achieve it as we follow Christ and draw on His strength. When we do, and others around us are weak and struggling, we can use our renewed strength to help and encourage them. We must rest in the knowledge that God's ways are perfect and His grace is all-sufficient. No matter what may come our way, His help is adequate.

People follow people. Others will follow our example. What legacy are you leaving behind? Does your walk with God make it easier for others to believe in Christ and want to follow Him? Does your faith in Christ stir up faith and make it easier for others to trust in God when the storms of life hit them? That is exactly what our reactions to life's circumstances should do. Live so others can see Christ in you, no matter what the season in your life may be. Allow the characteristics of Christ to shine through you, and watch others walk into victory because of it.

DECEMBER 30

By the word of the Lord the heavens were made,
and all the host of them by the breath of His mouth.

—Psalm 33:6

Words are powerful and no words are more powerful than words from God. By the power of His word, God created the world out of nothing. God's word has creative power and calls into existence the very thing of which it speaks (Isaiah 55:11). There is power in God's word. Don't underestimate the power of God's word in your life. God's word can turn any situation around for good. His word brings life, reviving the soul. His word can bring healing to your deepest hurts and calm any raging storm in your heart. God's word can bring comfort, healing, purification, insight, wisdom and truth. When we proclaim God's word, angels heed to the voice of His word (Psalm 103:20). They stand ready to do His word.

When you read the Bible, seek to understand what it is saying so that we can allow its truth to penetrate into your heart and soul. His word will transform you, changing how you think and how you live. Daily applying God's Word has a purifying effect on your mind and heart. The word of God has power to illuminate your darkness. Scripture points out your sin, motivates you to confess your sins, renews your relationship with Christ, and guides you back to the right path. Blessed are they that hear the word of God and put it into practice (Luke 11:28). We must not only hear the word of God but must also apply it to our lives. Study God's Word with determination to seek truth, find truth, and apply truth to your life. God's word is truth, and we must allow His truth to sanctify us (John 17:17). Believe that God's Word has omnipotent power to change you.

DECEMBER 31

My son, do not forget my law, but let your heart
keep my commands; for length of days and long life
and peace they will add to you. Let not mercy and
truth forsake you; bind them around your neck, write
them on the tablet of your heart, and so find favor
and high esteem in the sight of God and man.

—Proverbs 3:1–4

I thought it would be appropriate to end this year with some wise words from Proverbs. Throughout this year, the Lord has given us much wisdom and insight into His ways through the "Whispers of Hope" devotional. I thank the Lord for guiding me throughout the year to enlighten you all and hopefully bring you closer to God. Each day contains God's Word. We are to hide His Word deep within our hearts and follow Him that we might live long peaceful days. Wisdom is a gift from God. It starts with knowing God and digging into His Word—the source of knowledge and understanding (Proverbs 2:6)—and applying it to our lives. We gain wisdom by growing in His Word. Wisdom comes by making a lifelong series of right choices and avoiding moral pitfalls. When we do make sinful mistakes, we seek forgiveness and learn from our errors. It is a part of the growing process. Keeping God's Word deep in our hearts helps us to avoid making many unwise choices.

Notice that God tells us to not forsake mercy and truth; we are to bind them around our necks and write them on the tablet of our hearts. In other words, we are never to walk without them. We must always walk in truth and show mercy to all. Mercy without truth can lead to ungodly compromise. Truth without mercy can lead to legalism. When we pursue both simultaneously, we reflect the heart of the Father and bring Him great pleasure. Never judge people. Extend mercy to everyone. If they are in a moral pitfall, lead them to truth in love and you will win a friend forever.

About the Author

Patricia M. Riggie leads the prayer ministry at her local church in Morgantown, West Virginia. Her desire is to see others develop a deeper walk and faith in God through prayer and daily devotionals.

CPSIA information can be obtained
at www.ICGtesting.com
Printed in the USA
BVHW032128280120
570806BV00001B/8